Foreword

As a family we love to travel. We have been lucky enough to visit many places over the years both in Britain and abroad, and as our children have grown we have become more bold with our destination choices. It has given us hours of shared experiences to mull over and endless discussions about where or when our next adventure will be.

As a family we also adore our dogs. They bring an unquestionable loyalty and unending affection to our daily lives we could not be without. I firmly believe lives are enriched by animals and my childhood memories are peppered with names of long lost pets that can bring a smile to my face or a tear to my eye. In this respect our two Vizslas Dolly and Boo, along with newly acquired Collie Peg, are creating family history as I write.

For a dog lover there can hardly be a worse feeling than packing for a holiday, knowing that these loyal friends are staying behind. They seem to predict we are going away well before the cases bump down the stairs! I'm sure many of us will have looked into those sad eyes and felt dreadful at the thought of leaving them at home.

Despite these feelings of guilt we have rarely been away with our dogs and I'm not sure why. I think we have consoled ourselves with the thought that once we've actually managed to leave, our dogs will be happier staying in familiar surroundings. We live on a farm where we have access to acres of space so they aren't particularly used to interaction with others. Going away is bound to be a culture shock so why bother?

Last year however that all changed when we took the plunge and travelled to Cornwall with our beloved pets. From the minute they leapt into the car, almost in disbelief, I knew we had made the right decision. Coastal walks were a pleasure and hours of ball throwing on the beach, swimming in the sea and trips to dog-friendly pubs in the evenings became part of our daily routine. Our dogs were often the cause of conversations with like-minded people that led to new friendships for ourselves and our children. What more could you want from a holiday?

Sawday's *Dog-friendly Breaks in Britain* is a wonderful resource for dog owners. Flicking through the pages, it's heart-warming to find such a range of places where you can guarantee a genuine welcome for both you and your dogs. We will definitely be going away with our hounds again this year. I can't think of any reason not to.

Adam Henson

Third edition
Copyright © 2016
Alastair Sawday Publishing Co. Ltd
Published in 2016
ISBN-13: 978-1-906136-72-7

Alastair Sawday Publishing Co. Ltd,
Merchant's House, Wapping Road,
Bristol BS1 4RW, UK
Tel: +44 (0)117 204 7810
Email: info@sawdays.co.uk
Web: www.sawdays.co.uk

The Globe Pequot Press,
P. O. Box 480, Guilford,
Connecticut 06437, USA
Tel: +1 203 458 4500
Email: info@globepequot.com
Web: www.globepequot.com

Series Editor Alastair Sawday
Content Manager Wendy Ogden
Editorial Assistance Lianka Varga,
Louise Phipps
Canopy & Stars Editorial
Isabelle Gourlay
Senior Picture Editor Alec Studerus
Production Coordinators
Lianka Varga, Sarah Barratt
Marketing & PR
0117 204 7801
marketing@sawdays.co.uk

We have made every effort to ensure the accuracy of the information in this book at the time of going to press. However, we cannot accept any responsibility for any loss, injury or inconvenience resulting from the use of information contained therein.

Production: Pagebypage Co. Ltd
Printing: Pureprint, Uckfield
Maps: Maidenhead Cartographic Services
UK distribution: The Travel Alliance, Bath
Diane@popoutmaps.com

Cover photo credits.
Front 1. The Felin Fach Griffin, entry 202 2. Competition winner Oscar
3. 5 & 6 Porth Farm Cottages, entry 15
Back: 1. The Church Inn, entry 165 2. Harry & Monty
3. The Cholmondeley Arms, entry 7
Spine: Jago (Alec Studerus)

Alastair
Sawday's

Special Places
to Stay

Dog-friendly
Breaks in Britain

4   Contents

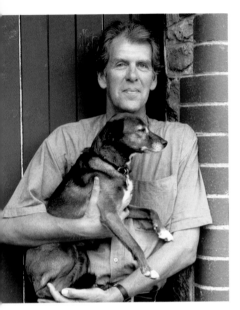

This delightful book has been one of our most successful ever. It all goes to show that the need is there, as I know from personal experience with Suky, our whippet cross. The stains on the carpets of my mother's house are a reminder, however, that much is asked of the owners of places to stay.

Curiously, a rare complaint about dogs was from an owner who found her guests' children riding her dog like a horse. The dog was large, but so too were the children, and the animal's back had to be operated on. The parents of the offenders were very 'liberal', and unfazed by their children's behaviour.

But all is well in the dog-owners' world. There are now many places that accept dogs as guests, though some are asked to stay downstairs, or sleep in a small room. You can go on dog-friendly walking tours, enjoy beaches that allow dogs and learn ahead which places to avoid. But a book like this is extra-useful, for it brings together Sawday places that will welcome you with your dog – and that is a treat indeed.

A reminder of how well-behaved a dog can be: I once ate a dauntingly posh meal in a French hotel, behaving with proper decorum. The sommelier oozed from table to table; the waiters hovered and preened. One exquisitely coiffed lady ate alone. Finally she arose, and sashayed from the restaurant, towing, to our amazement, a vast dog. It had lain under the table, soundlessly. And the restaurant was fully aware of it. Don't you love France?

My only request to the owners of the dogs that travel is that you kick-start a campaign to remove the decorations that one finds on trees and bushes where dogs promenade. Those little, laden, plastic bags are a gentle rebuke to a community that otherwise adds so much to the joy in our lives.

It is my own view, laden with prejudice, that places which welcome dogs with open arms and sagging sofas will probably welcome humans just as well. Do let us know how you get on.

Alastair Sawday

It's simple. There are no rules, no boxes to tick. We choose places that we like and we are subjective in our choices. We look for comfort, originality, authenticity, and a genuine welcome. The way guests — and their pets! — are treated comes as high on our list as the setting, the atmosphere and the food.

Inspections

Our inspectors know their patch. They don't take a clipboard and they don't have a list of what is acceptable and what is not. Instead, they chat with the owner and look round — closely — and if the visit happens to be the last of the day, they stay the night. It's all very informal, but it gives us an excellent idea of who would enjoy staying there; our simple aim is to match places with guests. Once in the book, properties are re-inspected every four years so that we can keep things fresh and up to date.

What to expect

This new edition of our best-selling Dog-friendly guide contains a wonderful mix of places that welcome you and your dog (or dogs — many allow more than one). Some have specific bedrooms that are set aside for guests with a dog in tow, others welcome dogs in all their rooms. In some places dogs may sleep downstairs but not in the bedroom; do check before you book. Dogs may not, anywhere, sleep on the bed!

The 'pub' entries welcome you for a pint with your dog; the 'inn' entries have dog-friendly bedrooms too. All have bar areas that welcome dogs, and often gardens too; most pubs draw the line at allowing dogs into dining rooms (although some have a special table set aside for visitors with a dog). If you want to check the details beforehand just give them a call. Dog treats

Photo: Isabelle Gourlay (Hebe)

at the pubs and inns might include a juicy bone, homemade biscuits or even dog 'beer' and birthday cakes!

There's a fascinating mix inside these pages of B&Bs, hotels, self-catering escapes, inns, pubs and Canopy & Stars outdoor retreats. Remote and simple, or wrapped in luxury, there's something for every pooch and its owner here.

Map

If you know which region you want to stay in, our maps are your best guide. Lozenges flag up properties in colours denoting whether they are catered (red), self-catering (blue) or pubs (dark grey). Our quirky outdoor retreats are also listed, under Canopy & Stars CANOPY&STARS . The maps are the perfect starting point for planning a stay – but please don't use them for navigation.

Photo above: Tess & Poppy, Orcheston Mill, entry 54
Photo right: The Cat, entry 138

Types of places to stay

B&Bs

B&Bs, however grand, are people's homes, not hotels. You'll most probably have breakfast and dinner with your hosts and/or fellow guests, and the welcome will be personal. Some owners give you a front door key so you may come and go as you please; others like to have the house empty between, say, 10am and 4pm.

Do expect
• a personal welcome
• a willingness to go the extra mile
• a degree of informality, and a fascinating glimpse into someone else's way of life

Don't expect
• a lock on your bedroom door
• your room cleaned and your bed made every day
• a private table at breakfast and dinner
• an immediate response to your booking enquiry
• a TV in your room

Hotels

Those we choose generally have fewer than 50 rooms; most are family-run with friendly staff; many are in historic buildings – perhaps a castle or two; others have a boutique feel. All those in this book like dogs!

Inns

Our one-page inns entries vary from swish suites with plasma TVs to sweet simple rooms overlooking the sea. Staying in

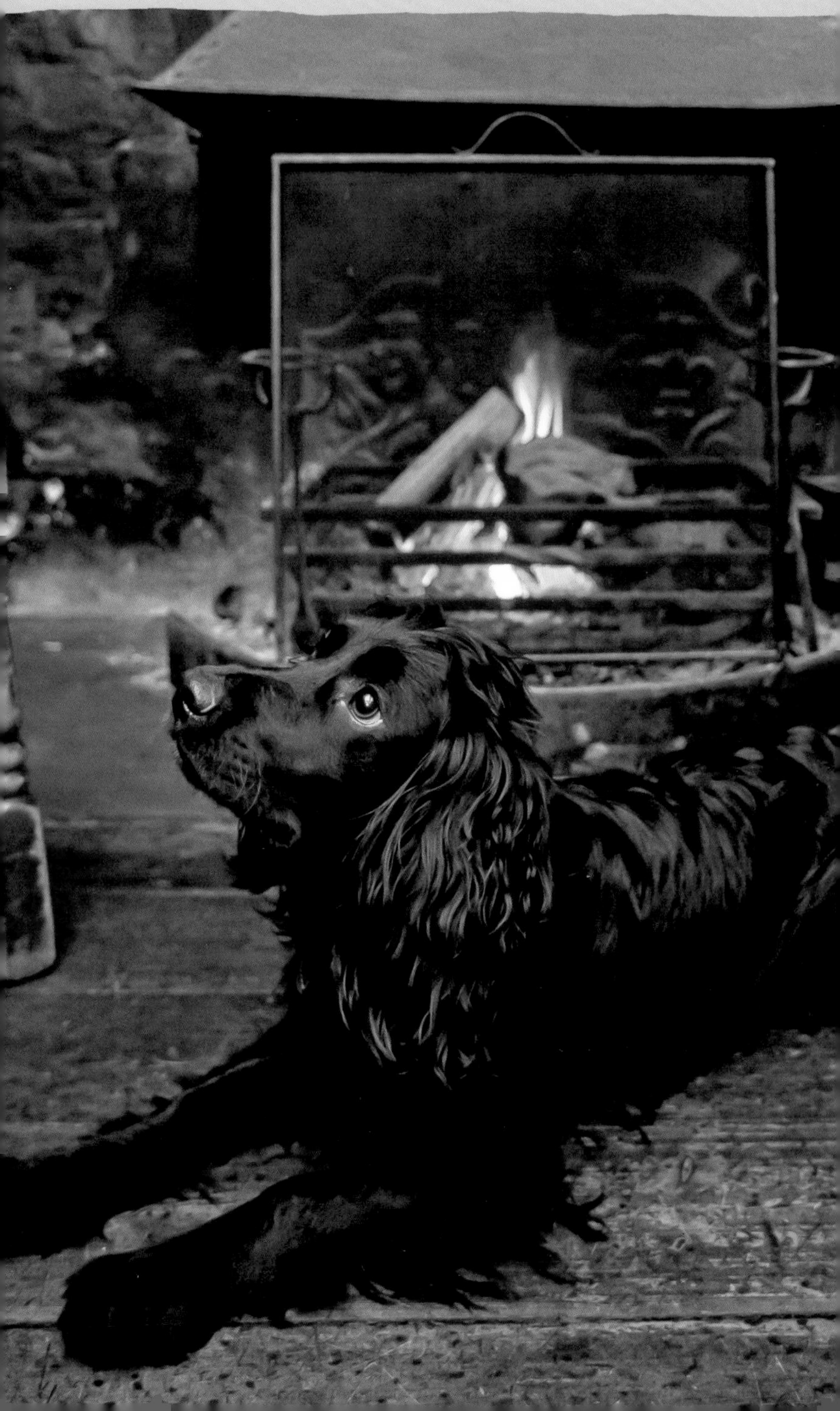

a pub – above the bar or in the converted barn behind – is often great value for money.

Self-catering places

Perfect independence for couples – and families – with dogs. Cottages, farmhouses, coach houses, studios, mills, barns – each and every one has been visited by us and found to be special. We don't include places we wouldn't stay in ourselves.

Canopy & Stars

For those who love to be at one with nature, welcome to our collection of beautiful, simple, quirky (and sometimes luxurious) places to sleep under the stars. Treehouses, shepherd's huts, yurts, gypsy caravans and romantic log cabins – the choice is inspiring.

Bedrooms

We tell you if a room is a single, double, twin/double (with zip and link beds), suite (a room with space for seating), family (a double bed + single beds), or triple (three single beds).

Bathrooms

The vast majority of bedrooms in this book are en suite. Only if a bedroom has a shared or a private-but-separate bathroom do we say so.

Sitting rooms

Most hotels have one or two communal areas, while most B&Bs offer guests the family sitting room to share, or provide a sitting room just for guests.

Meals

Unless we say otherwise, breakfast is included, simple or extravagant. Some owners are fairly unbending about breakfast times, others are happy just to wait until you want it, or even bring it to you in your room.

Many B&Bs offer their guests dinner, usually an opportunity to get to know your hosts and to make new friends among the other guests. Note that meal prices are per person. Always book in advance.

Prices

Self-catering prices are mostly quoted per week. Each other entry gives a price PER ROOM per night for two. The price range covers a night in the cheapest room in low season to the most expensive in high season. Some owners charge more at certain times (during regattas and festivals, for example) and some owners ask for a minimum two nights at weekends. Others offer special deals for three-night stays. Prices quoted are those given to us for 2016 but are not guaranteed. Double-check when booking.

At many of these places dogs go free, at others where there's a charge, we say so.

Bookings and cancellations

Sometimes you will be asked to pay a deposit. Some are non-refundable; some people may charge you for the whole of the booked stay in advance; and some cancellation policies are more stringent than others. It is also worth noting that some owners will take the money directly from your credit/debit card without contacting you to discuss it. So ask them to explain their cancellation policy clearly before booking to avoid a surprise. Always make sure you have written confirmation of all you have discussed.

Payment

All our owners take cash and UK cheques with a cheque card, and those who take credit cards have our credit card symbol. Check that your particular credit card is acceptable.

Tipping

Owners do not expect tips – but if you have been treated with extraordinary kindness, drop your hosts a line. If you are on Facebook or Twitter, you can sing their praises from our website www.sawdays.co.uk. Find their Special Place, then 'share' or 'tweet'.

Arrivals and departures

Say roughly what time you will arrive (normally after 4pm; for inns, after 6pm), as most hosts like to welcome you personally. Be on time if you have booked dinner. If, despite best efforts, you are delayed, phone to give warning.

Photo: Breedon Hall, entry 95

Closed

When given in months this means the whole of the month stated.

Feedback

The accuracy of our books depends on what you, as well as our inspectors, tell us. Your feedback is invaluable and we always act upon comments. Tell us whether your stay has been a joy or not, if the atmosphere was great or stuffy, the owners cheery or bored. Importantly, a lot of new places come to us via our readers, so keep telling us about new places you've discovered. Just visit our sites:

www.sawdays.co.uk

for hotels, inns, B&Bs and self-catering properties

www.canopyandstars.co.uk

for outdoor retreats.

Complaints

Please do not tell us if the bedside light was inadequate, the hairdryer was broken or the bedroom was cold. Tell the owner instead, and ask them to do something about it. Most owners are more than happy to correct problems and will bend over backwards to help. If you think things have gone seriously awry, do tell us.

Symbols

There is an explanation of the symbols used for our Special Places to Stay on the inside back cover of the book. Use them as a guide, not as a statement of fact. However, things do change: bikes may be under repair or a new pool may have been put in. If an owner does not have the symbol that you're looking for, it's worth discussing your needs.

Note that the ⬤ symbol shows places that are happy to accept children of all ages; it does not mean that they will have cots and high chairs. Many who say no to children do so not because they don't like them but because they may have a steep stair, an unfenced pond or they find balancing the needs of mixed age groups too challenging.

The ⬤ symbol is given when the owners have their own pet on the premises. It may not be a cat! But it is there to warn you that you may be greeted by a dog, serenaded by a parrot, or indeed sat upon by a cat.

The symbols used at the foot of the pub entries apply to the bar and not (should the pub have them) to its bedrooms.

Quick reference indices

At the back of the book we list properties

Photo above: Alec Studerus (Jax)
Photo right: Rhiannon Gardiner-Bateman (Lily)

that are wheelchair-friendly, have pets of their own or accept credit cards.

Treats

Dog treats provided by owners are shown on each entry and listed at the back of the book for a bit of fun. How about local sausage cooked to perfection with a splash of milk to wash it down, or a coastal walk straight from the door? Or a tour of the grounds from the resident lurchers, and a bone from the village butcher? Many dogs like to share their favourite treats and walks, and some owners are willing dog sitters so you can have a night out at a non-dog-friendly place.

Membership

Owners pay to appear in this guide. Their membership fee goes towards the costs of inspecting, publishing, marketing, and maintaining our websites. It is not possible for anyone to buy their way onto these pages as we only include places that we like. Nor is it possible for owners to write their own description.

We say if the bedrooms are small, the stairs are steep or if a main road is near. We aim not to mislead you!

Disclaimer

We make no claims to pure objectivity in choosing these places. They are here simply because we like them. Our opinions and tastes are ours alone and this book is a statement of them – we do hope you will share them. We have done our utmost to get our facts right but apologise unreservedly for any mistakes that may have crept in.

You should know that we don't check such things as fire regulations, swimming pool security or any other laws with which owners of properties receiving paying guests should comply. This is the responsibility of the owners.

We hope you enjoy our dog-friendly selection – we're almost 100% sure that you and your hound will have a brilliant holiday.

Photo above: Zomba & Zanzie, Combermere Abbey Cottages, entry 112
Photo right: Sky Den, entry 106

Alastair Sawday's

'More than a bed
for the night…'

Britain
France
Ireland
Italy
Portugal
Spain

www.sawdays.co.uk

Self-Catering | B&B | Hotel | Pub | Treehouses, Cabins, Yurts & More

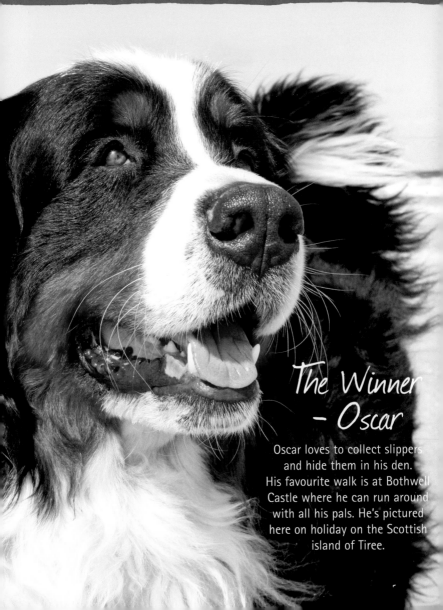

Cover Star Competition
#dogcoverstar

Our previous 'handsome hound' competitions have been so popular that we decided to continue the tradition for our third guide. And our readers didn't disappoint! We were once again overwhelmed with dapper looking dogs, pretty pooches and cute canines. As always, we had a tough time choosing just one favourite, so alongside our winner we picked five runners up and scattered some of our other favourites throughout the book.

The Winner
– Oscar

Oscar loves to collect slippers and hide them in his den. His favourite walk is at Bothwell Castle where he can run around with all his pals. He's pictured here on holiday on the Scottish island of Tiree.

This is Milo, he's a pedigree Golden Retriever affectionately known as the Golden Idiot. His favourite thing is cannonballing into lakes!

Ginny loves to run and play on the beach at Newport, north Pembrokeshire. But wherever she is, just loves to meet everyone.

Meet Wookie. His favourite place is anywhere that he can get mucky and chase his ball. Harlech Beach in North Wales is ideal, if a bit windy!

This is Daisy, a 7-year-old Soft Coated Wheaten Terrier. Here she is enjoying the fabulous ancient bluebell woods in Southwick Woods, Northamptonshire.

This is Doobi. Her favourite place is anywhere there's lots of snow, she just loves to eat it!

We had so many lovely pictures to choose from for this competition that we couldn't resist scattering a few more throughout the book, so keep your eyes peeled for some more of our favourites. You could also meet some of the other gorgeous entries on social media. Search for #dogcoverstar on Twitter or Facebook and be prepared to melt!

 twitter.com/sawdays   facebook.com/sawdays

Dogs don't appreciate cultural breaks. They want beaches, woods, puddles and fields. Here's our pick of places that welcome dogs with open paws.

ENGLAND

St Ives, Cornwall
Stride the coastal path to Zennor (six miles), on to The Gurnard's Head pub (three miles) for lunch, then bus it back to St Ives.

Bodmin Moor, Cornwall
Trek up to the two highest points in Cornwall (OS Exp 109) and look to both coasts on a clear day. The remains of an iron age hill fort reward you at the summit.

Daymer Bay, Cornwall
Lovely large sandy bay, one of the few open to dogs all year round, with proper waves.

Branscombe, Devon
Unspoilt pebble beach in pretty Branscombe where dogs can romp lead-free 50m in either direction of the car park and café. From here, a coastal walk.

Durdle Door, Dorset
Dogs on leads permitted all year round; also at Lulworth Cove and Worbarrow Bay. Dogs off-lead (except May-September) at Studland Shell Bay, a short drive east.

Camber Sands, East Sussex
When the tide is out dogs get a brilliant run on the sand. Well-managed beaches with Minnis Bay the favourite – but no dogs May-September.

Cotswold Water Park, Gloucestershire
Criss-crossed by miles of flat foot and cycle path, this massive water park has been created from dozens of quarries filled with water and linked by canals. Keep dogs on leads in the bird nesting areas, otherwise, let them bound.

Saxon Shore Way, Kent
On the long-distance footpath to the white cliffs of Dover you cross four wonderful nature reserves: Conver Creek, Harty Ferry, the village of Oare and Faversham. Dogs on leads please.

Botany Bay, Broadstairs, Kent
Big old-fashioned sandy beach with rock pools and famous chalk stacks, off limits to dogs in summer (May-September

10am-6pm). Dogs welcome all year on Dumpton Gap beach. And gallops on the top for drying wet dogs off.

Greenwich Park, London
A really old park (1427) stuffed full of heritage (Anglo-saxon burial mounds; the Meridian Line), with amazing views across the Thames to St Paul's. Open 6am-6pm (later in summer) for good dogs that are off-lead. Park near the Pavilion Tea House and Royal Observatory.

Groton Wood, Suffolk
Ancient woodland, enchanting walks: bluebells, nightingales, toads, newts and brimstone butterflies.

Wells-next-the-Sea, Norfolk
The Kennel Club's beacon 2014 winner is dog-friendly all year round but at nesting time dogs are on leads. Big dogs go mad for the wide open spaces of nearby Holkham; at low tide the sands reach to the horizon.

Worcester Woods Country Park, Worcestershire
Acres of oak woodland, wildflower meadows and two gentle, circular walks perfect for elderly pooches.

Danes Dyke, Yorkshire
A small, away-from-it-all, award-winning beach – sand, pebbles, rock pools, clean water – reached from the car park down a steep road one mile west of Flamborough Head.

Rievaulx to Byland, Yorkshire
Not one but two ruined and magnificent abbeys in the North York Moors with a beautiful and varied six-mile walk between them.

Cautley Spout, Cumbria
Take the obvious path behind the inn at Low Haygarth and walk downstream along the beck (passing the famous wild horses of the Howgill Fells) towards the magnificent 'spout'. Dogs must be under control at the top as there's a mighty drop down, and a bit of a scramble to get there. Short, wild, remote and exhilarating.

Keswick, Cumbria
Lots of wag-friendly shops, pubs and cafés in town, and fells, woodland and lakes beyond – meaning clever Keswick won the Kennel Club's 2012 Open for Dogs Awards in the Dog Friendly Town category.

Photo: Jules Richardson (Luna)

St Bees, Cumbria

A great family beach three miles from Whitehaven – be sure to scoop every poop. For serious walkers, link up with the Coast to Coast Walk that runs from St Bees on the west to Robin Hood's Bay on the east – glorious.

Bamburgh, Northumberland

A vast, big skies, dog-happy beach with dunes, overlooked by magnificent Bamburgh Castle.

Attingham Park, Shropshire

Luscious parkland for dogs with a nose for the high life, at this 18th-century, National Trust mansion. A hidden gem four miles south-east of Shrewsbury, it is blessed with large parkland that borders the river. Keep dogs on leads near the deer.

Baggeridge Country Park, Staffordshire

Between Wombourne and Sedgley, a much-loved Green Flag park, created over a former colliery. There are four trails in all, from a circular Easy Access trail, perfect for wheelchairs and buggies, to a 90-minute romp through Baggeridge Wood.

WALES

Conwy Mountain, Conwy

There's walking here as adventurous as anywhere in Snowdonia – but on a smaller scale.

Elan Valley, Powys

From Rhayader to Devil's Bridge, and some of the remotest hiking south of the Cairngorms. Miles of peaty plateaus, a few sheep, wheeling red kites and five larch-lapped Victorian reservoirs with associated viaducts and dams.

Rhossili Bay, Swansea

Miles of pristine sand at the tip of the Gower Peninsula, reached via many steps. There's enough space for dogs to run free all year – and a colourful selection of kites to bark at.

St David's Head Walk, Pembrokeshire

Circular three-hour walk from Whitesands Bay, the first bit inland, the second along the wind-buffeted coastal path. Thrill to the Hats and Barrels – the rocks and reefs that still pose a threat to boats passing through these tidal races.

Usk Valley Walk, Monmouthshire

One gorgeous stretch of this 48-mile route from Brecon to Caerleon and the sea, is along the fish-rich river bank between Usk and Abergavenny. Every bit as pretty as the Wye.

Glanusk Estate, Crickhowell

Luscious acres roll as far as the eye can see – plus ancient Celtic standing stones, a bridge over the river Usk, a private chapel, farm buildings and stables, 120 different species of oak, opera (though not for the dog), and country shows galore.

Broad Haven, Bosherston, Pembs

Beautiful sheltered sand and dune bay reached via boardwalks across the famous lily ponds. Bow-wow heaven.

SCOTLAND

Culzean Castle & Country Park, Ayrshire

A 'castle in the air' perched high above the crashing waves of the Firth of Clyde, with miles of woodland walks. Leads on please for the deer park and swan pond.

Craigower, near Pitlochry, Perthshire

High-up open heathland with stunning long views, rare butterflies and scattered Scots pines. Dogs on the lead when crossing the golf course.

Hermitage, near Dunkeld, Perthshire

A woodland walk though huge Douglas firs to a folly overlooking the crashing Black Linn waterfall – best keep dogs and toddlers on leads.

Barry Mill, Carnoustie, Angus

It is a lovely walk with the dog up to Barry Mill, for the splash of the waterwheel and the smell of grinding corn: milling demos on Sundays.

Calgary Bay, Isle of Mull

Silver sands and crystal waters, exquisite on a fine day, atmospheric on a misty one. Unrestricted romps for dogs – but please think of humans too. (And the gulls and waders.)

Photo: The Hayloft at Flamborough Rigg, entry 154

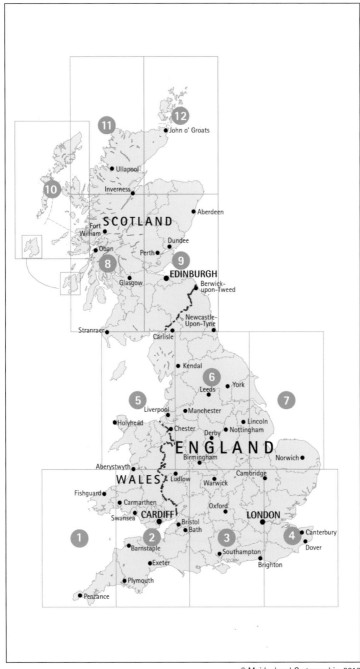

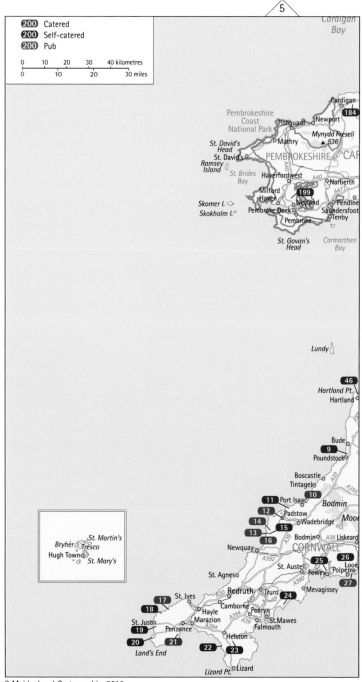

5

200 Catered
200 Self-catered
200 Pub

0   10   20   30   40 kilometres
0   10   20   30 miles

Cardigan
Bay

Pembrokeshire
Coast
National Park
Fishguard   Newport   **184**
St. David's   Mynydd Preseli
Head   Mathry   ▲ 536
St. David's   PEMBROKESHIRE   CAR
Ramsey
Island   St. Brides   Haverfordwest   Narberth
Bay   Milford
Haven   **199**
Skomer I.   Neyland   Pendine
Skokholm I.   Pembroke Dock   Saundersfoot
Pembroke   Tenby

St. Govan's   Carmarthen
Head   Bay

Lundy

46
Hartland Pt.
Hartland

Bude
9
Poundstock

Boscastle
Tintagel   **10**
11 Port Isaac   Bodmin
12
Padstow   Moor
14   Wadebridge
13   **15**
Bodmin   Liskeard
16   CORNWALL
Newquay
St. Austell   **25**   **26**
Fowey   Looe
Polperro
St. Agnes   Mevagissey   **27**

Redruth   Truro   **24**
17 St. Ives
18   Camborne   Penryn
Hayle   St. Mawes
Marazion   Falmouth
St. Just   Penzance   **19**
20   **21**   Helston
22   **23**
Land's End   Lizard
Lizard Pt.

St. Martin's
Bryher   Tresco
Hugh Town   St. Mary's

Map 2   27

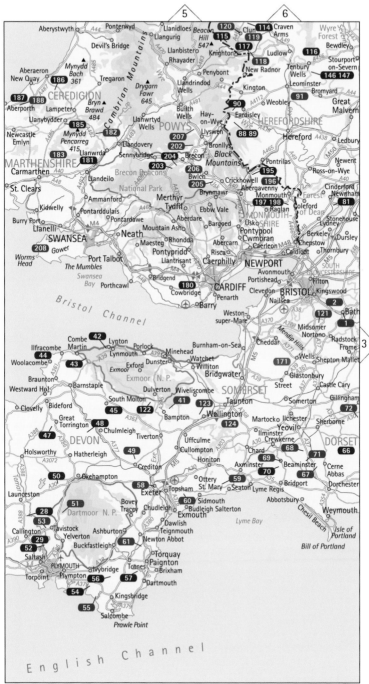

© Maidenhead Cartographic, 2016

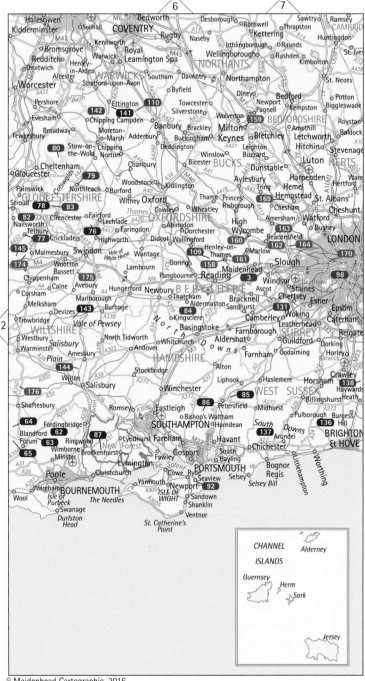

Map 4

29

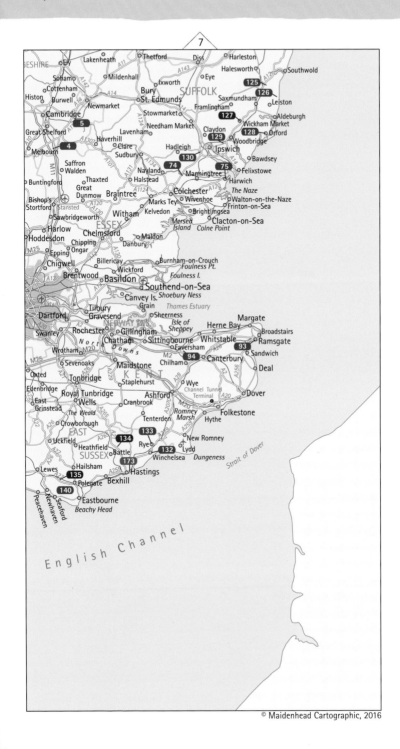

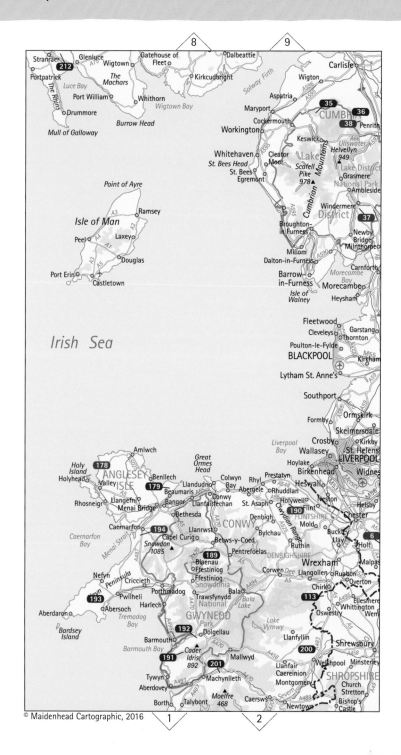

© Maidenhead Cartographic, 2016

Map 6   31

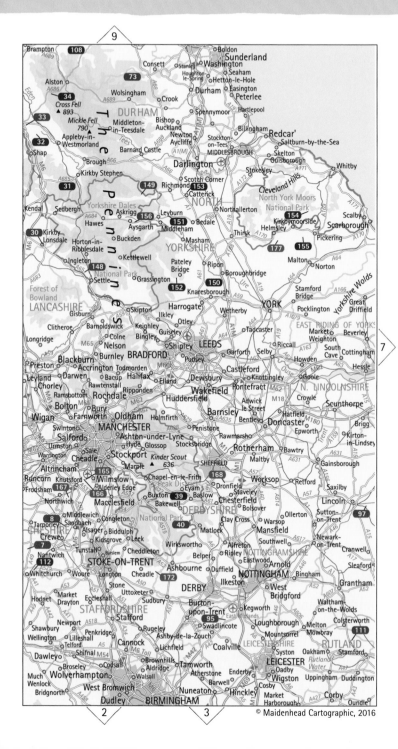

© Maidenhead Cartographic, 2016

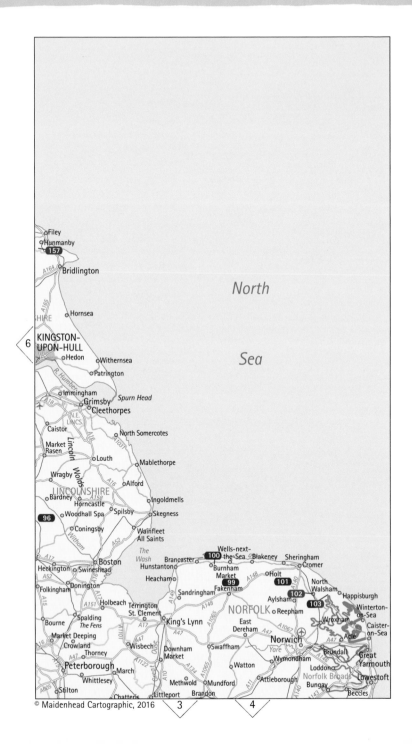

Map 8

33

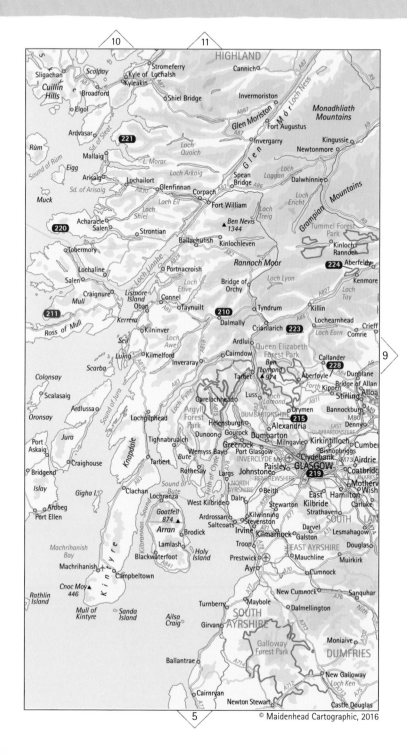

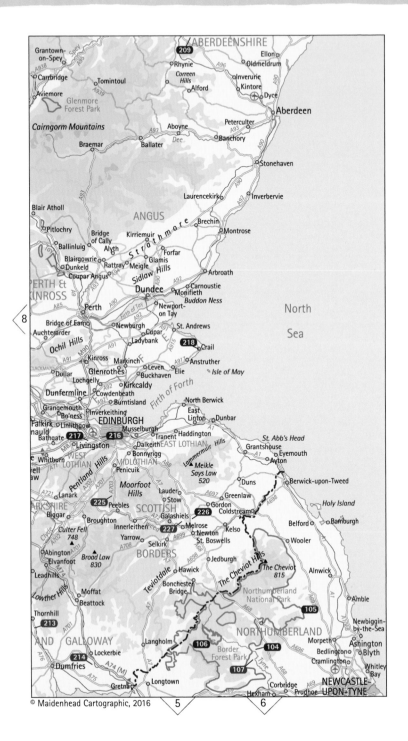

Map 10

35

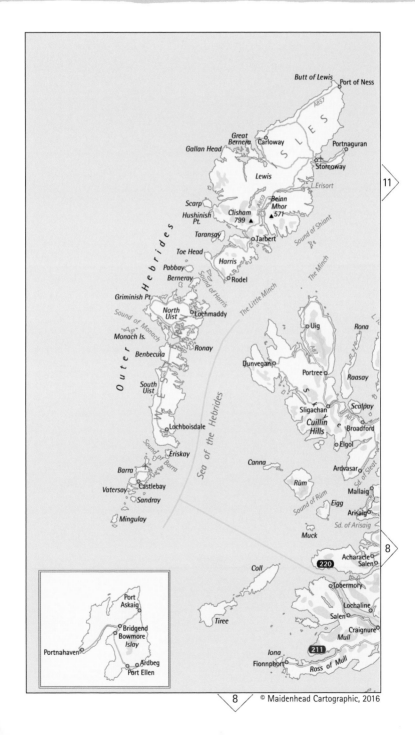

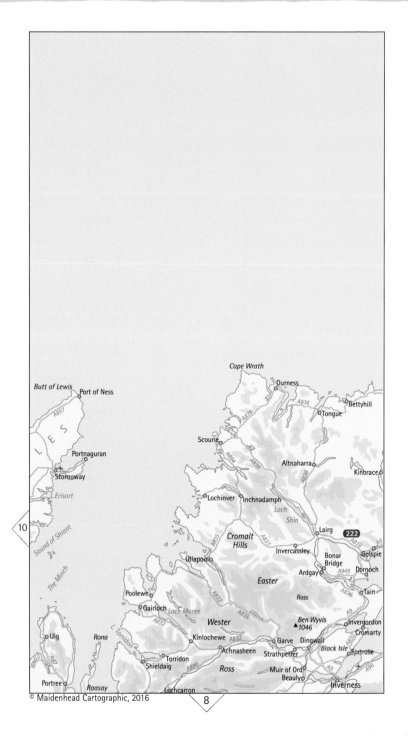

Cape Wrath

Butt of Lewis Port of Ness

Durness

A836

Bettyhill

A851

Tongue

L E S

Scourie

Altnaharra

Kinbrace

Portnaguran

Stornoway

A894

A838

A836

L.Erisort

Lochinver Inchnadamph

Loch

Shin

10

Sound of Shiant

Cromalt
Hills

Lairg 222

A837

A839

Invercassley

A835

Bonar
Bridge

Golspie

The Minch

Ullapool

Ardgay

A949

Dornoch

Easter

A836

Poolewe

A832

A835

Ross

Tain

A9

Gairloch

Loch Maree

A9

Invergordon

Uig

Rona

Wester

A833

Ben Wyvis
▲ 1046

Cromarty

L. Torridon

Kinlochewe

A832

Garve Dingwall

Black Isle

Fortrose

Portree

Torridon
Shieldaig

Achnasheen

Strathpeffer

A890

Ross

Muir of Ord

A9

A832

A96

Raasay

Lochcarron

Beauly

Inverness

8

© Maidenhead Cartographic, 2016

Map 12

37

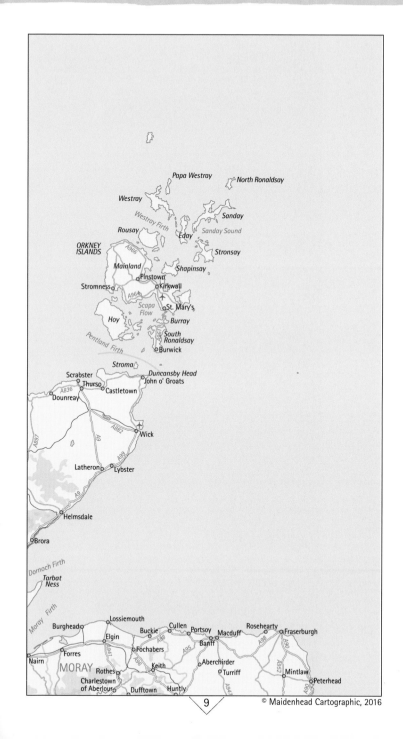

Papa Westray

North Ronaldsay

Westray

Westray Firth

Sanday

Rousay

Sanday Sound

Eday

ORKNEY
ISLANDS

A966

Stronsay

Mainland

Shapinsay

Finstown

Stromness

Kirkwall

A964

Scapa
Flow

St. Mary's

Hoy

Burray

South
Ronaldsay

Pentland Firth

Burwick

Stroma

Scrabster

Duncansby Head

Thurso

John o' Groats

A836

Castletown

Dounreay

A9

A882

A897

Wick

Latheron

A99

Lybster

A9

Helmsdale

Brora

Dornoch Firth

Tarbat
Ness

Moray Firth

Lossiemouth

Burghead

Buckie

Cullen

Portsoy

Rosehearty

Elgin

A98

Macduff

Fraserburgh

Forres

A941

Fochabers

A95

Banff

A90

Nairn

MORAY

Rothes

A96

Keith

Aberchirder

A952

Charlestown
of Aberlour

Dufftown

Huntly

Turriff

Mintlaw

A947

Peterhead

England

Abbey Hotel

You're in the epicentre of Bath, just behind the abbey, in one of the prettiest quarters in town. Parade Gardens waits across the road, the river Avon pours over the weir at Pulteney Bridge, Bath rugby club stands on the far bank. As for the hotel, in summer you take to the terrace café for coffee and watch the world go by; in winter it turns into an après-ski bar for mince pies and mulled wine. Inside, you find contemporary art in the sitting room, wine glasses hanging from the ceiling in the stylish bar, then Chris Staines lovely food in the theatrical restaurant, perhaps Thai mussels with lemongrass and ginger, whole roast spring chicken with herb gnocchi, salted peanut parfait with caramel popcorn and vanilla yoghurt. Smart rooms wait upstairs, where deeply comfy beds have woollen throws and colourful headboards. Some are small, others are big, all have iPads for room service, sparkling new bathrooms are beginning to emerge. Bath waits on your doorstep: rugby at the Rec, the Christmas market, all things Jane Austen. You're close to the station, too, so leave your car at home. *Minimum stay: 2 nights at weekends. Central Bath very near park areas – easy for dog-walking.*

Rooms	46 doubles, 14 twin/doubles: £105-£330. Dogs £10 per stay.
Meals	Breakfast £15. Lunch from £7.50. Dinner, 3 courses, £30-£35. Sunday lunch from £16.
Closed	Never.
	Advice on walks and a selection of treats.

Ian & Christa Taylor
Abbey Hotel,
North Parade,
Bath, BA1 1LF
Tel   +44 (0)1225 805615
Email   reception@abbeyhotelbath.co.uk
Web   www.abbeyhotelbath.co.uk

Entry 1 Map 1

Bath & N.E. Somerset

The Power House

On top of Bath's highest hill lies Rikki's Bauhaus-inspired home, its glass walls making the most of a magical spot and a sensational view; on a clear day you can see the Welsh hills. In the vast open-plan living space – homely, inviting, inspiring – are treasures from a lifetime of travels: ancient Tuareg camel sacks, kitsch Art Deco pots, gorgeous Persian chests. Bedrooms in the house are airy, with doors onto a huge balcony; the snug, colourful studio room has a wood-burner and little kitchen. Rikki is an incredible chef and uses the finest ingredients from Bath's farmers' market, ten minutes away. Breakfasts are superb – good coffee too. *Self-catering available in the studio. Exceptional walks with fields, woods, streams, in short – a dog paradise.*

Rooms	1 double: £100-£120.
	1 single: £70.
	1 studio for 2: £100-£120.
Meals	Dinner £25.
	Pubs/restaurants 3-minute drive.
Closed	Rarely.

Advice on walks, a Bonio and a pat on the back.

Rikki Howard
The Power House,
Brockham End, Lansdown,
Bath, BA1 9BY
Tel   +44 (0)1225 446308
Email   rikkijacout@aol.com

Entry 2 Map 1

Cover Star Competition

Some of our favourite handsome hounds

Harry (left) and Monty love holidays where they can explore the fields and footpaths or swim in the lakes or sea!

I'm Flow a working dog who loves places with sheep.

Georgie enjoys chasing birds around her owner's barn.

The Oakley Court

Now privately owned, this splendidly-intact Victorian house (with 70s wings mercifully ivy-covered) is hurling off its corporate shackles and turning itself into the friendliest of places. An enthusiastic and dedicated young team of people make sure you feel happy wherever you wander with your nurturing glass of bubbly: choose from the lively bar, elegant drawing and sitting rooms (with blazing fire on chilly days), a library full of interesting first editions, or sweeping lawn with deckchairs overlooking the Thames. Children will be charmed with their own dressing gowns and cookies with milk at bedtime; bustling butlers care for you. Pristine bedrooms (next for makeovers) will not raise any designer eyebrows (patterned carpets, reproduction furniture) but there are imaginative books, suggested walks/rides/runs and White Company goodies in immaculate bathrooms. Borrow a bike or wellies, hire a boat and grab a picnic, eat in Bray or just stay put and be thoroughly spoiled – fine food, honey from their own bees, homegrown veg. Ask about the horror film connections! *All rooms can sleep 1 child under 10. Interconnecting rooms available for families. 33 acres of river-facing grounds with a nature trail. Nearby parks include Virgina Water Lake, the Great Park, Home Park and Savill Garden.*

Rooms	81 doubles, 28 twins, 9 suites for 2: £145-£400. Dogs £20 per dog per stay. Max. 1 (2 small dogs can be allowed at manager discretion).
Meals	Dinner, 3 courses, £38. Tasting menu, 7 courses, £65.
Closed	Never.
	Blankets, dog treats, toys, bed and donation to Battersea Dogs Home.

Rachel Pearce
The Oakley Court,
Windsor Road, Water Oakley,
Windsor, SL4 5UR
Tel   +44 (0)1753 609988
Email   rachel.pearce@oakleycourt.co.uk
Web   www.oakleycourt.co.uk
Entry 3 Map 3

Red Lion Inn

In pretty, peaceful Hinxton, close to Cambridge, the rambling Red Lion is a popular stopover in an area deprived of good inns. And its secluded garden, replete with dovecote, arbour and patio, overlooks the church: a lovely spot for peaceful summer sipping. Another draw is the buzzy atmosphere Alex has instilled in the beamed bar with its deep green chesterfields, worn wooden boards, cosy log fire and ticking clock. Ales from City of Cambridge, Adnams and Woodforde's add to the appeal, as do eclectic menus that list a range of classic pub dishes and more inventive specials, all at good prices. Pop in for a beef and horseradish sandwich or linger over venison with blackberry jus or wild mushroom fettuccine; tuck into delicious roast Norfolk chicken on Sunday. Puddings are to die for: sticky toffee pudding with caramel sauce, lemon tart with mango coulis. Named after local beers and ciders, new-build rooms are comfortable and smart with a fresh, contemporary feel – lightwood furniture, wooden floors, crisp cotton on top-quality beds, fully tiled bathrooms. Breakfasts are a serious treat. *Garden. Field and recreation ground walk 5 minutes away.*

Rooms	3 doubles, 5 twin/doubles: £120–£140. Singles £95. Extra bed/sofabed available £30 per person per night. Dogs £10 per dog per night. Max. 2.
Meals	Lunch & dinner £11–£25. Bar meals £4.50–£10.50. Sunday lunch £12.
Closed	Rarely.
	Water and walks.

Alex Clarke
Red Lion Inn,
32 High Street, Hinxton,
Saffron Walden, CB10 1QY
Tel   +44 (0)1799 530601
Email   info@redlionhinxton.co.uk
Web   www.redlionhinxton.co.uk

Entry 4 Map 4

The Black Bull Inn

Buoyed by the success of the Red Lion at Hinxton, Alex has snapped up the 16th-century Black Bull in nearby Balsham. Unloved for years, it is back on track as a pretty thatched pub. The beamed and timbered bar is spruced up, a new bar servery has been added, wooden floors gleam and there's a smart mix of old dining tables and leather sofas fronting the glowing log fire; so cosy up with a pint of Rusty Bucket on a winter evening. The ancient, high-raftered and adjoining barn has been restored and refurbished to perfection and is the place to sit and savour some cracking pub food; try the lamb shank with roasted garlic mash and rosemary jus, or the smoked haddock with tarragon foam. In the bar, tuck into roast beef and horseradish sandwiches or a plate of Suffolk ham, plus eggs and hand-cut chips. Comfortable rooms in the annexe, some overlooking the car park, sport oak floors and handmade furniture, and huge duvets on king-size beds. Tiled bathrooms come with bath and shower. A peaceful backwater bolthole, handy for the A11/M11, and Cambridge and the Newmarket Races. *Big garden. River and field walk 5-minute walk from pub.*

Rooms	5 twin/doubles: £115–£135. Singles £95. Extra bed/sofabed available £30 per person per night. Dogs £10 per night. Max. 2.
Meals	Lunch & dinner from £12. Bar meals from £6. Sunday lunch £13.
Closed	Rarely.
	Water and walks.

Alex Clarke
The Black Bull Inn,
27 High Street, Balsham,
Cambridge, CB21 4DJ
Tel   +44 (0)1223 893844
Email   info@blackbull-balsham.co.uk
Web   www.blackbull-balsham.co.uk

Entry 5 Map 4

The Pheasant Inn

Pheasants scatter across the fields and the views, on a clear day, stretch to Liverpool. Gloriously positioned on a former farm in the Peckforton Hills, the Pheasant has been stylishly revamped. The old laid-back feel has survived the smartening up of dark beams in bustling bars where pots of jasmine scent the air and Weetwood Old Dog comes from the cask; for sheer cosiness, book a table by a fire (there are three). The food is more refined than your average pub grub, and is informally and delightfully served. Our lamb rump with broad beans, radish and apricots was full of flavour, our salmon with pancetta came with a creamy chive butter, and the sticky toffee pudding was pleasingly light. Deli boards and all-day hot beef sandwiches are also on the cards: just the job after hiking the Sandstone Trail. The staff are the best and if you stay the night – why wouldn't you! – the 12 bedrooms, some traditional (soft carpeting, sumptuous drapes, dark oak furniture), some contemporary (wide oak boards, exposed stone walls, atmospheric lighting) are split between the inn, the stone barn and the 'stables'; go for one with a view. *The inn is on the 34-mile Sandstone Trail. Dog-friendly dining areas.*

Rooms	8 twin/doubles: £95–£124.
	3 suites for 2: £105–£140.
	1 family room for 4: £135–£170.
	Singles from £85.
Meals	Lunch & dinner £6.75–£19.95.
	Bar meals £3.95–£8.50.
	Sunday lunch £12.50.
Closed	Open all day.
	Dog treats and advice on walks.

Andrew Nelson
The Pheasant Inn,
Higher Burwardsley, Tattenhall,
Chester, CH3 9PF
Tel   +44 (0)1829 770434
Email   info@thepheasantinn.co.uk
Web   www.thepheasantinn.co.uk

Entry 6 Map 6

The Cholmondeley Arms

As prim and proper as a Victorian schoolmistress on the outside, as stylish as Beau Brummell within: the sandblasted brick walls of this old school house rise to raftered, vaulted ceilings and large windows pull natural light into every corner. Shelves of gin hover above fat radiators, cartoons and photos nestle amongst old sporting paraphernalia, and oriental rugs sprawl beneath an auction lot of tables, pews and chairs. The glorious carved oak bar dominates the main hall and apart from the malted charms of Cholmondeley Best Bitter and Merlin's Gold there are a staggering 200 varieties of ruinously good gin to discover, with the aid of a well-thumbed guide or one of the many charming staff. And when the dinner bell goes study the menus on antique blackboards and opt for devilled lamb's kidneys on toast, followed by baked cod with brown shrimps and lemon butter, or a spicy sausage and butternut squash hash cake. Rooms in the old headmaster's house behind are calm and civilised with all the comfort you need. Seldom has going back to school been this much fun. *Land where a dog can exercise chasing a tennis ball. Many walks nearby: the Sandstone Trail, Cholmondeley Castle Gardens, Beeston Castle.*

Rooms	5 doubles, 1 twin: £60–£100.
	Dogs £10 per stay. Max. 2 per room.
Meals	Lunch & dinner £7.25–£17.95.
	Not Christmas Day.
Closed	Rarely.

Biscuits on the bar, water bowls, Doggie Beer and good walks. Dogs' dinner menu and dog basket as well for dogs staying in rooms.

Jess Turner
The Cholmondeley Arms,
Wrenbury Road, Cholmondeley,
Malpas, SY14 8HN

Tel   +44 (0)1829 720300
Email   info@cholmondeleyarms.co.uk
Web   www.cholmondeleyarms.co.uk

Entry 7 Map 6

The Bear's Paw

Tucked into a pretty village is a dazzlingly refurbished 19th-century inn. There's an almost baronial feel to the Bear's Paw, thanks to the polished oak panelling, the huge fireplaces, the sweeping floors, the leather bucket chairs, bookshelves and old prints and vintage photos. No stuffiness here, just cheery staff making sure you are well-watered and well-fed. Six cask ales, several from Weetwood, all local, take centre stage on the bar; there are also premium brand spirits, 12 malts and an excellent wine list. At well-spaced wooden tables are menus that blend classics with modern twists. Try game and root vegetable pie served with hand-cut chips and pickled red cabbage; vegetarian lasagne with wild mushrooms, spinach and toasted pine nuts; posh poached egg with truffle sabayon. There are deli boards and fabulous sandwiches too. Staying the night? You have 17 superb bedrooms to choose from, each boutiquey, each flaunting funky fabrics, contemporary wallpapers, media hubs and designer fittings. Bathrooms are sleek with granite tops, rain showers, and the softest towels and robes. *Dog-friendly dining areas.*

Rooms	10 doubles, 7 twin/doubles: £80–£170.
Meals	Lunch & dinner £5.95–£19.95.
Closed	Never.
	Dog treats and advice on walks.

Andrew Nelson
The Bear's Paw,
School Lane, Warmingham,
Sandbach, CW11 3QN
Tel   +44 (0)1270 526317
Email   info@thebearspaw.co.uk
Web   www.thebearspaw.co.uk

Entry 8 Map 6

The Look Out & Sheep to Shore Shepherd's Hut

You'll linger along the scenic route to this spot, a stone skim away from one of Cornwall's dog-friendly bays. Your greeting will be a warm one, perhaps by a pet donkey or curious Highland cow, as well as by bright and breezy owners. This is the perfect coastal hideout: barbecue, decking, and bright blue picnic table all await relaxed al fresco dinners after a day's surfing. Inside it couldn't be sweeter with a well-stocked wood-burner surrounded by sofas in an all-in-one living and dining space; the pine kitchen fits neatly along one wall, and there are quirky nautical touches to catch the eye. The seaside theme continues upstairs, the master double is a delight: a telescope will please stargazers, the remote lighting and sound system adding to the romance. The cutesy Shepherd's Hut is cosy, warm and perfect for two plus a waggy-friend; and best of all you're on the coastal path. Head out to see what's on the horizon: there are 20 acres of private land around you, Bude and Padstow are close and great walks start from the door. With all of this, you'll be as happy as a clam. *Minimum stay for The Shepherd's Hut: 2 nights. Short breaks available at The Look Out. Own beach, on SW Coastal Path, secure field, sun terrace & garden. Dogs to be kept on lead around farm animals.*

Rooms	1 cottage for 4 (1 double, 1 twin/double): £695–£1,250 per week. 1 shepherd's hut for 2 (1 double): £775 per week. £15 per dog per stay. Max. 2 large or 4 small in The Look Out; 1 large or 2 small in Sheep to Shore.
Meals	Self-catering.
Closed	Never.

 A Welcome Pack including dog sitting, a dog's own hot/cold outdoor shower, blankets/throws, towels and dog beach guide.

Jane Montague
The Look Out & Sheep to Shore Shepherd's Hut,
Wanson Mouth,
Bude, EX23 0DF

Mobile	+44 (0)7880 798111
Email	thelookoutincornwall@gmail.com
Web	www.thelookoutincornwall.co.uk

Entry 9 Map 1

The Mill House Inn

Coast down the steep winding lane to a 1760s mill house in a woodland setting. Trebarwith's spectacular beach – all surf and sand – is a ten-minute walk away. It's quite a spot. Back at the inn, the bar combines the best of Cornish old and Cornish new: big flagged floor, wooden tables, chapel chairs, two leather sofas by a wood-burning stove. The swanky dining room overlooking the burbling mill stream is light, elegant and very modern. Settle down to some rather good food: fish chowder; rib-eye steak with wild mushroom and pink peppercorn fricassée; rose, jasmine and orchid panna cotta. Bar meals are more traditional, they do great barbecues in summer and (be warned) a band often plays at the weekend. In keeping with the seaside setting, bedrooms are simple and uncluttered, with good shower rooms in the smaller standard rooms. Note that room character and comfort have been raised following some essential upgrading. Coastal trails lead to Tintagel, official home of the Arthurian legends, there's biking, surfing, crabbing... you couldn't possibly be bored. *Dogs to be kept on a lead please.*

Rooms	7 doubles,
	1 family room for 4: £75–£130.
	Singles £56–£97.
	Dinner, B&B £60–£90 per person.
	Extra bed/sofabed available £20 per person per night.
	Dogs £7.50 per night.
Meals	Lunch from £7.50. Dinner from £12.
	Sunday lunch, 3 courses, £17.85.
Closed	Rarely.

Guidance on local walks. Doc Martin's dog Dodger stays here!

Mark & Kep Forbes
The Mill House Inn,
Trebarwith,
Tintagel, PL34 0HD

Tel	+44 (0)1840 770200
Email	management@themillhouseinn.co.uk
Web	www.themillhouseinn.co.uk

Entry 10 Map 1

Mynford Cottage

At the end of the farm track find this: sweeping wood floors and fresh white walls, and the keel of an old rowing boat perched on the beams. Your one-storey cottage is as fresh as a daisy and everything sparkles: turquoise window frames, red and white striped blinds, chic log-burner, big sofas, an oak table with high-backed chairs, a bowl of fruit. The look is coastal chic and there's a great sense of space. The open-plan living area stretches to the kitchen, equally crisp with its white units, wooden surfaces, pretty blue tiles and mod cons; carry on and you come to a bathroom with a shower for two and locally made soaps, then the all-white bedroom with views to Friesian-flecked fields. Steep steps lead to a mezzanine landing (unsuitable for toddlers but super for little pirates – it makes the perfect crow's nest), and a twin with velux windows for spying from and balustrades to peep through. Outside are a south-facing furnished patio with views to the fields and a barbecue. Amanda and her family live next door, love this part of Cornwall, and are happy to point you in all the right directions. *Minimum stay: 7 nights in high season. Lovely coastal walks. Keep dogs in kitchen and utility rooms, not on sofas or beds.*

Rooms	1 cottage for 4
	(1 twin/double – en suite, 1 twin):
	£687–£1,419 per week.
	Dogs £30 per dog per week. Max. 2.
Meals	Self-catering.
Closed	Never.
	Advice on walks.

Amanda Woodward
Mynford Cottage,
Moyles Farm, St Minver,
Polzeath, PL27 6QT
Tel   +44 (0)1208 862331
Email   mail@moylesfarm.co.uk
Web   www.moylesfarm.co.uk

Entry 11 Map 1

The Seafood Restaurant

In 1975 a young chef called Rick Stein opened a restaurant in Padstow. These days he has four more as well as a deli, a pâtisserie, a seafood cookery school and 40 beautiful bedrooms. Despite this success, his homespun philosophy has never wavered: buy the freshest seafood from fisherman on the quay, then cook it simply and eat it with friends. It is a viewpoint half the country seems to share – the Seafood Restaurant is now a place of pilgrimage – so come to discover the Cornish coast, walk on the cliffs, paddle in the estuary, then drop into this lively restaurant for a fabulous meal, perhaps hot shellfish with garlic and lemon juice, Dover sole with sea salt and lime, apple and quince tartlet with vanilla ice cream. Book in for the night and a table in the restaurant is yours, though flawless bedrooms are so seductive you may find them hard to leave. They are scattered about town, some above the restaurant, others at the bistro or just around the corner. All are immaculate. Expect the best fabrics, stunning bathrooms, the odd terrace with estuary views. *Minimum stay: 2 nights at weekends. Walks along Camel Trail by Camel estuary, or across harbour and on to beautiful North Cornwall coast paths.*

Rooms	32 doubles, 8 twin/doubles: £110–£330. Dogs £20 for 1st night, £5 thereafter, per dog. Max. as many as can comfortably fit.
Meals	Lunch £38.50. Dinner £58.50.
Closed	25–26 December.
	Fleecy Chalky's pal blanket, guide to dog walks in Cornwall, personal dog bowls, and 100% natural dog treats from Green & Wilds with selected breaks.

Jill & Rick Stein
The Seafood Restaurant,
Riverside,
Padstow, PL28 8BY

Tel	+44 (0)1841 532700
Email	reservations@rickstein.com
Web	www.rickstein.com

Entry 12 Map 1

Bedruthan Hotel & Spa

A family friendly hotel that delights adults and children alike. It has beautiful interiors, delicious food, sea views and an inexhaustible supply of distractions. There's a football pitch, a surf school, a zip wire, then a cool spa with a couple of pools. If you can think of it, it's probably here, and younger children can be supervised by lovely, qualified staff. There's lots for adults, too, who get the run of the place during school time: a sitting room that hogs the view, a wood-burner to keep things cosy, a terrace in good weather for sea views. There are three restaurants (one for children's parties). Younger children have early suppers, adults return later for a slap-up meal, perhaps hand-picked crab, chargrilled steak, hazelnut tart with pistachio ice cream. There's a beach below, but you may spurn it for the indoor pool or a game of tennis. Lovely bedrooms have warm retro colours, blond wood, sparkling bathrooms, then separate rooms for children. Some open onto private terraces, lots have sea views, a few overlook the car park. Impeccable eco credentials and fantastic staff, too. *Easy access to the coast path; Mawgan Porth beach below allows dogs year round and has a shallow river.*

Rooms	38 twin/doubles: £135–£270.
	27 suites for 4: £205–£490.
	30 family rooms for 4: £175–£305.
	6 singles: £75–£125.
	Dinner, B&B from £95 per person.
	Dogs £12. Max. depends on breed and size.
Meals	Lunch from £7. Dinner £30–£35.
	Sunday lunch from £15.
Closed	Christmas & 3 weeks in January.
	Biscuits, bedding and bowls.

Janie White
Bedruthan Hotel & Spa,
Mawgan Porth,
Newquay, TR8 4BU

Tel	+44 (0)1637 860860
Email	stay@bedruthan.com
Web	www.bedruthan.com

Entry 13 Map 1

The Scarlet

A super-cool design hotel which overlooks the sea; a vast wall of glass in reception frames the view perfectly. The Scarlet does nothing by halves – this is a serious contender for Britain's funkiest bolthole – but it also offers a guilt-free destination as it's green to its core. Cutting-edge technology includes a biomass boiler, solar panels and state-of-the-art insulation. You'll find a couple of indoor swimming pools to ensure against the weather, then hot tubs in a garden from which you can stargaze at night. There's a cool bar, a pool table in the library, a restaurant that opens onto a decked terrace, where you eat fabulous Cornish food while gazing out to sea. Exceptional bedrooms come with huge views: all have balconies or terraces, private gardens or viewing pods. Expect oak floors from sustainable forests, organic cotton, perhaps a freestanding bath in your room. Some are enormous, one has a dual-aspect balcony, another comes with a rooftop lounge. If that's not enough, there's an ayurvedic-inspired spa, where tented treatment rooms are lit by lanterns. Amazing. *Minimum stay: 2 nights at weekends. Easy access to South West Coast Path. Mawgan Porth beach, just below, open to dogs all year round; a small shallow stream runs down one side.*

Rooms	21 doubles, 8 twin/doubles: £195-£405. 8 suites for 2: £270-£460. Dogs £15. Max. depends on breed and size (check with hotel).
Meals	Lunch, 3 courses, £22.50. Dinner, 3 courses, £42.50.
Closed	4 January to 12 February.
	Bowls, water, biscuits and an information leaflet about dogs at the hotel.

Meeche Hood
The Scarlet,
Tredragon Road,
Mawgan Porth, TR8 4DQ
Tel   +44 (0)1637 861800
Email   stay@scarlethotel.co.uk
Web   www.scarlethotel.co.uk

Entry 14 Map 1

5 & 6 Porth Farm Cottages

The beach is a five-minute stroll, the cliff path crosses National Trust coastline, the quiet village has a surf school, shop and fish 'n' chips: all the ingredients for a terrific seaside holiday. The cottages are part of a horseshoe of stone barns with communal gardens, art hut, swings and zip wire, all tucked into a hillside with views over the Vale of Lanherne and out to sea. The conversions are impressive, with underfloor heating, elm floorboards and wonderful woodwork. No. 5's staircase spirals up to a gallery landing, comfy bedrooms and a large slate-tiled bathroom. Soak in a roll top bath; blast away sand under a huge shower head. Downstairs: cosy up by the fire in an open-plan living room; the kitchen and dining table catch the morning sun. Outside: sit with a sunset drink and gaze up at the 'living roof' of flowers. It's a short drive to the Eden Project or St Ives, but mostly you can leave the car behind. The coastal path stretches to Newquay, Watergate Bay and Padstow (good bus service, too), there are farm shops and horse riding, and you can head down the valley to St Mawgan's convent and a gastropub lunch. *Minimum stay: 3 nights, 7 nights in high season. Short breaks available.*

Rooms	1 cottage for 4 (1 double, 1 twin; 1 bathroom), 1 cottage for 6 (1 double, 2 singles, 1 bunkroom; 1 bathroom, 2 shower rooms): £400–£1,200 per week. Dogs £20 per stay. Max. 2.
Meals	Self-catering.
Closed	Rarely.

Underfloor heating, advice on walks and dog poop bags by the door.

Carol & Peter Misch
5 & 6 Porth Farm Cottages,
Mawgan Porth,
Newquay,

Mobile	+44 (0)7812 574131
Email	enquiries@5and6porthfarmcottages.com
Web	www.5and6porthfarmcottages.com

Entry 15 Map 1

Watergate Bay Hotel

Watergate Bay is one of those lovely Cornish landscapes where nature rules the roost, a world of sand, sea and sky and nothing but. The few buildings that have taken root here don't qualify as a village and have no name, they're just chattels of the beach, a sandy beach that runs for a mile and is one of the best in Cornwall. The hotel sits directly above it, making the most of the view, with walls of glass in the café/bar, a smart terrace strewn with sun loungers, a swimming pool that looks out to sea. Outside, the hotel's surf school will kit you out to ride the waves and you can kite surf and paddle board, too, while beach polo and music festivals come in summer. As for the hotel, it mixes cool design with an informal vibe. Coastal light floods the café, there's a cute sitting room with an open fire, then a cool pool with treatment rooms and a hot tub. Airy bedrooms – some with sea views, others with balconies – have seaside colours and fancy bathrooms. As for the food, you can eat in the café or the grill, or walk 50 paces to the Beach Hut for a burger, or head for Jamie Oliver's Fifteen. *A year round dog-friendly beach, and 2 dog-friendly public areas/restaurants.*

Rooms	47 twin/doubles: £145-£345. 2 suites for 2, 20 suites for 4: £230-£405. Singles £109-£259. Extra bed/sofabed available. Dogs £15. Max. 2.
Meals	Lunch from £5.75. Dinner, 3 courses, about £35.
Closed	Never.
🐕	Runs on the beach all year round, and advice on other dog-friendly beach walks.

Mark Williams
Watergate Bay Hotel,
On the Beach,
Watergate Bay, TR8 4AA

Tel	+44 (0)1637 860543
Email	reservations@watergatebay.co.uk
Web	www.watergatebay.co.uk

Entry 16 Map 1

The Gurnard's Head

The coastline here is utterly magical and the walk to St Ives is full of surprises. Secret beaches appear at low tide, cliffs tumble down to the water and wild flowers streak the land pink in summer. As for this inn, you couldn't hope for a better base. It's earthy, warm, stylish and friendly, with airy interiors, colour-washed walls, stripped wooden floors and fires at both ends of the bar. Logs are piled up in an alcove, maps and art hang on the walls, books fill every shelf; if you pick one up and don't finish it, take it home and post it back. Rooms are warm, cosy and spotless, with Vi-Spring mattresses, crisp white linen, throws over armchairs, Roberts radios. Downstairs, super food, all homemade, can be eaten wherever you want: in the bar, in the restaurant or out in the garden in good weather. Snack on rustic delights – pork pies, crab claws, half a pint of Atlantic prawns – or tuck into more substantial treats, maybe salt and pepper squid, braised shoulder of lamb, pineapple tarte tatin. Picnics are easily arranged, there's bluegrass folk music in the bar most weeks. Dogs are very welcome. *Large back garden. Beautiful coastal path, and a sandy beach as well if you time the tides right.*

Rooms	3 doubles,
	4 twin/doubles: £110–£175.
	Dinner, B&B £80 per person.
Meals	Lunch from £12.
	Dinner, 3 courses, £25–£35.
	Sunday lunch from £13.
Closed	Christmas.

🐕 Doggie biscuits, blanket, towels, advice on walks, black bags and dog bowls. Very friendly staff too.

Charles & Edmund Inkin
The Gurnard's Head,
Zennor,
St Ives, TR26 3DE
Tel   +44 (0)1736 796928
Email   enquiries@gurnardshead.co.uk
Web   www.gurnardshead.co.uk

Entry 17 Map 1

Wheal Rose

Just above the sandy cove of Portheras, on Britain's most scenic coast, a tiny lane leads down to a beautifully refurbished, detached farmhouse with stunning views. The old part of the cottage has all the charm you would expect: a cosy but surprisingly spacious sitting room with painted beams in muted colours, a log-burner and Cornish art in alcoves and on walls and window sills. This is a great cottage for family get-togethers as there is plenty for everyone to do: take the 15-minute walk down to the cove for a bracing early morning dip, or idle away an afternoon watching the seals. If you fancy spoiling yourself with a Cornish cream tea, take a gentle stroll across the fields to The Old School House and Gallery at Morvah. Or stride out along wild stretches of coastal path through historic mining landscapes dotted with ancient field systems towards Zennor and St Ives. As the sun begins to sink in the sky, light the barbecue, pour a glass of your favourite tipple, and watch the sun's descent into the Atlantic Ocean and the comforting presence of the Lighthouse at Pendeen Watch. *Short breaks available. Pets are welcome downstairs. Secure garden, beautiful year round dog-friendly beach and very close to Cornish Coastal Path.*

Rooms	1 cottage for 7 (1 double, 1 twin/double, 1 twin, 1 single; 1 bath/shower room, 1 shower room, separate wc): £615–£1,570 per week. Dogs £20 per dog per week. Max. 2.
Meals	Self-catering.
Closed	Rarely.
	Towels for drying and advice on walks and dog-friendly beaches.

Nicky Gregorowski
Wheal Rose,
Higher Chypraze, Morvah, Pendeen,
Penzance, TR19 7TU

Tel	+44 (0)1386 881454
Email	gregorowski@hotmail.com
Web	www.whealrose.co.uk

Balleswidden Cabin

Walk up the path to Balleswidden Cabin and you will feel like you've discovered an uninhabited island. Outside, the cabin looks like a funky shack but inside, it surprises you at every turn with stylish luxury. Originally built as a writer's lodge, it's stocked with books which you're welcome to swap, and a big, red leather chesterfield to curl up on. Laze on the deck and enjoy the sunset with a glass of something chilled. Up a ladder, tucked under the eaves is a mezzanine bedroom perfect for two to snuggle into (but not stand up in!). The bathroom is minty and relaxing with a full-size claw-foot tub. Through here, there's a small single room for a child. The cabin traps the light all day long, flooding the high-ceilinged living area. Set in a private garden, there is a timeless quality to this place, so peaceful you can almost hear the greenery growing. From the deck, you have uninterrupted views over the wild moors and down to the Longships off Land's End. Wild and wonderful is the only way to describe this part of Cornwall, known for its ruined tin mines, ancient wells and standing stones, enchanting fishing villages and dramatic coastline of high cliffs and long, golden beaches... there's so much to do, from surfing to seafood. *Free-range chickens – keep dogs on lead!*

Rooms	Cabin for 3: (1 double, 1 2ft child's bed): from £102 per night. Max. 1 dog.
Meals	Self-catering.
Closed	Never.

🚶 Dog towels, homemade biscuits and a list of dog-friendly activities.

Canopy & Stars
Balleswidden Cabin,
The Count House, Balleswidden,
St Just, Penzance TR19 7RY

Tel	+44 (0)117 204 7830
Email	enquiries@canopyandstars.co.uk
Web	www.canopyandstars.co.uk/balleswiddencabin

Entry 19 Map 1

Sennen Summerhouse

The Sennen Summerhouse doesn't need ostentation. The glass walls let in light and the dramatic Atlantic views negate the need for interior design. Though the main house is nearby, the facing wall is covered to give privacy and you can set the deckchairs up in your private piece of garden and bask uninterrupted, watching the sun set over the sea. Inside the summerhouse you'll find the sofabed, a big armchair, lamps, lanterns, gas hobs in the kitchen corner and… not much else. While there's no power, you can charge devices in the house, where you'll also find the shower and bath. There is a compost loo in a lean-to attached to the hut. The cabin was created entirely from recycled materials and is the perfect place to give yourself a new lease of life as you indulge in breezy coastal walks (access the path without driving anywhere), beach day trips, maybe a little surfing and everything else that Cornwall has to offer. Kind owner Naomi will happily lend you water sport equipment, you can visit St Ives, Penzance and Mousehole, but this is a peaceful place, you may just want to stay and rest. *Amazing cliff walks and dog-friendly beaches within easy walking distance; fields all around.*

Rooms	Cabin for 2 (1 fold-out double): from £60 per night. Max. 1 dog (well-behaved!).
Meals	Self-catering.
Closed	November – March.
	Lots of advice for dog-friendly days out.

Canopy & Stars
Sennen Summerhouse,
Mayon Vean, Marias Lane, Sennen,
Penzance, TR19 7BX

Tel	+44 (0)117 204 7830
Email	enquiries@canopyandstars.co.uk
Web	www.canopyandstars.co.uk/sennensummerhouse

Entry 20 Map 1

The Old Coastguard

The Old Coastguard stands bang on the water in one of Cornwall's loveliest coastal villages. It's a super spot and rather peaceful – little has happened here since 1595, when the Spanish sacked the place. Recently, the hotel fell into the benign hands of Edmund and Charles, past masters at reinvigorating lovely small hotels; warm colours, attractive prices, great food and a happy vibe are their hallmarks. Downstairs, the airy bar and the dining room come together as one, the informality of open plan creating a great space to hang out. There are smart rustic tables, earthy colours, local ales and local art, then a crackling fire in the restaurant. Drop down a few steps to find a bank of sofas and a wall of glass framing sea views; in summer, doors open onto a decked terrace, a lush lawn, then the coastal path weaving down to the small harbour. Bedrooms are lovely: sand-coloured walls, excellent beds, robes in fine bathrooms, books everywhere. Most have the view, eight have balconies. Don't miss dinner: crab rarebit, fish stew, chocolate fondant and marmalade ice cream. Dogs are very welcome. *Secure garden with sea views. Pebbled beach a stone's throw away and plenty of walks nearby.*

Rooms	10 doubles, 3 twin/doubles: £130–£220. 1 suite for 2: £185–£235. 1 family room for 4: £170–£200. Dinner, B&B from £90 per person.
Meals	Lunch from £6. Dinner, 3 courses, about £30. Sunday lunch from £12.50.
Closed	1 week in early January.
	Doggie biscuits, blanket, towels, advice on walks, black bags and dog bowls. Very friendly staff too.

Charles & Edmund Inkin
The Old Coastguard,
The Parade, Mousehole,
Penzance, TR19 6PR

Tel	+44 (0)1736 731222
Email	bookings@oldcoastguardhotel.co.uk
Web	www.oldcoastguardhotel.co.uk

Entry 21 Map 1

Halzephron Cabin

Up the hill from the village, behind Lucy and Roger's landmark B&B (you won't miss the white crenellations) and across the walled garden, you'll find your snug, seaside hideaway. An unassuming white shack on the outside, the compact interior has been given a full, contemporary makeover. There's a romantic wood-burner for the cooler evenings as well as electric radiators throughout, and a mini kitchen with oak breakfast bar and views of the bay – when it's too dark to admire them you can just turn to the flat screen TV. The bathroom has a beautiful double-ended bath and a nautical porthole window that reminds you of your coastal surroundings, although with the faint sound of the waves lapping below as you drift off, you probably won't have forgotten. French windows open onto the lawn, and if you go for a little wander you'll find the secret garden overlooking the cove below. From here you can see all the way to St Michael's Mount on a clear day! For more sea and golden sand, Halzephron is a perfect launch pad for miles of secluded beaches and a selection of local fishing villages that offer delicious, fresh seafood. *Secure walled garden. Right on coastal path, by the beach; 2 all year dog-friendly beaches (Dollar Cove and Gunwalloe fishing cove) within 5 minutes.*

Rooms	Cabin for 2 (1 double): from £100 per night. Max. 1 dog.
Meals	Self-catering.
Closed	Never.
	Advice on walks, river to swim in, dog-friendly beaches, and lovely dog-friendly pub 5-minute walk.

Canopy & Stars
Halzephron Cabin,
Gunwalloe, Helston, TR12 7QD

Tel   +44 (0)117 204 7830
Email   enquiries@canopyandstars.co.uk
Web   www.canopyandstars.co.uk/ halzephroncabin

Entry 22 Map 1

Trelowarren

'A jewel in the palm of your hand', wrote Daphne du Maurier of Trelowarren. It remains one of Cornwall's finest estates. The entrance drive brings you in past a long row of evergreen Holm oaks that emerge from an ancient Cornish 'hedge'. The main house, 500 years old, belongs to the Vyvyan family and is at the heart of this vast project. There's a gorgeous swimming pool, a spa treatment centre, the courtyard restaurant and a pop-up pizza house in the old stables; the whole place is yours to explore. These old estate houses have been handsomely restored to be as modern as possible inside, and they are just around the corner from the courtyard and the newly-converted restaurant. (Here you might linger all day, so exquisite and cosy is it.) The estate is a wonderful place for families – deep in the great outdoors yet so close to much else. The lush south coast is nearby, the Helford River too; the Lizard wraps around Trelowarren, and Penzance is a short drive away. Neither adults nor children can fail to enjoy themselves here; it is a paradise for those who love Cornwall. *Minimum stay: 2 nights on weekdays, 3 nights at weekends, 7 nights in high season. Short breaks available. 1,000 acres of woodland walks.*

Rooms	1 cottage for 4, 6 cottages for 6, 1 cottage for 8, all with a sofabed available: £595-£2,595 per week. Max. 2 dogs.
Meals	Restaurant on site. Lunch from £6.95. Dinner, 3 courses, from £22.95. Wine from £15.50.
Closed	Never.

 Dog-friendly beach map – there are lots of beaches and walks all year round.

Kerenza Cooksey
Trelowarren,
Mawgan,
Helston, TR12 6AF

Tel   +44 (0)1326 221224
Email   info@trelowarren.com
Web   www.trelowarren.com

Entry 23 Map 1

Round House East

Standing like sentries guarding the village pub and green below are two whitewashed 1820s roundhouses with thatched roofs and crosses – believed to keep the devil away. Ingenious how everything fits so neatly within the curving walls, from solid wood floors to fitted wardrobes, in this warm, quirky bolthole. Local art and retro touches – a tide clock, a 50s sideboard, sky blue upholstery – rub shoulders with a vast TV (in both sitting room and cosy upstairs bedroom). In the kitchen extension, past the lime green fridge, find a glass dining table and windows to the pretty cottage garden. Take a morning espresso out to your lounger and watch the seagulls swoop. When night falls, soak in the roll top bath, then retire to a super king-sized bed under a vaulted ceiling; Art Deco mirror, quirky lamps and pink-and-purple rug continue the fun retro theme. Bring bicycles, dogs, flip flops for the beach and walking boots for the South West Coast Path; the Roseland Peninsula is awash with secret coves and seaside restaurants. The boat to Truro is voted one of the world's most scenic ferry routes. No wonder guests book again and again. *The nearby beaches are dog-friendly.*

Rooms	1 cottage for 2
	(1 double; 1 bathroom):
	£420-£940 per week.
	Dogs £20 per stay.
	Contact owner if you wish to bring
	more than 2 dogs.
Meals	Self-catering.
Closed	Never.

Little cupboard filled with tug toys.

Ian Rose
Round House East, Pendower Road,
Veryan, Truro, TR2 5QL

Tel	+44 (0)1494 774290
Mobile	+44 (0)7480 198040
Email	iprose@btinternet.com
Web	www.roundhousecornwall.co.uk

Entry 24 Map 1

Coriander Cottages

No shortage of natural entertainment here: a gaggle of waddling ducks, a buzzard hovering overhead, a night-time display by bats, a terrace for a ringside view: for a deep-country setting, these converted farm buildings are surprisingly lively! Both cottages combine ultra-green credentials with rustic luxury. Solar panels and geothermal heat ensure energy is renewable, rainwater is harvested, and natural textiles create harmony. Open-plan living spaces are sleek with limestone flooring, wooden beams and stone walls; there are comfortable leather sofas, rugs, leafy plants and toasty wood-burning stove; super kitchens are well-equipped; bedrooms are cosy and inviting; bathrooms are fabulous with TVs, candles and aromatherapy oils. Balconies and terraces have valley views to Fowey, a gentle mile downhill, and charming owner Colin, who lives next door, will drive you if you're not happily mobile. Beaches, the Coast Path and Saint's Way are close, the Eden Project and Lostwithiel are not much further. Superb. *Pets welcome in White Willow only. Due to local wildlife dogs to be kept on lead within the grounds.*

Rooms	1 cottage for 2
	(1 twin/double; 1 bath & shower room),
	1 cottage for 2
	(1 double; 1 bathroom):
	£450–£780 per week.
	Max. 2 dogs.
Meals	Self-catering.
Closed	Rarely.

Coastal, country lane and riverbank walks.

Colin King
Coriander Cottages,
Penventinue Lane,
Fowey, PL23 1JT

Tel	+44 (0)1726 834998
Email	stay@coriandercottages.co.uk
Web	www.coriandercottages.co.uk

Entry 25 Map 1

Treworgey Farm

The shepherd's huts at Treworgey Farm are a wonderful way to explore a fabulous area of Cornwall. The farm is Holly and Andy's family business, spread over 150 acres overlooking the Looe river valley. It's a lively place, with a riding school on site that runs on weekdays and a few holiday cottages dotted about. The Hideaway Hut sits in its own corner of the farm and The Lambing Hut is on the west with uninterrupted views. Both come with a private shower and loo twenty metres off. From here you can hit the coastal path or ramble down in the woodlands, but you're more than welcome to use the games room, the pool, and the tennis court, which you'll share with the cottages. Tea and cake, light suppers or Cornish cream teas can be delivered to your door. There's a wood-burner in the hut to keep you warm and a gas hob for cooking along with all the basics, but why not hike out to the local (forty minutes uphill on the way out) and try the local sparkling cider and some good pub food. During the day, the beach is only a few minutes by car and the many attractions of Cornwall await. *Babies welcome. Secure private garden. Bluebell woods, open fields and riverside walks from the door. Great dog-friendly pub within walking distance.*

Rooms	2 shepherd's huts for 2 (1 double, space for 2 in tent alongside hut): from £69 per night. Dogs £15 per stay. Max. 1.
Meals	Self-catering.
Closed	December/January.

Throws for furniture, private fenced garden for dog to play in, empty field for running free. Advice and maps for fantastic dog walks, dog-friendly beaches, pubs and days out.

Canopy & Stars
Treworgey Farm,
Duloe, Liskeard, PL14 4PP

Tel   +44 (0)117 204 7830
Email   enquiries@canopyandstars.co.uk
Web   www.canopyandstars.co.uk/
treworgeyfarm

Entry 26 Map 1

Talland Bay Hotel

The position here is magical. First you plunge down rollercoaster lanes, then you arrive at this lovely hotel. Directly in front, the sea sparkles through pine trees, an old church crowns the hill and two acres of lawns end in a ha-ha, then the land drops down to the bay. In summer, sun loungers and croquet hoops appear on the lawn and you can nip down to a beach café for lunch by the water. Back at the hotel there's a conservatory brasserie, a sitting room bar, and a roaring fire in the half-panelled dining room. Masses of art hangs on the walls, there are vast sofas, polished flagstones, a terrace for afternoon tea. Follow the coastal path over the hill, then return for a good dinner, perhaps John Dory and squid, Bodmin lamb with black olives, carrot cake with candied walnuts and cinnamon ice cream. As for the bedrooms, they've been nicely refurbished and pamper you rotten. Expect rich colours, vast beds, beautiful linen, the odd panelled wall. One has a balcony, a couple open onto terraces, all have lovely bathrooms. Gardens, beaches, pretty villages and the coastal path all wait.

Rooms	15 twin/doubles: £100-£240. 4 suites for 2: £180-£260. 3 cottages for 2: £140-£230. Dinner, B&B £95-£155 per person. Dogs £10.
Meals	Lunch from £5.95. Dinner £32-£38.
Closed	Never.
	Biscuits and blanket.

Stephen Waite
Talland Bay Hotel,
Porthallow, Looe PL13 2JB

Tel	+44 (0)1503 272667
Email	info@tallandbayhotel.co.uk
Web	www.tallandbayhotel.co.uk

Entry 27 Map 1

Spring Park

The five gleaming wagons at Spring Park each have an individual charm. There's Duke, a classic 1940s showman's wagon, with bright vibrant paintwork on the outside and interior furnishings to match. Next, Maiden, a restored railway wagon has been paired up with a large modern cabin, Wisteria Cottage. Then there's Pip and Pip's Cabin, a sturdy 1930s steamroller living van with spacious cabin alongside. Next is The Duchess, bright blue and complete with her own wood-fired hot tub to soak in. Finally, Hercules, a large cedar living van, holds an eclectic mix of antique and vintage finds put together by owners Kitty and Paddy. They used to own two vintage boutiques, so this is right up their street! Each wagon has its own kitchen and a fifth of an acre of private garden, perfect for just lying back and daydreaming in the Cornish countryside. If you do want to go adventuring, pack up a picnic and go off for the day, maybe down to the beach for surfing, scaling the Dartmoor peaks or wandering through the local villages and visiting the markets. *Babies welcome. In the Tamar Valley — an area of outstanding natural beauty, with loads of walks and rivers.*

Rooms	3 wagons for 2 (1 double): from £66 per night. 2 wagons for 4 (1 double, 1 sofabed): from £60 per night. Dogs £20 per pet per stay. Max. 2.
Meals	Self-catering.
Closed	Never.

Treats, biodegradable dog bags, towels for drying and advice on the surrounding walks and some of our favourites.

Canopy & Stars
Spring Park,
Rezare, Launceston, PL15 9NX

Tel	+44 (0)117 204 7830
Email	enquiries@canopyandstars.co.uk
Web	www.canopyandstars.co.uk/springpark

Entry 28 Map 1

Okel Tor Mine

It's not often you sleep in a World Heritage Site in an AONB, where flora and fauna – badgers, kingfishers, otters, rare mosses – also mark it as an SSSI. The two cottages – converted buildings of a former Victorian copper and tin mine – sit in a fairytale landscape of ivy-clad chimneys and tree-covered hillsides. Totally hidden, even from each other, with sweeping views over the river Tamar, their small but thoughtful layouts are perfect for a romantic retreat. Open-plan living areas are country-cottage cosy with wood-burning stoves, deep red sofas, rugs on flagstone floors and a table by the window for those views. A simple kitchen and, for wet-weather days, books, games and DVDs. Bedrooms are fresh and unfussy country-pine, with equally neat shower rooms with handmade soaps. Stroll to the village shop and pubs in Calstock, walk along the river to the National Trust's Cotehele House, enjoy walks on the Bere Peninsula or visit Morewell Ham Quay port and copper mine. Within 30 minutes you could be enjoying Dartmoor, Bodmin Moor or Whitsand Bay. Return to your private decking, birdsong, watery views and serenity. *Min. stay: 2 nights, 7 in high season. River to swim in, woodland and heathland walks from doorstep, far from any roads. Short walk from 2 dog-friendly pubs.*

Rooms	2 cottages for 2 (1 double; 1 bathroom): £315-£645 per week. Extra bed/sofabed available at no charge. Dogs £25 per stay. Max. 2 large or 3 small due to cottage size.
Meals	Self-catering.
Closed	Never.

Throws provided, doggy towels available and wonderful road-free walks.

Greg Smith
Okel Tor Mine,
Calstock, PL18 9SQ

Email greg1971@mac.com
Web www.tinmine.com

The Sun Inn

This lovely old inn sits between the Dales and the Lakes in an ancient market town, one of the prettiest in the north. It backs onto St Mary's churchyard, where wild flowers flourish, and on the far side you'll find 'the fairest view in England', to quote John Ruskin. Herons fish the river Lune, lambs graze the fells, a vast sky hangs above. Turner came to paint it in 1825 and benches wait for those who want to gaze upon it. As for the Sun, it does what good inns do – looks after you in style. There's lots of pretty old stuff – stone walls, rosewood panelling, wood-burners working overtime – and it's all kept spic and span, with warm colours, flowers and the daily papers on hand. You find leather banquettes, local art and chairs in the dining room from Cunard's Mauretania, so eat in style, perhaps mussels with cider, saddle of venison, Yorkshire rhubarb and ginger sponge trifle. Bedrooms upstairs are stylishly uncluttered with Cumbrian wool carpets, robes in smart bathrooms and earplugs to ward off the church bells. Car park permits come with your room and can be used far and wide. Brilliant. *Minimum stay: 2 nights at weekends. Fabulous dog-friendly town – lots of bars, shops and cafés accept dogs. Great riverside and woodland walks from the door, river to jump in.*

Rooms	8 doubles, 2 twin/doubles: £110–£183. 1 family room for 4: £170–£203. Dogs £20 for 1 dog, £30 for 2, per stay. Max. 2.
Meals	Bar snacks & lunch from £5.95. Dinner, 4 courses, £32.95. Sunday lunch from £13.95.
Closed	Never.
	Towel, dog bowl, biscuits, walking information and dog shower outside for muddy paws.

Mark & Lucy Fuller
The Sun Inn,
6 Market Street, Kirkby Lonsdale,
Carnforth, LA6 2AU

Tel	+44 (0)15242 71965
Email	email@sun-inn.info
Web	www.sun-inn.info

Entry 30 Map 6

The Burton

Selina's gorgeous showman's wagon dates back to 1940 and was originally pulled by four horses. These days it sits behind the farmhouse with views up Clouds Fell and a fire pit in the garden for starry nights. It's a brilliant feat of interior engineering with a Nordic, chalet feel. You get everything you need wrapped up in oodles of rustic chic: rugs on wooden floors, chairs at a pretty table and a wood-burner to keep you cosy. There are books on shelves, fresh flowers and a welcoming tipple waiting for you as well. A sweet little kitchen bar comes with a microwave and a hob, and a tiny shower room does the trick in style. The bed is fabulous: lovely linen, a good mattress and drawers below. There's a decked terrace at the front, then a drying room, a fridge/freezer and piles of logs in the shed behind, home to the boiler that assures hot showers. Selina is happy to take delivery of supplies before you arrive, but she also manages a lovely local inn, so a slap-up meal is on hand if you don't want to cook. Great walking to be had straight from the door; return to your romantic space, get yourself a cup of tea and be glad you're here. *Surrounded by livestock so advise dogs on leads, but many different walks all within a 4-mile radius: woodland, riverside and fells.*

Rooms	Wagon for 2 (1 double): from £95 per night. Dogs £5 per stay, payable directly to Selina on arrival. Max. 1.
Meals	Self-catering.
Closed	Never.

Wonderful walks from the doorstep up and onto the Cumbrian fells.

Canopy & Stars
The Burton,
Stennerskeugh, Ravenstonedale,
Kirkby Stephen, CA17 4LL
Tel   +44 (0)117 204 7830
Email   enquiries@canopyandstars.co.uk
Web   www.canopyandstars.co.uk/theburton

Entry 31 Map 6

Steele's Mill

There's been a working grain mill here since 1327; this one was built in the 1800s. Fragments of the past remain: staircases and floors of oak grown on the estate, grinding stones set into the floor, and the old apple-wood cogs encased in glass. There's a lovely approach to this stunning conversion, a hugely comfortable retreat for four, with the master bedroom positioned grandly at the top, and below the tiny twin. Cook just-caught brown trout from the river Lyvennet on a shiny black Rangemaster, dine at a handmade oak table furnished with welcoming flowers and a bottle of wine, lounge on a leather sofa by the gas wood-burner, idle with a book on the balcony. By day, venture out on the snaking road past fields of cattle to King's Meaburn village, to Appleby for delis, pubs and a country fair in summer, to Lowther Castle for those seeking gothic revival grandeur. Nature is embraced indoors, too: the mill has a hidden bat loft with an aperture only accessible to the pipistrelle! Colours are cream and duck-egg blue melting into pale oak, mattresses are superb, shower heads drench you and the peace is supreme. *Secure garden, woodland walks and safe rivers.*

Rooms	1 house for 4 (1 double, 1 twin): £540–£820 per week. Dogs 1 free; 2nd £30 per stay. Max. 3.
Meals	Self-catering.
Closed	Never.
	Advice on walks.

Karen Addison
Steele's Mill, King's Meaburn,
Penrith, CA10 3BU

Tel	+44 (0)1931 714017
Mobile	+44 (0)7831 865749
Email	karenaddison@karenaddison.co.uk
Web	www.steelesmill.co.uk

Entry 32 Map 6

George and Dragon

Charles Lowther has found a chef who does perfect justice to the slow-grow breeds of beef, pork and lamb produced on the Lowther Estate – and you'll find lovely wines to match, 16 by the glass. Ales and cheeses are local, berries and mushrooms are foraged, vegetables are home-grown… and his signature starter, twice-baked cheese soufflé with a hint of spinach – is divine. As for the long low coaching inn, it's been beautifully restored by craftsmen using wood, slate and stone, and painted in colours in tune with the period. Bare wooden tables, comfy sofas, intimate alcoves and crackling fires make this a delightful place to dine and unwind; old prints and archive images tell stories of the 800-year-old estate's history. Outside is plenty of seating and a lawned play area beneath fruit trees. Upstairs are 11 bedrooms of varying sizes (some small, some large and some above the bar), perfectly decorated in classic country style. Carpeting is Cumbrian wool, beds are new, ornaments come with Lowther history, showers are walk-in, baths (there are two) are roll top, and breakfast is fresh and delicious. *Dogs welcome in the bar dining area and bedrooms (not the main restaurant).*

Rooms	11 twin/doubles: £95–£155. Singles £79. Dogs £10 per stay. Max. 3.	
Meals	Lunch from £7.95. Dinner from £12.95. Sunday lunch from £12.95.	
Closed	Boxing Day.	
	Doggy welcome pack including treat, map of local walks and doggy bag.	

Charlie Lowther
George and Dragon,
Clifton,
Penrith, CA10 2ER

Tel   +44 (0)1768 865381
Email   enquiries@georgeanddragonclifton.co.uk
Web   www.georgeanddragonclifton.co.uk

The Lodge

Splendidly located on a wide bend of the river Eamont, The Lodge is frontier living at its finest. While the exterior of this timber log cabin blends perfectly into its natural surroundings, the interior comes as a surprise: simple and homely, but beautifully furnished with several stylish touches. From the upstairs 'master' bedroom – with views that make the most of the spot – a wrought-iron spiral staircase drops down into the centre of the well-equipped kitchen/sitting room. Find comfy armchairs around a wood-burner, another double bedroom, and sliding doors that open to a veranda and the hot tub; occasionally deer come to the river bank for a drink. You can catch trout for your supper, then cook up a storm on the four-hob gas oven. Edenhall estate offers plenty of scope for hiking and cycling as well as private stretches of river fantastic for salmon. You can arrange for your supper to be waiting in the oven, book a full hamper before you arrive, or arrange a massage to ease away hiker's pains. You're also on the very edge of the Lake District, great yomping territory for you and your dog. *Babies welcome. The area is very secluded with no traffic. Lots of walks from the door and around the area.*

Rooms	Cabin for 4 (2 doubles): from £171 per night. Dogs £15 per stay. Max. 1.
Meals	Self-catering.
Closed	Never.
🐕	Outdoor bed, blanket, water bowl and dog lead.

Canopy & Stars
The Lodge, Edenhall Estate,
The Courtyard, Edenhall,
Penrith, CA11 8ST
Tel   +44 (0)117 204 7830
Email   enquiries@canopyandstars.co.uk
Web   www.canopyandstars.co.uk/thelodge

Entry 34 Map 6

High Houses

Tucked away at the quieter end of the Lake District National Park is this beguiling 17th-century hilltop house – all lime-plastered walls, rustic beams, open fires and original flagstones. Its delightful owners, who live in the house's other half, have resisted smoothing out the rough edges; 1920s graffiti still adorns the stable dividers. The hardships of country living have, however, been banished: find lovely new pink and soft-green 'pineapple' covers on sitting room chairs, delicious bed linen and towels, handmade soaps and piping hot radiators. Bedrooms may prompt some tough decisions – do you choose the room with the roll top bath (semi en suite) and the cockloft for kids, or the four-poster with the sofabed and the log fire? The farmhouse kitchen is cosy with Aga, big fridge and gadgets aplenty, but reluctant cooks can book Jill's homemade meals in advance. Beautiful views reach out from every fine sash window to wildlife-rich farmland beyond – 350 private acres, yours to explore. Venture further and you reach the Lakes and the Solway Plain. Heaven for sybarites and walkers. *Great place for walking with your dog: totally surrounded by fields, bridle path right behind house and no traffic.*

Rooms	1 house for 6 (3 doubles; 2 bathrooms): £600-£800 per week. Max. 3 dogs.
Meals	Self-catering.
Closed	Never.
	Water bowl and perfect walks from the door.

Jill Green
High Houses,
Snittlegarth, Ireby, Carlisle, CA7 1HE

Tel	+44 (0)1697 371549
Mobile	+44 (0)7929 397273
Email	enquiries@highhouses.co.uk
Web	www.highhouses.co.uk

Entry 35 Map 5

Scales Plantation

High in the wilds of the North Lakes, in the woods around Scales Farm, Tabitha and Rob have created a selection of fabulous boltholes. Three shepherd's hut camps with timber kitchens are set in semicircular clearings on the edge of the forest; there's a family safari tent, and a bell tent and cabin camp too. The sites are sheltered and peaceful, with views out towards Bowscale Fell and Mount Skiddaw. As part of the regeneration of the woodland, the once thick canopy has been thinned to allow wildlife such as the resident red squirrels to flourish. The camps have already come to feel like natural extensions of the Lake District, with beautiful walks across the fells on your doorstep. You can get trail advice or hire bikes just down the road and head into the hills, then come back to the rustic comfort of the hut and your toasty wood-burner. Groceries can even be supplied by your hosts: simply choose from the list of supplies in advance and they'll be waiting on your arrival. Keep dogs on leads when sheep are about! *Babies welcome. The whole of the Lake District on the doorstep for dogs to drag their owners around!*

Rooms	3 shepherd's huts for 4 (1 double, 2 bunks): from £70 per night. 1 safari tent for 6 (1 double, 2 singles, 2 bunks): from £108 per night. Camp for 4 (1 double, 2 singles): from £90 per night. Max. 2 dogs.
Meals	Self-catering.
Closed	Never.

Advice on walks, dog-friendly activities and pubs in the area.

Canopy & Stars
Scales Plantation, Scales Farm, Berrier, Penrith, CA11 0XE
Tel +44 (0)117 204 7830
Email enquiries@canopyandstars.co.uk
Web www.canopyandstars.co.uk/scalesplantation

Entry 36 Map 5

Linthwaite House Hotel & Restaurant

It's not just the view that makes Linthwaite so special, though Windermere sparkling half a mile below with a chain of peaks rising beyond does grab your attention. There's loads to enjoy here – 15 acres of gardens and grounds, a fantastic terrace for sunny days and interiors that go out of their way to pamper your pleasure receptors. The house itself is beautiful, one of those grand Lakeland Arts & Crafts wonders, with original woodwork and windows in all the right places. Logs are piled high by the front door, fires smoulder, sofas wait in the conservatory sitting room, where big views loom. Gorgeous country-house bedrooms are coolly uncluttered with warm colours, chic fabrics, hi-tech gadgetry, fabulous bathrooms. Those at the front have lake views, a couple have hot tubs, you can stargaze from one of the suites. Downstairs, ambrosial food waits in the dining rooms (one is decorated with nothing but mirrors), perhaps seared tuna with pickled ginger, chargrilled pigeon with beetroot purée, caramelised banana tart with peanut butter. Sunbeds wait on the terrace. Fabulous.

Minimum stay: 2 nights at weekends. The dog-friendly rooms have private external access; 14 acres of grounds for walks. Dogs not allowed in main hotel building; kennel in the grounds.

Rooms	22 doubles, 5 twin/doubles: £202-£490. 3 suites for 2: £410-£630. Singles £136-£195. Dinner, B&B £135-£315 per person. Dogs £10. Max. 1 medium size or 2 small.
Meals	Lunch from £6.95. Dinner for non-residents £52.
Closed	Rarely.
	Dog treats, dog toy, bowls, mat and bed.

Mike Bevans
Linthwaite House Hotel & Restaurant,
Crook Road, Bowness-on-Windermere,
Windermere, LA23 3JA
Tel   +44 (0)15394 88600
Email   stay@linthwaite.com
Web   www.linthwaite.com

Entry 37 Map 5

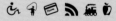

Cumbria

Johnby Hall

You are ensconced in the quieter part of the Lakes and have independence in this Elizabethan manor house – once a fortified Pele tower, now a family home. The suites are airy and each has its own sitting room with books, children's videos, squashy sofas, pretty fabrics and whitewashed walls. Beds have patchwork quilts, windows have stone mullions and all is peaceful. Henry gives you sturdy breakfasts, and good home-grown suppers by a roaring fire in the great hall; he and Anna can join you or leave you in peace. Children will have fun: hens and pigs to feed, garden and woods to roam, garden toys galore. Walks from the door are sublime. *Please keep dogs who aren't trustworthy with chickens under control within in the garden; sheep fields nearby too.*

Rooms	1 twin/double, 1 family room for 4, each with sitting room: £125. Singles £87. Extra bed/sofabed available £20 per person per night.
Meals	Supper, 2 courses, £20. Pub 1 mile.
Closed	Rarely.

Acres of garden and woodland sniffs; one room has an enclosed garden that's dog-proof for most breeds!

Henry & Anna Howard
Johnby Hall,
Johnby,
Penrith, CA11 0UU
Tel   +44 (0)17684 83257
Email   bookings@johnbyhall.co.uk
Web   www.johnbyhall.co.uk

Entry 38 Map 5

Cover Star Competition

Some of our favourite handsome hounds

Buster loves going to Westonbirt Arboretum for a good sniff round. Woods are generally good, but he likes the beach too!

Merlin is rising 7 years old and loves everyone!.

Walter – half lab, half setter – likes beaches, sofas and apples.

The Corner House

A delightful 18th-century cottage opposite Tideswell church – the 'Cathedral of the Peak'. Bells ring on the hour while voices from the Tideswell Male Voice Choir drift blissfully over the garden. Oak beams and flagstone floors recall the cottage's fascinating past, while John and Nikki have introduced modern comforts from an Aga to White Company towels, Laura Ashley bed linen and country antique furniture. A generous welcome hamper including tea, coffee, local handmade sausages, chutney, bread and a Tidza pud awaits in the kitchen, which has a sociable table for six. Plump sofas surround a wood-burner stocked with logs in the cosy sitting room. Head up the wide, carpeted staircase to sleep in peaceful bedrooms; doubles have comfy king-size or super king-size beds, while the twin overlooks the church. There's a spacious bathroom on the first floor and a small shower room up the next flight of stairs. In sunny weather, you can breakfast al fresco in the pretty garden alongside the churchyard. Stroll to pubs and cafés from the front door, or put on your walking boots to explore the Peak District. *Minimum stay: 3 nights, 7 nights in high season. Short breaks available. Separate garden that is partly walled and gated to path. Please keep dogs on leads as lane outside has passing cars sometimes.*

Rooms	1 cottage for 6 (2 doubles, 1 twin; 1 bathroom, 1 shower room): £560–£975 per week. Max. 2 dogs.
Meals	Self-catering. Pubs 5-minute walk. Restaurants 15-minute drive.
Closed	Rarely.
	Dog bed, bowls and treats, towels for drying and dog bags. Advice on local dog-friendly cafés, pubs and walks.

Nikki Turton
The Corner House,
1 Pursglove Road, Tideswell,
Buxton, SK17 8LG

Mobile	+44 (0)7876 763730
Email	info@thecornerhousetideswell.co.uk
Web	www.thecornerhousetideswell.co.uk

The Peacock at Rowsley

The Peacock sits between two fine houses, Haddon Hall and Chatsworth House. You can follow rivers up to each – the Derwent to Chatsworth, the Wye to the hall – both a stroll through beautiful parkland. As for the hotel, it was built in 1652 and was home to the steward of Haddon. Inside, old and new mix gracefully: mullioned windows, hessian rugs, aristocratic art, then striking colours that give a contemporary feel. You'll find Mouseman tables and chairs in the restaurant, where French windows open onto the terrace. Elsewhere, a fire smoulders in the bar every day, the daily papers wait in the sitting room, the garden lawn runs down to the river. Stylish bedrooms have crisp linen, good beds, Farrow & Ball colours, the odd antique; one has a bed from Belvoir Castle. Good food waits in the restaurant, with meat and game from the estate, perhaps venison terrine, roast partridge, Bakewell Tart with buttermilk ice cream. There's afternoon tea in the garden in summer and you can fish both rivers, with day tickets available from reception. Guests also receive a discount on entry to Haddon Hall. *Minimum stay: 2 nights at weekends. Lots of walking in woodland and fields. Peak Park area – follow countryside code. Derwent & Wye rivers.*

Rooms	10 doubles,
	2 four-posters: £180–£280.
	1 suite for 2: £220–£280.
	2 singles: £110–£125.
	Dogs £10 per dog per night. Max. 2.
Meals	Lunch from £4.50.
	Sunday lunch £22.50–£29.50.
	Dinner £60.
Closed	Rarely.
	Dog biscuits at turndown, towels available and lots of walking information.

Laura Ball
The Peacock at Rowsley,
Bakewell Road, Rowsley,
Matlock, DE4 2EB

Tel	+44 (0)1629 733518
Email	reception@thepeacockatrowsley.com
Web	www.thepeacockatrowsley.com

Entry 40 Map 6

Loyton Lodge

You get the impression the tiny lanes that wrap around this small estate act as a sort of fortification, one designed to confuse invaders and protect this patch of heaven. And heaven it is – 280 acres of rolling hills and ancient woodland, with wild flowers, pristine rivers, strutting pheasants and the odd red deer commuting across the fields. It's England circa 1964 with nothing but birdsong to break the peace and glorious walks that start at the front door. As for Loyton, it's a great little base for a night or two deep in the hills. It mixes contemporary interiors with an old-school feel – roaring fires, comfy sofas, wonderful art, even a snooker room. Bedrooms have warm colours and smart fabrics, perhaps a sleigh bed or a claw-foot bath, then books and robes and crisp white linen. Breakfast is a treat – bacon and sausages from home-reared pigs, eggs from estate hens – and there's dinner by arrangement, perhaps local asparagus, lemon sole, walnut and fruit crumble. Take the whole house and bring the family or come for the odd night of live jazz. Exmoor waits, as do good local restaurants. *Woodland, extensive lawns and streams to discover. Farmland beyond with livestock so leads on dogs encouraged.*

Rooms	7 doubles, 2 twin/doubles, 1 twin: £95–£130. Singles from £80. Extra beds £20 (under 12s free). Max. 3 dogs.
Meals	Dinner, 3 courses, about £30 by arrangement.
Closed	Rarely.
	Towels, water bowl, bedding, dog treats and lovely walks from the door.

Isobel, Sally & Angus Barnes
Loyton Lodge,
Morebath,
Tiverton, EX16 9AS
Tel   +44 (0)1398 331051
Email   thelodge@loyton.com
Web   www.loyton.com

Entry 41 Map 2

Garden Studio, North Walk House

Ramblers may feel they've reached nirvana: a clifftop apartment overlooking the sea that sits on the coastal path to Exmoor. There's a collection of guest houses on the North Walk promenade and Ian and Sarah snapped up a B&B and transformed it into a calm retreat, building in a self-catering space at the same time. Inside is sweet and simple. The walls have been freshly painted in white and the shower room is bedecked in gleaming red tiles. The bedroom sits behind a wooden half wall, brightened cheerfully in blushing pink, in contrast with the dark brass bed. Living and kitchen spaces come together, one corner stocked with all the white goods you could need, the other hosting a sofabed, stacks of books and a library of walking maps. Wind-blasted wanderers can return to privacy, take a drink to the terrace or get cosy with a DVD. In the morning you may prefer to seek out Sarah's fabulously local and organic breakfasts in the B&B above (your hosts couldn't be nicer). There are miles of coast, wood and moorland to explore, so come to discover your inner Akela. *Minimum stay: 4 nights on weekdays, 3 nights at weekends. Short breaks available. Lovely walks – join the coastal path.*

Rooms	1 apartment for 2 (1 double, sofabed; 1 shower room): £305-£395 per week. Further flat available for 2 (1 double, sofabed): check with owners for prices. Dogs £5 per night per stay. Max. 2.
Meals	Self-catering.
Closed	Rarely.

Edible dog treats.

Ian & Sarah Downing
Garden Studio,
North Walk House, North Walk,
Lynton, EX35 6HJ
Tel   +44 (0)1598 753372
Email   walk@northwalkhouse.co.uk
Web   www.northwalkhouse.co.uk

Entry 42 Map 2

Longlands

The five Longlands lodge tents jut impressively out of the hillside on raised wooden decks, in a wide open field near the North Devon coast. They're the perfect haven for big family escapes, sleeping six each. The lodge tents are beautifully made, with a king-sized bed, two single beds and a cabin double, all with thick duvets, spare blankets and hot water bottles. Each has a fully equipped kitchen, private loo and shower and a spacious living area. Tire the little ones out on beach excursions or coastal walks, or explore the enticing 'blanket box', full of games and other treasures. The on-site honesty shop can take care of the basics, you can have meals organised for your arrival or those occasional lazy evenings, the games room has plenty to offer in any weather and there are even two boats on the lake for racing round the island! The area is packed full of every kind of adventure: outdoor sports on Exmoor, coastal villages and towns full of galleries. *Babies welcome. Dogs on leads except in wood please. Details of dog-friendly beaches and pubs given.*

Rooms	5 safari tents for 6 (1 double, 1 double cabin bed, 2 singles): from £144 per night. Dogs £30 per pet per stay, payable on departure. Max. 2.
Meals	Self-catering.
Closed	November – March.

🚶‍🦮 Towels, beds and bowls. Also hose and poo bin provided under lodges.

Canopy & Stars
Longlands,
Coulsworthy,
Combe Martin, EX34 0PD
Tel   +44 (0)117 204 7830
Email   enquiries@canopyandstars.co.uk
Web   www.canopyandstars.co.uk/longlands

Entry 43 Map 2

The Quarry

Skip back from seaside rock pools to your giant Victorian house, built for an Admiral, now a fantastic place for messing around with friends and family. So much space: in the vast living room, find a huge dining table, log fire, bright paintings and cushions, funky lamps, 42-inch Sky TV, a trunk of games. The yellow-walled kitchen has colourful Victorian tiles and is kitted out to cook up a feast: two-oven Aga, separate cooker, heaps of pots and pans. On sunny days, spill out to the terrace, from which you can spy the sea. Seven simple, uncluttered bedrooms are scattered about the two upper floors, two with their own showers, others sharing big bathrooms with deep baths and sparkling showers. With mostly wooden or Victorian-tiled floors, no precious ornaments, a safe, fenced terrace and large natural garden (with Wendy house) you can let kids loose. Escape to the 'vine room' conservatory (dripping with grapes and nectarines in season) or a secluded garden halfway up the drive. The South West Coast Path runs right past; Ilfracombe is on your doorstep; Woolacombe beach is a ten-minute drive; the moors just a little further. *Min. stay: 4 nights on weekdays, 2 at weekends, 7 in high season. Booklet given showing the dog-friendly beaches and dates when other beaches can be used.*

Rooms	1 house for 13 (2 doubles – en suite, 3 doubles, 1 twin, 1 single, 2 single sofabeds; 2 bathrooms): £1,750–£3,650 per week. 3 night weekends from £1,200. Max. 4 dogs.
Meals	Self-catering.
Closed	Never.
	Advice on walks.

Kirstie Jackson
The Quarry,
Torrs Park,
Ilfracombe, EX34 8AZ
Mobile   +44 (0)7979 306079
Email   info@bighousedevon.co.uk
Web   www.bighousedevon.co.uk

Entry 44 Map 2

Little Comfort Farm Cottages

Deep in Devon hills and way way down a grass-tufted lane is a slice of green heaven. The usual dose of urban din is replaced by the sound of a gurgling stream and odd squeak of very happy children. Five sturdy stone cottages blend into the landscape and have been gently updated over the years. You're made very welcome on Jackie and Roger's working organic farm; their passion makes this place. Slip off walking boots at your door and escape into a homely haven – an easy mix of lived-in sofas, wooden furniture, log-burner, TV and DVD for lazy nights in. Bathrooms are simple, bedrooms cosy with flowery curtains and country views. The local shop will stock your fridge and freezer, and you can buy the farm's organic sausages, bacon, lamb, beef, eggs and apple juice (Jackie also makes delicious homemade meals). This place is a gift for young families: morning trailer rides, lamb feeding and a barn filled with toys and crafty stuff. A blissful retreat for couples too, outside of the busiest times. Walk miles, fish in the lake, switch off… Remote, yet close enough to Barnstaple and the endless sands of Saunton, Putsborough and Woolacombe. *Fully enclosed gardens; riverside walks through the farm with opportunities for doggy swims; close to dog-friendly beaches and fantastic walks.*

Rooms	2 cottages for 4, 1 cottage for 5, 1 cottage for 6: £320-£1,153 per week. 1 house for 10: £481-£1,604 per week. Dogs £25 per dog per week, £15 per dog per short break.
Meals	Self-catering.
Closed	Never.

🚶‍🐕 Lots of advice on dog-friendly walks, beaches and places to eat out. Towels for drying soggy dogs, and plenty of doggy accessories (bowls, crates etc) can be provided if needed.

Roger & Jackie Milsom
Little Comfort Farm Cottages,
Braunton, EX33 2NJ

Tel	+44 (0)1271 812414
Email	info@littlecomfortfarm.co.uk
Web	www.littlecomfortfarm.co.uk

Entry 45 Map 2

Loveland Farm

On the border of Devon and Cornwall – beautifully remote yet close to surfing and dog-friendly beaches, and the wildly dramatic south west coast path – Loveland Farm is a place that celebrates modern simplicity and, thanks to Jeff's tree planting, is carbon neutral. It's home to chickens, pigs, ducks, a pair of Asian water buffaloes, Karina and Jeff's original creation Loveland Pod and now four more bubble-shaped pods with clear sides for the moon and stars to shine through at night, shiny copper rain showers, ghost chairs, and cashmere blankets. The Griffins' world travels with their fashion line inspired the ingenious, stylishly quirky design here and two of their domes welcome dogs. Welcombe Pod has space too for four humans – with a 4-poster and sofabed, and two wooden huts out on the elevated deck for the kitchenette, shower and eco loo. Hartland Pod sleeps six in a double and two sofabeds, it has space to sit and stare and suspended from its strong steel skeleton, mini chill out tents for children! People love to unwind here with woodland, river and meadow views by day, star-gazey skies by night. *Babies welcome. Hartland is the perfect place to bring your dog: fields for running and local dog-friendly beaches only a mile away.*

Rooms	Geodome for 5 (1 double, 1 sofabed, 1 travel cot): from £125 per night. Geodome for 5 (1 double in tipi, 1 sofabed, 1 travel cot): from £133 per night. Dogs £30 per stay. Max. 1.
Meals	Self-catering.
Closed	Rarely.

 Pig's ears and advice on dog walks and local dog-friendly beaches.

Canopy & Stars
Loveland Farm,
Hartland, EX39 6AT

Tel	+44 (0)117 204 7830
Email	enquiries@canopyandstars.co.uk
Web	www.canopyandstars.co.uk/ lovelandfarm

Entry 46 Map 1

The Woodland Retreat

From the welcome cream tea to the moment you leave, you'll find The Woodland Retreat fits its name perfectly. The shack is one of our wilder retreats, small and rustic but with a big double bed and bunks occupying each wall. The wood-burner in the middle does its best to keep out the chill but don't forget your chunky jumper if you're going in spring or autumn. A few steps away is a converted wood-panelled bus with optional extra sleeping space. The kitchen and shower are outdoor but covered meaning the terrace with its sofas and table acts as a lounge and dining room. The bell tent is an extra day space, perfect for taking yourself off to read or nap. Owners Lydia and Alex have a long history in the arts and their record label is run from the on-site recording suite which you can hire if you book their other cabin too, Candyland Studios. They built this 8 person cabin themselves with timber from the woodland, straw bales from the land and a reclaimed tin roof. If you don't feel like making music, head out to the coast at nearby Bude or rack up some miles hiking the stunning surrounding scenery. *Babies welcome. 4 acres of woodland to walk in.*

Rooms	Cabin for 6 (1 double, 2 bunks, 1 double in bus): from £80 per night. Cabin for 8 (2 doubles, 2 bunks, 2 singles): from £160 per night. Max. 2 dogs.	
Meals	Self-catering.	
Closed	November – March.	
	Blankets and dog biscuits.	

Canopy & Stars
The Woodland Retreat, Stapleton Farm,
Langtree, Torrington, EX38 8NP

Tel   +44 (0)117 204 7830
Email   enquiries@canopyandstars.co.uk
Web   www.canopyandstars.co.uk/
         thewoodlandretreat

Entry 47 Map 2

Horry Mill

In deepest Devon where the birds chirrup, the river flows and the stars shine brightly at night is the much-loved Horry Mill. Here, award-winning mixed woodland is carefully managed, bees, birds and bluebells are encouraged, and a small herd of beef cattle, pigs, ducks and hens merrily thrive. The guardians of this special place are Sonia and Simon, welcoming hosts both, who live in the Millhouse and are on hand should you need them. Inside the miller's cottage is all you need: an inviting dining room with a creamy Rayburn, a vintage iron bedstead up wide oak stairs, a wonderful old fireplace with limitless logs. Who needs web or mobile when there are books, games and a flat-screen TV? Holing up in bad weather is sheer pleasure here. A pretty window seat upstairs overlooks the cottage garden – secluded and south-facing, with a barbecue for summer meals. If you're feeling lively you can hot-foot it to Winkleigh (three shops, two pubs); if you're not, you can discover the gardens at Rosemoor, or plan a delicious lunch in Chagford. Your hosts know all the best places. *Woodland for walks. Chickens and ducks nearby.*

Rooms	1 cottage for 4 (1 double, 1 twin; 1 bath/shower room): £330–£625 per week. Max. 1 dog.
Meals	Self-catering.
Closed	Rarely.
	Woodland walks, maps and dog towels.

Simon & Sonia Hodgson
Horry Mill,
Hollocombe,
Chulmleigh, EX18 7QH
Tel   +44 (0)1769 520266
Email horrymill@aol.com
Web   www.horrymill.com

Entry 48 Map 2

The Lamb Inn

This 16th-century inn is adored by locals and visitors alike. It's a proper inn in the old tradition with gorgeous rooms and the odd touch of scruffiness to add authenticity to its earthy bones. It stands on a cobbled walkway in a village lost down tiny lanes, and those lucky enough to chance upon it leave reluctantly. Inside there are beams, but they are not sandblasted, red carpets with a little swirl, sofas in front of an open fire. Boarded menus trumpet irresistible food – carrot and orange soup, haunch of venison with a port jus, an excellent rhubarb crumble. You can eat wherever you want: in the bar, in the fancy restaurant, or out in the walled garden in good weather. There's a cobbled terrace, a skittle alley, maps for walkers and well-kept ales. The seven rooms have a chic country style: two have baths in the room; those in the barn have painted stone walls, the suite has a wood-burner and a private terrace. All are lovely with comfy beds, white linen, good power showers and flat-screen TVs. Kind staff chat with ease. Dartmoor waits, but you may well linger. Brilliant. *Secure garden and friendly staff who love dogs; all dogs must be on a lead and well-behaved if eating in the bar area with their owners.*

Rooms	5 doubles, 1 twin/double: £69-£130. 1 suite for 3: £150. Dogs £5 per dog per night.
Meals	Lunch from £9. Dinner, 3 courses, £20-£30. Sunday roast from £8.90.
Closed	Open all day.
🐕	Advice on local walks, and fresh water bowl.

Mark Hildyard & Katharine Lightfoot
The Lamb Inn,
Sandford,
Crediton, EX17 4LW
Tel   +44 (0)1363 773676
Email   thelambinn@gmail.com
Web   www.lambinnsandford.co.uk

Entry 49 Map 2

CANOPY&STARS

Eversfield Safari Tents

Complete canvas comfort in a quiet wildlife-filled valley. A double room, twin room and a double cabin bed in each means plenty of space for families or groups of friends. There's a sofa, dining table, a blanket box full of games, and a wood-burning stove in the kitchen but, being pitched on a big wooden deck, you can cook outside on the BBQ too and make the most of the lovely views across the lake. You can buy delicious organic stuff from the owners Anna and Jon's farm shop. No need to tramp up through the fields either as each tent has its own en suite shower pod and separate loo – just stoke the wood-fired boiler to heat up your water. Eversfield sits on the edge of Dartmoor National Park, and is a perfect base for walkers who want to discover this famously wild wilderness. At home there's also plenty on offer – row the boat around the lake or try your hand at fly fishing. If you catch rainbow trout you can cook it for your campfire supper whilst spotting constellations. If the wind blows in a certain direction you may hear a faint noise from the road but otherwise you'll likely forget all about 'life outside'. *Babies welcome. Dartmoor National Park on doorstep, forests and sandy beaches for walks. Organic farm with sheep, pigs & cattle in fields so dogs need to be kept on leads.*

Rooms	2 safari tents for 6 (1 double, 1 twin, 1 double cabin bed): from £136 per night. Dogs £20 per pet per stay. Max. 2.
Meals	Self-catering.
Closed	Nov – March.

 Advice on walks.

Canopy & Stars
Eversfield Safari Tents, Water Meadow, Ellacott Barton, Bratton Clovelly, Okehampton, EX20 4LB
Tel +44 (0)117 204 7830
Email enquiries@canopyandstars.co.uk
Web www.canopyandstars.co.uk/eversfield

Entry 50 Map 2

The Elephant's Nest Inn

Travellers look happy as they enter the main bar, all dark beams, flagstone floors and crackling fires... you almost imagine a distant Baskerville hound baying. This is an atmospheric inn that serves delicious home-cooked food – local, seasonal and British with a twist. Tuck into antipasto of pastrami, rosette saucisson and Black Forest ham; South Devon sirloin with mushrooms, vine tomatoes and French fries; and Mrs Cook's fabulous lemon posset with blueberry compote. When suitably sated, slip off to the annexe and a nest of your own in one of three peaceful, very comfortable rooms, with gleaming oak floors heated underfoot; one room has its own private patio. Wake to a pretty garden with views to Brentor church and the moor, an exceptional breakfast and perhaps a cricket match to watch: the pub has its own ground and club. Settle back to the thwack of willow on leather with a pint of Palmer's IPA. There's Doom Bar too, Jail Ale from Princetown, and guest ales from Otter, Cotleigh, Teignworthy, Butcombe. What's more, the pub is a dog-friendly zone – check out their website for photos of the residents. *Lovely walks; be careful about sheep.*

Rooms	3 twin/doubles: £88.
	Dogs £5 per dog per night. Max. 3.
Meals	Lunch & dinner £8.95–£19.95.
Closed	Never.
	Dog biscuits.

Hugh & Denise Cook
The Elephant's Nest Inn,
Horndon, Mary Tavy,
Tavistock, PL19 9NQ
Tel +44 (0)1822 810273
Email info@elephantsnest.co.uk
Web www.elephantsnest.co.uk

Entry 51 Map 2

South Hooe Count House

It's lovely here, so peaceful in your own private cottage perched above the Tamar; the views over the river are glorious and steep steps lead to the shore and a little jetty – borrow a canoe and paddle up stream. Rowers, geese and herons glide by on misty mornings; the woodland garden is full of spring bulbs, vegetables you can pick, free-range hens, chatting guinea fowl and Arabella and Willow the donkeys. Settle on the cushioned window seat in the pretty sitting room with toasty wood-burner, books, art and family photos; copper urns and pewter jugs on a deep slate sill brim with flowers. The cosy kitchen has a lived-in, charming feel with old pine, pretty china, coffee grinder, Belfast sink and cosy Rayburn. Sip coffee on the sheltered terrace that catches the morning sun. The light-filled bedroom has a comfortable bed, thick curtains and that view to wake to; the double ended rolltop bath is a treat. Delightful Trish can give you routes for good walks, lend you a map and suggest places to visit, boat trips to take. Nearby Tavistock has independent shops, galleries and a lively Saturday market. Live by the tide and emerge refreshed. *Babes in arms very welcome. Short breaks of 3 nights or more. Lovely woodland walks with no sheep. Tamar river below: lots of fun.*

Rooms	1 house for 3 (1 double, 1 single in attic – access via ladder; 1 bath/shower room): £495-£595 per week. Max. 2 dogs.
Meals	Self-catering.
Closed	Rarely.

Towels, bowls and advice on walks. A river to swim in and resident wonder dog Rags to entertain. Plans afoot for special dog-proof run with kennel and shade.

Trish Dugmore
South Hooe Count House,
South Hooe Mine,
Hole's Hole, Bere Alston,
Yelverton, PL20 7BW

| Tel | +44 (0)1822 840329 |
| Email | trishdugmore@googlemail.com |

Entry 52 Map 2

The Horn of Plenty

The Horn of Plenty is one of those clever hotels that has survived the test of time by constantly improving itself. This year's contribution is six gorgeous new rooms, four of which have terraces or balconies that give 40-mile views over the Tamar Valley. Potter about outside and find six acres of gardens, then a path that leads down through bluebell woods to the river. Inside, beautiful simplicity abounds: stripped floors, gilt mirrors, fine art, fresh flowers everywhere. Bedrooms in the main house come in country-house style, those in the garden have a contemporary feel. All have smart colours, big comfy beds, perhaps a claw-foot bath or a ceiling open to the rafters; ten have a terrace or a balcony. Despite all this, the food remains the big draw, so come to eat well, perhaps beetroot mousse with goat's cheese parfait, grilled duck with chicory and orange, chocolate cannelloni with banana sorbet; views of the Tamar snaking through the hills are included in the price. Afternoon tea is served in the shade of a magnolia tree in summer. Tavistock, Dartmoor and The Eden Project are close. *The Tamar Valley (2 minutes) provides woodland and rivers. Dartmoor (10-minute drive) offers everything a dog dreams of!*

Rooms	16 twin/doubles: £110–£245. Singles from £100. Dinner, B&B from £135 per person. Extra bed/sofabed available £25 per person per night. Dogs £10 per night.
Meals	Lunch from £19.50. Dinner, 3 courses, £49.50. Tasting menu £65.
Closed	Never.

🐕 Dog snacks, 5-acre gardens, loads of great local walks.

Julie Leivers & Damien Pease
The Horn of Plenty,
Gulworthy,
Tavistock, PL19 8JD

Tel	+44 (0)1822 832528
Email	enquiries@thehornofplenty.co.uk
Web	www.thehornofplenty.co.uk

Entry 53 Map 2

Orcheton Mill

Kids and dogs will love free-ranging in five lush acres: apple orchard, wildflower-strewn meadow, burbling leat. Grown-ups can fire up the barbecue on the suntrap terrace and enjoy a sundowner at the garden table – made from the old mill wheel. Inside, this converted 300-year-old watermill, is equally delightful. Enter the hall, off here is a sublime beamed living room with a coffee table, slouchy sofas and a wood-burner (first basket of logs on the house). The fantastic country-style kitchen will keep cooks happy (note the gorgeous Gothic style mirror), eat at the scrubbed table here or decamp to the more formal flagged stone dining room. Upstairs to four über comfy, prettily dressed bedrooms; the master double has beams and an en suite. The fifth bedroom is in the separate barn annexe accessed outside via stone steps – totally private and with its own pretty terrace. Find a homemade cream tea to welcome you. The nearest pub is a five-minute drive, the secluded Erme estuary and Wonwell beach are two miles and the walking is excellent. Boaty Salcombe and arty Totnes are close. *Min. stay: 7 nights high season. Short breaks available. Dogs downstairs only. Water areas & steep banks. Estuary is dog heaven for a crazy run or quiet amble. SW coast path accessible.*

Rooms	1 house for 9 (3 doubles, 1 twin, 1 single): £1,000–£1,950 per week. Discounts for parties of 4 or less out of peak season. Dogs £20 per dog per stay. Max. 2 well-behaved.
Meals	Self-catering. Pub 5-minute drive.
Closed	Rarely.
	Dog bowl, treats, advice on walks and best seat in the house (cushion in front of the wood-burner).

Caroline Beardsworth
Orcheton Mill,
Modbury,
Ivybridge, PL21 0TG

Mobile	+44 (0)7989 586547
Email	cbeardsworth@outlook.com
Web	www.orchetonmill.tumblr.com

Entry 54 Map 2

Devon

The Henley Hotel

A small house above the sea with fabulous views, super bedrooms and some of the loveliest food in Devon. Despite these credentials, it's Martyn and Petra who shine most brightly, their kind, generous approach making this a memorable place to stay. Warm interiors have wooden floors, Lloyd Loom furniture, the odd potted palm, then big windows to frame the view. Below, the Avon estuary slips gracefully out to sea. At high tide surfers ride the waves, at low tide you can walk on the sands. There's a pretty garden with a path tumbling down to the beach, binoculars in each room, a wood-burner in the snug and good books everywhere. Bedrooms are a steal (one is huge). Expect warm colours, crisp linen, tongue-and-groove panelling and robes in super little bathrooms. As for Martyn's table d'hôte dinners, expect to eat very well. Fish comes daily from Kingsbridge market, you might find grilled figs with goat's cheese and Parma ham, roast monkfish with a lobster sauce, then hot chocolate soufflé with fresh raspberries. Gorgeous Devon is all around. Better than the Ritz! *German spoken. Minimum stay: 2 nights at weekends. Beach right below for swimming and playing (only minor restrictions during summer months). South West Coast Path just outside, garden to relax in after walks.*

Rooms	2 doubles, 2 twin/doubles: £120–£137. 1 suite for 2: £150. Singles from £85. Dinner, B&B £87–£97 per person (2 night minimum). Dogs £5 per night. Max. 2 per room.
Meals	Dinner £36.
Closed	November – March.
	Maps and advice on walks, towels for drying on request, entertainment and company from resident Labrador Kasper.

Martyn Scarterfield & Petra Lampe
The Henley Hotel,
Folly Hill, Bigbury-on-Sea,
Kingsbridge, TQ7 4AR

Tel	+44 (0)1548 810240
Email	thehenleyhotel@btconnect.com
Web	www.thehenleyhotel.co.uk

Entry 55 Map 2

The Batman's Summerhouse

The 1930's Batman's Summerhouse at Riverleigh has been beautifully restored with natural materials – wood, cotton, glass – in a clean yet comfy Scandinavian style. Find a snuggly double on a mezzanine up steep steps and a bunk room for three downstairs. With one wall of glass looking out to the spectacular riverbank setting, the open-plan living area has a super kitchen with gas hobs and store cupboard staples. Stacks of well-thumbed cookbooks give you a clue to the owner: Miranda is a food writer and can have supper waiting for you when you arrive. You're 10 metres from the main house so quite independent. Fling open the double doors to bring in the summer, catch salmon and trout in the river. You're nestled in English native woodland in the Avon valley of South Devon; home to dippers, wagtails, buzzards, otters, deer, hares and the greater horseshoe bat. Fetch morning croissants from the garden centre, a pleasant stroll along the river bank; there are great local pubs, and lovely beaches nearby – Bigbury-on-Sea, Blackpool Sands, and Bantham for surfing are all a short drive. *Babies welcome. Miles of beautiful riverside walks, 8 acres of private English woodland. Dog-friendly beaches nearby – even in summer months.*

Rooms	Cabin for 5 (1 double, 3 bunks, 1 sofabed): from £109 per night. Dogs £25 per pet per stay. Max. 2.
Meals	Self-catering.
Closed	Never

Organic dog biscuits, dog towels, and acres of private woodland for walks in your pyjamas and wellies.

Canopy & Stars
The Batman's Summerhouse,
Riverleigh,
Kingsbridge, TQ7 4DR

Tel   +44 (0)117 204 7830
Email   enquiries@canopyandstars.co.uk
Web   www.canopyandstars.co.uk/batmans

Entry 56 Map 2

Fingals Barn

Unusual, quirky and fun. Loyal fans return year after year for Fingals' laid-back charm. In a rolling green valley half a mile from the river Dart, all you need is here: the hotel has snooker, grass tennis, croquet and a pool. You can self-cater in the oak-framed barn where your kitchen is simple, or (occasionally) eat convivially in the atmospheric restaurant. Reached from an outside stair, your huge private space has massive beams and floor-to-ceiling windows overlooking the gardens. Polished oak floors with faded oriental rugs, well-snuggled-in sofas, a rocking horse, grand piano and books and games will suit families and friends. The main bedroom, with pine bed and Indian throw, sloping roof and skylight windows, hides behind a sliding Japanese screen; the second bedroom is much smaller; the bathroom has a green-footed roll top tub. Children can knock a ball about, swim, make friends, as you order your favourite tipple and loll on a steamer chair. Golfers can golf (ask Richard about discount at the local club), and everyone can head off to the beach, the river, the pub… the area is a treat to discover. *Min. stay: 3 nights, 7 in high season. Secure garden, woodland and river. Goats, ducks and chickens in walled garden so please keep dogs under control in and around the gardens.*

Rooms	1 barn for 4-6 (1 double, 1 twin; 1 bath/shower room): £400-£1,200 per week. With Garden Room, sleeps up to 6: £500-£1,400 per week. Dogs £5 per dog per night. Max. 3.
Meals	Self-catering (restaurant occasionally open).
Closed	Never.

Advice on walks, dog towels, resident friendly lurchers to play with – and plenty of love and attention!

Richard & Sheila Johnston
Fingals Barn,
Old Coombe, Dittisham,
Dartmouth, TQ6 0JA
Tel   +44 (0)1803 722398
Email   info@fingals.co.uk
Web   www.fingalsapart.co.uk

Entry 57 Map 2

Magdalen Chapter

Where do we start? It might be simpler to confine ourselves to a bald statement of facts to describe this contemporary wonderland. An open fire, terrazzo floors, big warm colours and the odd sofa greet you in the entrance hall. Contemporary art hangs on every wall. There's a curated library, where you can sit and flick through glossy pages; a stunning sitting room bar with a Zen fireplace and a Hugo Dalton mural; an interior courtyard with walls of glass that looks onto an attractive garden. The brasserie is magnificent, open to the rafters with white pods of light hanging from on high and an open kitchen on display. In summer, glass doors fly open and you eat on the terrace, perhaps roast monkfish with wild garlic or a good steak. There are deckchairs on the lawn, a small kitchen garden, treatment rooms for stressed-out folk; there's even a small swimming pool that comes with a wood-burner. Bedrooms have an uncluttered, contemporary feel: iPads, flat-screen TVs, black-and-white photography, handmade furniture. Bathrooms are excellent; expect power showers, REN lotions and white bathrobes. *Dogs are very much welcomed in and around the hotel. For those seeking an adventure: maps are available from reception for discovering great dog walks, and a bounty of beaches are nearby.*

Rooms	52 doubles, 2 twin/doubles: £120–£250. 5 singles: £105. Max. 2 dogs per room; no more than 6 in hotel at one time.
Meals	Lunch from £8. Dinner from £12.95; à la carte about £30.
Closed	Never.

Don't leave your four-legged family member at home! They will have a bed and bowl in the room, and a snooze in front of the roaring log fires in winter.

Fiona Moores
Magdalen Chapter,
Magdalen Street,
Exeter, EX2 4HY

Tel	+44 (0)1392 281000
Email	magdalen_ge@chapterhotels.com
Web	www.themagdalenchapter.com/

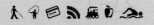

Entry 58 Map 2

Devon   B&B

Devon   B&B

Glebe House

Set on a hillside with fabulous views over the Coly valley, this late-Georgian vicarage is now a heart-warming B&B. The views will entice you, the hosts will delight you and the house is filled with interesting things. Chuck and Emma spent many years at sea – he a Master Mariner, she a chef – and have filled these big light rooms with cushions, kilims and treasured family pieces. There's a sitting room for guests, a lovely conservatory with vintage vine, peaceful bedrooms with blissful views and bathrooms that sparkle. All this, two sweet pygmy goats, wildlife beyond the ha-ha and the fabulous coast a hike away. *Minimum stay: 2 nights July & August weekends & bank holidays. The East Devon Way can be joined from the door and there's a river nearby to splash in. Emma has heaps of local knowledge on the walks.*

The Dairy Loft

The lovely East Devon Way brings you almost to the door of this smart, new B&B for the independent-minded. Up the exterior stair is your bright, refreshingly opinionated room with its clever corner kitchen and double-headed shower room. The funky red leather sofa and big bed (or twins) opposite French windows invite lazing, star-gazing, Merlin-spotting. You're free to concoct your own lavish breakfast and eat beneath the Italian lamp. Oak-floored inside, larch clad out and with kind, interesting owners across the flowered yard who'll advise on all things local, from sea and river fishing to Exe Trail cycling. Great! *Minimum stay: 2 nights. Single night stays considered. Arrive after 3pm, leave before 10am please. Secure courtyard.*

Rooms	1 double, 1 twin/double: £80. 1 family room for 4: £80–£110. Singles £50.
Meals	Dinner, 3 courses, £25. Pubs/restaurants 2.5 miles.
Closed	Christmas & New Year.
	Entertainment from the friendly resident terrier lurcher, Miss Cocofit, advice on walks and a Bonio at bedtime.

Rooms	1 twin/double: £120. Dogs £20.
Meals	Pubs/restaurants 2 miles.
Closed	Rarely.
	Lots of long walks in the open country – join the East Devon Way.

Emma & Chuck Guest
Glebe House,
Southleigh, Colyton, EX24 6SD
Tel   +44 (0)1404 871276
Mobile   +44 (0)7867 568569
Email   emma_guest@talktalk.net
Web   www.guestsatglebe.co.uk

Entry 59 Map 2

Rob & Annie Jones
The Dairy Loft, Valley Barn,
Hawkerland, Colaton Raleigh,
Sidmouth, EX10 0JA
Tel   +44 (0)1395 568411
Email   robertjones@eclipse.co.uk
Web   www.thedairyloft.co.uk

Entry 60 Map 2

Devon

Bulleigh Barton Manor

Tea and scones will be waiting. Find long, leafy views to wake up to, a pool for lazy summer days, ponds and a big colourful garden with a summerhouse. Liz and Mark have restored their house with care, uncovering beams and lovely bits of old wood and filling it with original art and books. Bedrooms are inviting: sink-into beds, china pieces on white window sills, a pot of garden flowers, local fudge and homemade cake. They are keen on sourcing the best local produce and their host of hens lay your breakfast eggs. Dartmoor and the south coast are at your feet; return to a friendly hello from Zennor the dog and dinner by the fire. *Large garden; sheep in neighbouring fields. Lots of walks nearby. Garden suite has direct access to garden.*

Rooms	2 doubles: £70–£115. 1 suite for 2 with kitchenette: £80–£95. Dogs £5 per dog per night, to a max. of £15 per dog per stay. Max. 2 in Garden suite, 1 in Brooking Room.
Meals	Dinner (Sept–May), 3 courses, £30–£35. Pubs/restaurants 0.5 miles.
Closed	Rarely.

Homemade biscuits, towels, blanket, shampoo, guides and pet shop voucher.

Liz & Mark Lamport
Bulleigh Barton Manor,
Ipplepen,
Newton Abbot, TQ12 5UA
Tel   +44 (0)1803 873411
Email   liz.lamport@btopenworld.com
Web   www.escapetosouthdevon.co.uk

Entry 61 Map 2

Cover Star Competition

Some of our favourite handsome hounds

This is Murphy a 4-month-old Cocker. He loves bounding through the woods chasing all the new smells.

Woody's favourite place is any hill he can roll his ball down. He then chases after it to repeat the game, over and over!

Brio loves to spend time at Nidd Gorge, racing in and out of the water and following all the exciting new scents.

2 Old Down Cottages

Wend your way through woodland and hit big skies and harvested fields. You're in the heart of Thomas Hardy country with Horton Tower on the horizon where scenes from *Far from the Madding Crowd* were filmed. Approach this semi-detached cottage through swathes of anemone and towering purple verbena. Once an 18th-century barn, now a well-decorated and uncluttered space. An open fire steals the show in a cosy sitting room with squidgy sofas and TV. Seat six around a farmhouse table in a smart kitchen groaning with good quality cutlery and pristine white china. Pretty country bedrooms have beams and fabulous views of fields. You're spoilt for spotless and contemporary bathrooms – three in all. Sit long enough on the small terrace out the back or in the pretty front garden and you're sure to spot a deer or an owl. Walk to Cranborne Chase, once King John's hunting ground and one of England's last ancient woodlands. Expect a thoughtful welcome from garden-loving Pip who lives in the nearby farmhouse: homemade cake and flowers. A bucolic bolthole within easy reach of Dorset's market towns and beaches. *Short breaks available (minimum 3 nights). Secure garden, woodland nearby for walks. Lots of walking from front door into open farmland.*

Rooms	1 cottage for 6
	(1 double, 1 twin – both en suite,
	1 twin; 1 bath/shower room):
	£456–£1,221 per week.
	Dogs £25 per stay. Max. 1.
Meals	Self-catering.
Closed	Never.

 Advice on walks.

Phillipa Davidson
2 Old Down Cottages,
Horton,
Wimborne, BH21 7HL
Tel   +44 (0)1258 840969
Email   olddown@btinternet.com
Web   www.olddown.co.uk

Entry 62 Map 3

The Bothy, Launceston Farm

Want to escape, just the two of you? Wend your way through the Tarrant Valley, past grazing cattle and thatch, to Launceston Farm. In the former groom's quarters of her Dorset farmhouse, enterprising Sarah has carved out two sanctuaries for loved-up couples. Step into open-plan living rooms-cum-kitchens; modern sofas hug wood-burning stoves, dainty tables for two sit opposite. Bedrooms feel fresh and airy, with large beds and views over the walled garden and outdoor pool (which you can use in summer). You'll find provisions; whip up eggs and coffee and breakfast al fresco. Entirely private, paved courtyards are bounded by a wall with windows to let the landscape in. And here's the showstopper: close the wooden shutters and slip into steaming water in your very own outdoor bateau bath, nothing between you and the heavens. There are things to do in all directions, but the Tarrant Valley is a gem rarely stumbled upon. Forget the car; ramble about, picnic, whip up a barbecue, stroll to the local inn and if the weather turns, why not just stay in bed... *Minimum stay: 3 nights. Short breaks available. Secure outdoor private courtyard and farmland walks.*

Rooms	2 barns for 2 (1 double): £600 per week. Short 3 night breaks available from £350. Dogs £25 per stay. Max. 2.
Meals	Self-catering.
Closed	Rarely.
🚶🐕	Towels for drying, and advice on walks, dog-friendly beaches and local attractions. Walks through surrounding farmland from the door.

Sarah Worrall
The Bothy, Launceston Farm,
Tarrant Launceston,
Blandford Forum, DT11 8BY
Tel   +44 (0)1258 830528
Email   info@launcestonfarm.co.uk
Web   www.launcestonfarm.co.uk

Entry 63 Map 3

Giddy Acre Barn

Escape to a pretty Dorset village where locals leave doors unlocked, pubs and post office thrive, and walks and bike paths spider through wooded hills and horse paddocks towards the coast. Simple, unspoilt and great for families – as is this chunky wood-clad barn which Tim and Kelly revived next to their cottage. From a young garden, lavender-scented with hints of honeysuckle and jasmine, views shoot to Hambledon Hill, a prehistoric hill fort and local beauty spot. Dine out among gambolling bunnies or loll back on the swing watching buzzards circle. Plenty to keep kids happy in the open-plan sitting room, with books and games in wicker chests, modern leather sofas, a toasty wood-burner (free logs). The organic eggs in your welcome pack are from the local farm shop, the contemporary art from Kelly's gallery. Relax – nothing is too precious: kids, dogs are welcome. Bedrooms – two cosy doubles (one is en suite) and a simple bunk – are compact, as are bathrooms. But cathedral ceilings and tall glass doors make all feel large and light. Tim and Kelly are relaxed, generous, and the views stretch for miles. *Secure garden. Possibly sheep in field in front, but they can be moved on request.*

Rooms	1 barn for 6 (1 double – en suite, 1 twin/double, 1 bunk room for 2; 1 bathroom): £450-£870 per week.
Meals	Self-catering.
Closed	Rarely.
	Advice for walks – there are many directly from the barn.

Tim & Kelly Evans
Giddy Acre Barn,
Ridgeway Lane, Child Okeford,
Blandford Forum, DT11 8HB
Tel   +44 (0)1258 863411
Email   kelly@giddyacrebarn.co.uk
Web   www.giddyacrebarn.co.uk

Entry 64 Map 3

53 Durweston

Rural chic at its best! A thatched 18th-century cottage bursting with character and clutter-free style. Dreamy window seats, an inglenook fireplace, oak floorboards and latch doors, exposed beams, cob walls, wood-burners, a rustic antique dining table, a vintage leather armchair... fresh flowers, soft furnishings, candles and contemporary artwork complete the picture. Picasso print line drawings dot the kitchen – a long, narrow Victorian addition with stone flooring, a painted dresser and all you'll need. Up the cottagey stairs to the oh-so-pretty bedrooms, light and luxuriously carpeted with views of church, water meadows and woods beyond. Both have king-size, French style, cream iron beds, crisp white cotton and chests of drawers; the larger gets a buttonback chair, the smaller, a cast-iron fireplace, and the spacious bathroom between them has sumptuous towels and toiletries. All this, and a herb and flower-planted garden, in the quietest part of a most attractive village in Dorset. Fantastic for cycling and chalk ridge walks, and a ten-minute drive from Georgian Blandford. It'll be hard to leave. *Secure garden and miles of beautiful country walks right on the doorstep.*

Rooms	1 cottage for 4 (2 doubles; 1 bathroom): £590–£1,450 per week Dogs £10 per dog per stay. Max. 2.
Meals	Self-catering.
Closed	Never.

Water bowl, food bowl and a doggie treat.

Emma Perry
53 Durweston,
Blandford Forum, DT11 0QA

Mobile	+44 (0)7966 490836
Email	info@53durweston.com
Web	www.53durweston.com

Entry 65 Map 3

Stock Gaylard

Down a farm track, around the corner from the deer park you'll find the three sturdy yurts on a raised wooden deck that make up Withy Bed Camp, one of three camps at Stock Gaylard. It's a ten-minute walk from, well, anything, so you have the camp and its surrounds to yourself. Owners Andy and Josie had these yurts built using the estate's own ash by a local carpenter, who also made all the bespoke furniture. The two sleeping yurts contain madly comfy beds and the one in the middle has a kitchen and seating area. The camp faces west so whether you're lying in bed or toasting marshmallows over the fire, you'll get the best of the setting sun. There's a compost loo and outdoor shower on the edge of the deck, but those needing to be eased in to the camping adventure can use the flushing toilet and electric shower in the farm buildings (just over the hill). Don't miss the chance to give the 'bath under the stars' a go though — you heat your own water in the wood-fired heater. There are 1,800 acres to explore and plenty of wildlife to spot. Lots to do nearby too: fishing and archery, llama trekking and paintballing. *Babies welcome. Lots of woodland walks on the estate and surrounding area. Animals are in nearby fields so owners asked to keep dogs on leads when out walking.*

Rooms	2 camps for 8 (2 doubles, 4 singles): from £128 per night. 1 camp for 4 (1 double, 2 bunks): from £76 per night. Max. 1 dog.
Meals	Self-catering.
Closed	October – March.
	Advice on walks.

Canopy & Stars
Stock Gaylard,
Sturminster Newton, DT10 2BG

Tel +44 (0)117 204 7830
Email enquiries@canopyandstars.co.uk
Web www.canopyandstars.co.uk/stockgaylard

Entry 66 Map 2

The Greyhound

It's hard to fault this little inn. It sits in one of Dorset's loveliest villages, lost in a lush valley with country views that shoot uphill. Outside, there's a colourful terrace that draws a crowd in summer. Inside, cool, rustic interiors mix old and new to great effect. You find stone walls, old flagstones, gilt mirrors and a wood-burner to keep things cosy. There's a lively locals' bar where you can grab a pint of Butcombe, then a chic little restaurant where you dig into delicious food. The feel throughout is informal and you can eat wherever you want, so spin onto the terrace in good weather and try seared scallops, boeuf bourguignon, sticky toffee pudding. Six lovely rooms wait in an old skittle alley. They're not huge, but nor is their price, and what they lack in space, they make up for in comfort and style, with crisp linen, airy colours and pretty furniture. There's a DVD library, too, and Wellington boots if you want to walk. The Cerne Abbas giant is close, while the coast is on your doorstep: Lyme Regis for fossil hunters, West Bay for fine walking and fabulous Chesil Beach. *Minimum stay: 2 nights on bank holidays. Lovely outdoor garden area for dogs to enjoy. Long country walks. Chalk Valley stream running directly behind – ideal for a cool down after a long walk!*

Rooms	6 doubles: £89-£99.
	Singles from £69.
	Dogs £5. Max. 1.
Meals	Lunch from £5.50.
	Dinner, 3 courses, about £30
	(not Sunday evening).
Closed	Never.
	Biscuits, blankets, dog-friendly dining area and advice on local walks.

Matthew Martinez
The Greyhound,
26 High Street, Sydling St Nicholas,
Dorchester, DT2 9PD

Tel   +44 (0)1300 341303
Email info@dorsetgreyhound.co.uk
Web   www.dorsetgreyhound.co.uk

Entry 67 Map 2

The Acorn Inn

Perfect Evershot and rolling countryside lie at the door of this 400-year-old inn in Thomas Hardy country. Red Carnation Hotels, under the guidance of Alex and chef Jack, are reviving its fortunes. It's very much a traditional inn; locals sup pints of Otter Ale in the long flagstoned bar and guests sample good food sourced within 25 miles. In the dining room, the atmosphere changes to rural country house with smartly laid tables, terracotta tiles, soft lighting and elegant fireplaces. Good gastropub fare is taken seriously, be it a roast beef and horseradish sandwich or a twice-baked cheese soufflé followed by grilled spatchcock and warm treacle tart. The service is helpful and friendly. Bedrooms creak with age and style; there are antiques and fabric wall-coverings, super little bathrooms, perhaps a wonky floor or a lovely four-poster. It's worth splashing out on a larger room if you want space. *Footpath through 900-acre parkland in village, and countless other footpaths in all directions. Coastal path within 20-minute drive.*

Rooms	3 doubles, 3 twins, 3 four-posters: £99–£160. 1 suite for 2: £160–£205. Dogs £10.
Meals	Lunch & dinner £5.25–£22.95. Bar meals from £4.95.
Closed	Rarely.
🐕	Dog-friendly guide to the area, water bowl, towel and treats. Walking map and dog treats in the bar too.

Jack & Alexandra Mackenzie
The Acorn Inn,
Evershot,
Dorchester, DT2 0JW
Tel   +44 (0)1935 83228
Email   stay@acorn-inn.co.uk
Web   www.acorn-inn.co.uk

Entry 68 Map 2

BridgeHouse Hotel

Beaminster – or Emminster in Thomas Hardy's *Tess* – sits in a lush Dorset valley. From the hills above, you drop through glorious country, rolling down to this old market town, where the church tower soars towards heaven. As for this lovely hotel, it's a 13th-century priest's house and comes with original trimmings: stone flags, mullioned windows, old beams and huge inglenooks. It's intimate, friendly and deeply comfortable, with something beautiful at every turn. There are rugs on parquet flooring, a beamed bar with an open fire, a splendid dining room with Georgian panelling and a Robert Adam's fireplace. Beautiful lighting sets the mood for excellent food, perhaps Witchampton snails, an imperious steak and kidney pie, pear and rosemary tart tatin. Rooms in the main house are bigger and smarter, those in the coach house are simpler and less expensive; all are pretty with chic fabrics, crisp linen, flat-screen TVs and stylish bathrooms. Breakfast is served in the conservatory, so watch the gardener potter about as you scoff your bacon and eggs. Chesil Beach at West Bay is close. *Minimum stay: 2 nights at weekends. Secure walled garden (with poo dustbin & bags); public bridleway walks along the river Brit Valley Way (occasionally horses in nearby fields).*

Rooms	6 doubles, 3 twin/doubles, 2 four-posters, 2 family rooms for 4: £95-£200. Dogs £15 per dog per night. Max. 2 per room.
Meals	Lunch from £8.50. Dinner, 3 courses, £25-£35.
Closed	Never.
	Dog treats on arrival. Special menus on request, drying towels and best walks advice.

Mark & Jo Donovan
BridgeHouse Hotel,
3 Prout Bridge,
Beaminster, DT8 3AY,
Tel   +44 (0)1308 862200
Email   enquiries@bridge-house.co.uk
Web   www.bridge-house.co.uk

Camping Coach

The quirky train carriage gleams inside and out. Turn the chunky brass handle on the door of this ancient London Brighton & South Coast Railway carriage and enter another era. Find original fittings (luggage racks, rounded windows, leather straps and brass work), but the tradition gives way slightly in the presence of a fully equipped kitchen and adjoining loo and shower at one end. In the main saloon there is a long bench seat that converts into a double bed and at the other end a wonderful antique French stove will keep you warm. Of course, you could spend your days in the living van a few steps from the coach, which is gaily decorated and equally comfortable. The van's seating can also convert into two single beds (ideal for children), so you can sleep four people in the whole camp together and then invite each other over for tea! There are pubs and restaurants, markets and teashops where you can explore the area's varied produce. You're a fossil's throw from the Jurassic Coast for some lovely beach walks and surrounded by endless fields and hills. *Children over 5 welcome. Fabulous walking area.*

Rooms	Train carriage for 4 (1 double, 2 singles): from £100 per night. Max. 1 dog – please call before booking.
Meals	Self-catering.
Closed	Never.
	Towels and advice for walking.

Canopy & Stars
Camping Coach, High Cross Cottage,
Whitecross, Netherbury, Bridport, DT6 5NH

Tel	+44 (0)117 204 7830
Email	enquiries@canopyandstars.co.uk
Web	www.canopyandstars.co.uk/campingcoach

Entry 70 Map 2

Old Forge

Snug in a stream-tickled hamlet, deep in Hardy country, this B&B is as pretty as a painting and wonderfully peaceful. Judy is charming and friendly – this is a happy place, a real country home, a no-rules B&B. The one guest double, sharing the former forge with a self-catering pad for two, is inviting and cosy with yellow hues, thick carpets and trinkets from travels. Sit outside in a sunny patch by a beautiful copper beech. The 17th-century farmhouse opposite is where you breakfast: Judy, ex Prue Leith, serves a neighbour's eggs, a friend's sausages and good coffee in an eclectically furnished room with bucolic views to garden, meadows and hills. *Large garden – almost secure except for stream, which an adventurous young dog could jump across.*

Rooms	Old Forge – 1 double: £100. Singles £60–£70.
Meals	Restaurant 1.5 miles.
Closed	Rarely.

 Towels for drying and protective covers for chairs etc.

Judy Thompson
Old Forge, Lower Wraxall Farmhouse,
Lower Wraxall,
Dorchester, DT2 0HL
Tel   +44 (0)1935 83218
Email   judyjthompson@hotmail.co.uk
Web   www.lowerwraxall.co.uk

Entry 71 Map 2

Lawn Cottage

In a quiet village in Blackmore Vale, the path to this spacious cottage is lined with tulips and vegetables. Easy-going June is a collector of pretty things; art, antiques and china blend charmingly with soft colours and zingy kilims. Bedrooms are sunny – one is downstairs (en suite) with a private entrance; there's a sweet very comfy shepherd's hut too if you fancy a night under the stars and sunset views. Breakfasts are generous; hut dwellers can come in to the dining room or have a hamper delivered. Visit Sherborne (abbey, castle, smart shops), walk from the gate to Duncliffe Wood. Return to a tiny snug sitting room. Perfect Dorset B&B! *Secure garden.*

Rooms	1 twin/double; 1 double with separate bathroom: £80. 1 shepherd's hut for 2 with separate bathroom in main house: £90.
Meals	Pub/restaurant 1 mile.
Closed	Rarely.

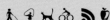 Village footpaths and 250-acre Woodland Trust wood within easy walking distance.

June Watkins
Lawn Cottage, Stour Row,
Shaftesbury, SP7 0QF
Tel   +44 (0)1747 838719
Mobile +44 (0)7809 696218
Email   enquiries@lawncottagedorset.co.uk
Web   www.lawncottagedorset.co.uk

Entry 72 Map 3

Lord Crewe Arms at Blanchland

Originally the abbot's lodge and kitchens (and its garden the cloisters), the Lord Crewe Arms has become a Grade II*-listed inn. The village, in a sheep-clad valley on the moors' edge, was built with stone from the abbey's ruins. Inside: ancient flags, inglenook fireplaces, fortress walls and a classy country décor. Public areas range from lofty to intimate and the atmospheric bar is in the vaulted crypt. With a head chef from Mark Hix's 'stable', the robust modern British menu includes steaks, chops and spit-roasted meats, fresh crab salad and ruby beets. Puddings hark back to ancient times: sea buckthorn posset, rhubarb fumble. Wines include great burgundies and clarets, ales range from Allendale's Golden Plover to Nel's Best from High House Farm, and there are water bowls for dogs in the garden. If you stay, you're in for a treat. Most rooms are divided between The Angel, a simple, beautiful, listed ex-inn across the way, and in the former tied cottages. Some bedrooms have exposed stone walls and real fires, all have soft carpets, fine fabrics, divine beds and deep baths. *Rivers to jump in. Sheep in fields so dogs to be kept on leads.*

Rooms	19 doubles: £106-£170. 1 suite for 2: £135-£180. 1 family room for 4: £165-£220. Dogs £10. Max. 3.
Meals	Starters from £4.95. Mains from £10.45. Sunday lunch, 2 courses, £21.
Closed	Open all day.
	Dog bed, towel, bowl and suggested walks.

Tommy Mark
Lord Crewe Arms at Blanchland,
Blanchland,
Consett, DH8 9SP
Tel +44 (0)1434 675469
Email enquiries@lordcrewearmsblanchland.co.uk
Web www.lordcrewearmsblanchland.co.uk

Entry 73 Map 6

Maison Talbooth

An outdoor swimming pool that's heated to 29°C every day, a chauffeur on hand to whisk you down to the hotel's riverside restaurant, a grand piano in the golden sitting room where those in the know gather for a legendary afternoon tea. They don't do things by halves at Maison Talbooth, a small-scale pleasure dome with long views across Constable country. The house, an old rectory, stands in three acres of manicured grounds, the fabulous pool house a huge draw with its open fire, honesty bar, beautiful art and treatment rooms. Interiors are equally alluring. There are no rooms, only suites, each divine. Some on the ground floor have doors onto terraces where hot tubs wait, but all pamper you rotten with flawless bathrooms, fabulous beds, vintage wallpapers, hi-tec excess. At dinner you're chauffeured to the family's restaurants (both within half a mile): Milsoms for bistro food served informally; Le Talbooth for more serious fare, perhaps roasted scallops with a Sauternes velouté, fillet of halibut with walnuts and apple, banoffee soufflé with caramelised banana crumble. A great escape. *Lots of walks nearby, through woods and by river. Livestock around part of the year on some walks.*

Rooms	12 suites for 4: £210-£420. Singles from £170.
Meals	Dinner at Milsoms £25; at Le Talbooth £35-£50.
Closed	Never.
🐕	Biscuits, blankets, towels and dog walks.

Paul & Geraldine Milsom
Maison Talbooth,
Stratford Road, Dedham,
Colchester, CO7 6HN
Tel   +44 (0)1206 322367
Email   maison@milsomhotels.com
Web   www.milsomhotels.com

Entry 74 Map 4

The Pier at Harwich

This attractive hotel was built in 1862 in the style of a Venetian palazzo and has remained in continuous service ever since. It sits above the historic Ha'Penny Pier with big skies above and watery views that shoot across the Stour estuary to Felixstowe. Inside you find a contemporary feel: boarded floors, a granite bar, deco travel posters framed on the wall, big arched windows to bring in the view. You can eat informally in the bistro downstairs (fish soup, rib-eye steak, warm treacle tart), or head upstairs to the beautiful first-floor restaurant, where you can watch the ferries glide past while tucking into Mersea rock oysters, rack of lamb, bitter chocolate pudding. Bedrooms are scattered about, some in the main house, others next door in a former inn. All are pretty, with padded bedheads, seaside colours, crisp white linen, and super bathrooms; if you want the best view in town, splash out on the Mayflower suite. Don't miss the coastal walks, the blue flag beach at Dovercourt, the ferry over to Felixstowe or the Electric Palace, the second oldest cinema in Britain. *Beach and promenade to walk on, sea to swim in.*

Rooms	10 doubles, 3 twins: £120–£170.
	1 suite for 2: £200–£230.
	Singles from £95.
	Dinner, B&B from £100 per person.
Meals	Lunch from £6.50.
	Sunday lunch from £19.50.
	Dinner à la carte £25–£40.
Closed	Never.

Blankets, towels, advice on walks, doggy dinners, water bowls and treat.

Paul & Geraldine Milsom
The Pier at Harwich,
The Quay,
Harwich, CO12 3HH
Tel   +44 (0)1255 241212
Email   pier@milsomhotels.com
Web   www.milsomhotels.com

Entry 75 Map 4

Great Farm

Wend your way along the leafy path through the trees and cross the narrow footbridge over the river – young-at-heart adventurers will find it idyllic. Otter Camp, Nightingale Camp and Barn Owl Camp are close together but secluded with a private clearing. Cross the water again and you'll have The Island at Great Farm all to yourself. Otter and Nightingale are intimate and off-grid, though the swish bathrooms are a step above camping. The river Coln forms a boundary to the front, there's woodland at the rear, and sheep and cattle nearby – keep the dogs on leads! Each spot has its own campfire, kitchen with gas hob (some outdoors), flushing loo and shower and many thoughtful touches besides. Leonie can provide a hamper of local ingredients for breakfast and picnics; dinner too can be delivered. If the river is too chilly, Otter and The Island have their own hot tubs. You're on a family-run working farm in the rural heart of the Cotswolds, with pretty villages, pubs galore and great walks. Go down river to Lechlade, or the Cotswold Water Park – Leonie will give you a map. If you're lucky, you'll spot an otter... *Babies welcome. Great walks, river to play in. Dogs need to be on a lead near farm livestock.*

Rooms	Cabin for 2 (1 double): from £100. Shepherd's hut for 2 (1 double, space for 2/own tent): from £90. Camp of 2 gypsy wagons for 6 (2 doubles, 2 5ft child singles, space for 10/own tents): from £125. Train carriage for 2 (1 double, space for own travel cot): from £90. All prices per night. Max. 2 dogs.
Meals	Self-catering.
Closed	October – March.
	Advice on walks.

Canopy & Stars
Great Farm,
Whelford, Fairford, GL7 4EA
Tel +44 (0)117 204 7830
Email enquiries@canopyandstars.co.uk
Web www.canopyandstars.co.uk/greatfarm

Entry 76 Map 3

The Royal Oak Tetbury

Resplendent after a full refurbishment this 17th-century coaching inn is abuzz with enthusiasm. Inside, reclaimed floorboards have been artfully fitted together, a salvaged carved oak bar has its own little 'Groucho snug' at one end. Exposed stone and a real fire co-exist with a pretty Art Deco piano whose ivories are often tinkled. Cheery staff will pull you a pint of Uley or Stroud ale – or perhaps an Orchard Pig cider – and on certain days you can even mix your own Bloody Mary. Treats in store on the menu from head chef Richard Simms feature pub classics with a twist: sharing or small plates, hearty salads, 'oak pots' with a veggie or meat option served with crusty bread or brown rice and plenty of choice for vegans. Up in the roof beneath massive beams is a more formal restaurant with a spacious, calm atmosphere. Across the cobbled yard are six bedrooms – three are dog-friendly – with a restful elegance, dreamy beds and bathrooms to linger in. And if a special occasion is the reason for your visit then the Oak Lodge room will not fail to get things off to a very good start. Enjoy the view from the garden, glass of wine in hand. *Minimum stay: 2 nights at weekends & in high season. Secure garden, and great walks on the doorstep.*

Rooms	6 doubles: £75–£160. Extra bed/sofabed available £20 per person per night. Dogs £10. Max. 2.
Meals	Lunch & dinner £5–£13.
Closed	Never.

Biscuits, advice and walks from the door as well as dog-friendly dining.

Kate Lewis
The Royal Oak Tetbury,
1 Cirencester Road,
Tetbury, GL8 8EY

Tel	+44 (0)1666 500021
Email	stay@theroyaloaktetbury.co.uk
Web	www.theroyaloaktetbury.co.uk

Entry 77 Map 3

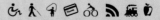

Asphodel Cottage

Asphodel stands out from the well-heeled houses in this quiet village: a hobbity stone shepherd's cottage with a bushy cap of thatch and trim garden behind. It's listed – early 1600s – and little has changed outside, but step in to a warm, bright living area of soft violet sofas, Indian rug on flagstone floors, a Moroccan lamp, original art. No TV downstairs to blight conversation, but a stone fireplace, wood-burner and coffee table with books. In one corner, a modern kitchen with vintage china and crystal glasses; in the other, steep stone stairs spiral to the bedroom. This is hugely romantic: chandelier dangling from open rafters, Laura Ashley bed on a rug-strewn wooden floor; centre stage in the bathroom, a claw-foot bath with fluffy towels and Molton Brown products. Hard to drag yourself out… but do, for outside are rattan seats hugged by Cotswold stone walls, a scented path over the lawn, a mini wild meadow, apples, plums, herbs to pick. Some asphodels, too — symbols of romance. Stroll to the Tunnel House Inn; close by are Roman Cirencester, Tetbury, the source of the Thames. Or roam as the deer do among endless fields. *Short breaks welcome. Big private garden, walled and secure (for most dogs!). Bathhurst estate woodlands 15-minute walk. All local pubs dog-friendly.*

Rooms	1 cottage for 2 (1 double): £560–£750 per week. Dogs £30 per pet per stay. Max. 1 large, 2 medium or 3 small.
Meals	Self-catering.
Closed	Never.
	Dogs treats, and walking maps in an information file. (Please bring your own dog bed, towels and bowls.)

Martin Jenner
Asphodel Cottage,
Tarlton,
Cirencester, GL7 6PA

Mobile	+44 (0)7951 681571
Email	reservations@asphodelcottage.co.uk
Web	www.asphodelcottage.co.uk

The Wheatsheaf

The Wheatsheaf stands at the vanguard of a cool new movement: the village local reborn in country-house style. It's a winning formula with locals and travellers flocking in for a heady mix of laid-back informality and chic English style. The inn stands between pretty hills in this ancient wool village on the Fosse Way. Inside, happy young staff flit about, throwing logs on the fire, ferrying food to diners, or simply stopping for a chat. Downstairs, you find armchairs in front of smouldering fires, noble portraits on panelled walls, cool tunes playing in the background. Outside, a smart courtyard garden draws a crowd in summer, so much so it has its own bar; English ales, jugs of Pimm's and lovely wines all wait. Back inside, beautiful bedrooms come as standard, some bigger than others, all fully loaded with comfort and style. Expect period colours, Hypnos beds, Bang & Olufsen TVs, then spectacular bathrooms with beautiful baths and/or power showers. As for the food, you feast on lovely local fare, perhaps devilled kidneys, coq au vin, pear and almond tart. Don't miss it. *Beautiful walks in the Cotswolds.*

Rooms	14 doubles: £120–£180.
	Extra bed £25 child, £50 adult.
	Dogs £10 per dog per night.
Meals	Continental breakfast included;
	cooked extras £5–£12.
	Lunch from £9.
	Dinner, 3 courses, about £30.
Closed	Never.

Dog bed in room with dog biscuits in a bowl. Pig's ears too.

James Parn
The Wheatsheaf,
West End,
Northleach,
Cheltenham, GL54 3EZ
Tel   +44 (0)1451 860244
Web   www.cotswoldswheatsheaf.com

Entry 79 Map 3

The Lion Inn

Annie's determination to restore an old inn's charms has been a joyous success. Push open the heavy oak door to reveal a beautiful main bar: rugs on pale-painted floors, candles at mullioned windows, rough stone walls, and a log fire crackling in a 15th-century inglenook. Jugs of fresh flowers, battered leather armchairs and grand gilt-framed paintings enhance the authentic feel. Review the papers over a pint of real ale, play scrabble, cards or one of the selection of games. Order from the seasonal menu: perhaps slowly braised brisket of Wagyu beef with mashed potato, followed by plum pudding with Earl Grey and armagnac prunes and a cassis sorbet. Country-chic rooms upstairs – one with its own small balcony, three with private staircases, one above the noisy snug bar – are toasty-warm and TV-free, with inviting beds and soothing colours, upholstered armchairs and antique furniture. Bathrooms are just as good, with Bramley products and en-suite showers. Winchcombe is on the Cotswold Way; Chipping Campden, Broadway and Cheltenham are a short drive. *Garden, river and lake short walk away. Cotswold Way and Cleeve Hill for walking; all sheep fields adequately signed.*

Rooms	5 doubles: £110–£160.
	2 suites for 3: £150–£185.
	Extra bed/sofabed available £25 per person per night.
	Dogs £25. Max. 3 per room.
Meals	Lunch & dinner £9.50–£24.50.
Closed	Never.

Dog beds in bedrooms, treats and biscuits on request. Towels, water in the gardens and lots of walking maps of the Cotswold Way.

Annie Fox-Hamilton
The Lion Inn, North Street,
Winchcombe,
Cheltenham, GL54 5PS
Tel   +44 (0)1242 603300
Email   sarah@thelionwinchcombe.co.uk
Web   www.thelionwinchcombe.co.uk

Entry 80 Map 3

The Priory Cottages

Down the one-mile lane, left over the cattle grid and onto an unmarked track – keep going! The owners' white farmhouse and the lovely cottages soon pop into view. The position is special and the bird life is extraordinary – so much so that Peter Scott set up Slimbridge on the other side of the water. This well-insulated home is a single-storey outbuilding divided into two wood-clad cottages, and inside has a charming simplicity. Step into a living room with a creamy sofa and armchair, a dining table, a cosy wood-burner and a TV; there are river views, too. To the side is a galley kitchen, brand new and nicely equipped; the white bathroom and separate wet room are simple but appealing. Expect cream bedspreads, white cotton, old pine, fresh paintwork and toasty terracotta floors. To the front are two grassed areas divided by a willow screen and a lovely old orchard; skirt around the Cowans' house and you reach the river beyond. Wonderful walks start from the door, you can visit the ancient village of Awre, and cycle in the nearby Forest of Dean. Come for the peace of it all – and the birds. *Minimum stay: 3 nights. Short breaks available. Surrounded by fields and several footpaths within 50 yds.*

Rooms	1 cottage for 2-4 (1 twin/double, sofabed), 1 cottage for 4 (1 double, 1 twin/double): £260-£547 per week. Dogs £20 per pet per stay. Max. 2 per cottage.
Meals	Self-catering.
Closed	Never.
	Hose for mucky dogs, towels for drying off, stock-proof orchard for dogs to run free. Advice on walks and where farm animals are; attention drawn to Countryside Code.

Ian Cowan
The Priory Cottages,
Awre,
Newnham, GL14 1EQ
Tel   +44 (0)1594 516260
Email   rigc@onetel.com
Web   www.thepriorycottages.co.uk

Entry 81 Map 2

The Close

Up a hill of pretty Cotswold-stone houses, this large Queen Anne house with handsome sash windows delivers what it promises. Step into a stone-flagged hall with grandfather clock and Georgian oak staircase; take welcoming tea with Karen in the drawing room — all gracious sofas and charming chandelier; then upstairs to three light and airy bedrooms softly furnished with antiques. Window seats, shutters and views over garden or pretty street add to the restful atmosphere. Karen, as gracious and relaxed as her house, serves excellent breakfasts in the polished dining room. An elegantly hospitable base for exploring the Cotswolds. *Minimum stay: 2 nights at weekends. Garden, lots of public footpaths and dog walks on beautiful Minchinhampton Common. Many dog-friendly pubs/cafés nearby.*

Rooms	2 doubles, 1 twin: £85-£95. Singles £65-£75. Dogs £10 per stay.
Meals	Pubs/restaurants 1-minute walk.
Closed	January.

 Advice on walks and large dog-friendly garden.

Karen Champney
The Close,
Well Hill, Minchinhampton,
Stroud, GL6 9JE

Tel   +44 (0)1453 883338
Email   theclosebnb@gmail.com
Web   www.theclosebnb.co.uk

Entry 82 Map 3

The Guest House

Your own timber-framed house with masses of light and space, a sunny terrace, and spectacular valley and woodland views... A peaceful secluded place, it's full of books and mementoes of Sue's treks across the world; the large living room has wooden floors, lovely old oak furniture and French windows onto the rose-filled garden. Sue brims with enthusiasm and is a flexible host: breakfast can be over in her kitchen with delicious farm shop sausages and bacon, or continental in yours at a time to suit you. There's a wet room downstairs, and you hop up the stairs to your charming up-in-the-eaves bedroom with oriental rugs and a big comfy bed. Wonderful! *2.5-acre fenced garden in glorious rural Cotswolds with walks straight from the door. Dogs must be completely sheep-proof as surrounded by breeding ewes.*

Rooms	1 double with sitting room & kitchenette: £140-£160. 3-6 night breaks £133-£152 per night; 7 nights £935.
Meals	Dinner, 2 courses, from £15; 3 courses, from £20. Pub 1 mile.
Closed	Christmas.

 Dog-sitting, towels for drying and advice on walks – or walks with Manor Cottage dogs.

Sue Bathurst
The Guest House,
Manor Cottage, Bagendon,
Cirencester, GL7 7DU

Tel   +44 (0)1285 831417
Email   thecotswoldguesthouse@gmail.com
Web   www.cotswoldguesthouse.co.uk

Entry 83 Map 3

The Wellington Arms

Lost down a web of lanes, the 'Welly' draws foodies from miles around. Cosy, relaxed and decorated in style – old dining tables, crystal decanters, terracotta floor – the newly extended bar-dining room fills quickly, so make sure you book to sample Jason's inventive modern cooking. Boards are chalked up daily and the produce mainly home-grown or organic. Kick off with home-grown courgette flowers stuffed with ricotta, parmesan and lemon zest, follow with rack of home-reared lamb with root vegetable mash and crab apple jelly, finish with elderflower jelly, strawberry and raspberry sorbet. Migrate to the huge garden for summer meals and views of the pub's small holding: seven little pigs, nine woolly sheep, a few bees and almost 100 assorted hens; buy the eggs at the bar. Stay over and get cosy in either one of the three rooms, housed in the former wine store and pig shed. Expect exposed brick and beams, vast Benchmark beds topped with goose down duvets, fresh flowers, coffee machines, mini-fridges, and slate tiled bathrooms with underfloor heating and walk-in rain showers. Breakfast too is a treat. *Open fields and woodland walks; public footpath from the pub.*

Rooms	3 doubles: £100–£200.
	Dogs £10.
Meals	Set lunch £15.75 & £18.75.
	Dinner £11–£21.
Closed	Rarely.

Lily's Kitchen Bedtime Biscuits, bones, sheepskin rug, water bowl, towels for drying, maps and advice on walks.

Jason King & Simon Page
The Wellington Arms,
Baughurst Road,
Baughurst, RG26 5LP
Tel   +44 (0)118 982 0110
Email   hello@thewellingtonarms.com
Web   www.thewellingtonarms.com

Entry 84 Map 3

The Rother

The Rother yurt at Adhurst, in the ancient woodland of the South Downs National Park, just an hour and a half from London, is a perfect place for getting back to nature. Owners Guy and Alison are passionate about sustainable living and invite you to set the fire, tramp through the woods and immerse yourself in a slower, more basic, way of life. The site is completely off-grid and the yurt, made from local wood, has been decked out with solar fairy lights, wood-burners, storm kettles and wind-up radios. It shares a camp kitchen with three other yurts, a gas-powered hot shower and the compost loo. A wood-burner keeps the yurt warm, and can be used to make tea, but there is also a storm kettle which can be lit with nothing more than twigs, leaves and a match. Once you've had a cuppa, you'll be ready to explore the woods (look out for the zip wire), try a bit of horse riding or fly fishing, head over to Cowdray to watch the polo, or admire the beautiful scenery of the South Downs Way. *Babies welcome. Yurts are spaced far enough away from each other to not confuse dogs about their territory. River and woods.*

Rooms	Yurt for 4 (1 double, 2 camp beds for children): from £137 per night. Max. 2 dogs – please call before booking.
Meals	Self-catering.
Closed	November – April.
	Advice on walks, and river swims!

Canopy & Stars
The Rother,
Steep,
Adhurst, GU31 5AD
Tel   +44 (0)117 204 7830
Email   enquiries@canopyandstars.co.uk
Web   www.canopyandstars.co.uk/rother

Entry 85 Map 3

Wriggly Tin

Wriggly Tin shepherd's huts was born out of a family holiday where Alex Evans and his two daughters got out into the countryside and never looked back. Although that defining stay was actually in tipis, Alex's love of all things mechanical has lead him to hand build these lovely off-grid huts in a wooded corner of Hampshire. Butser, a hut named after the highest point in the area, sleeps 2 people and there are 4 other huts, varying in size up to Boundary that can accommodate up to 5 guests but all have space for a dog to sleep in comfort. Showers and loos are shared and housed in, unsurprisingly, an even more cunningly converted shepherd's hut. You're far enough apart to feel on your own, with your personal fire pit, tripod, cast iron griddle and plenty of wood and kindling for some daring experiments in campfire cooking. 100-year-old Old Winchester even has a private wood-fired hot tub to soak in. Wriggly Tin gives you a chance to settle in to the slow lane. Keep a pan of water on the wood-burner for tea and stroll through the surrounding bluebell woods with your canine companion. *Dogs to be kept on a lead or tether while on site. Think twice before bringing a wolfhound, as space is limited! Butser, Barrow and Old Winchester have the most space for a dog bed.*

Rooms	3 shepherd's huts for 2 (1 double): from £90 per night. 1 shepherd's hut for 3 (1 double, 1 single bunk): from £90 per night. 1 shepherd's hut for 5 (1 double, 3 single bunks): from £90 per night. Max. 2 dogs.
Meals	Self-catering.
Closed	Never.
	Advice on the best places for walks and days out.

Canopy & Stars
Wriggly Tin,
Brook Lane, Hambledon,
Hampshire PO7 4TF
Tel   +44 (0)117 204 7830
Email   enquiries@canopyandstars.co.uk
Web   www.canopyandstars.co.uk/wrigglytin

Entry 86 Map 3

Waterfall Cottage

The 1840 cottage is set in gardens planted by a Chelsea gold-medallist; embraced by stream, waterfall and trees, its lawns lead directly to New Forest heathland and forest dotted with ponies and deer... it is quintessentially English, a magical place. John used to paddle in the stream as a boy – his aunt (the gardener) used to live here – now there's a lovely new summer house too, perfect for curling up in with a good book. Inside, the cottage is light and sunny and full of family antiques and some of Naomi's paintings and John's photographs. Restored parquet floors, velvet drapes, fresh flowers, Aga and working coal and log fire create cottage cosiness. Off a big landing are three eiderdowned bedrooms: the master with its own dressing room and tiny, wisteria-clad balcony, the second double with hugely wide floorboards and goatskin rugs, the little single with sloped ceiling and Victorian bed. Pubs, shops, bike-hire and horse-drawn carriages are a mile off; walks are on the spot. And everywhere, the song of birds and stream: it's like stumbling upon a hidden corner of England. *Doggie Heaven: miles of open country in all directions.*

Rooms	1 cottage for 6 (2 doubles, 1 single, 1 single on landing, sofabed, cot available; 1 bath/shower room): £400–£1,350 per week.
Meals	Self-catering.
Closed	Never.

Dust sheets, large dog crate, Aga, wood-burning stove, direct access onto New Forest heathland and woods, and fully fenced 2-acre garden and paddock.

Naomi King
Waterfall Cottage,
Burley,
Ringwood, BH24 4HR
Tel   +44 (0)1722 334337
Email   naomi4law@btinternet.com
Web   www.newforestcottage.biz

Entry 87 Map 3

Drover's Rest

The magic starts as you pass through the farmyard of Llan y Coed, and across a sheep-grazed common high above the Wye. Then the roof of your cottage, a restored drover's home, appears – to a backdrop of the distant Black Mountains. Buzzards wheel, black sheep bleat, ducks skim the ponds: it's a haven for wildlife! (Badgers, squirrels, foxes, rabbits and chickens, too.) The whole ethos of farmer/owners Kesri and Paul is one of harmony with nature, reflected in the limewashed interiors. The big open-plan living room and kitchen are deliberately spare; there's a cosy sitting room with an open fire; and, upstairs, an uncluttered bathroom and a double and a twin bedroom with wonderful views. Robins, woodpeckers, chaffinches, greenfinches, cuckoos, kestrels and more share these 130 acres; wild orchids flourish. The owners may cook you a curry for your arrival, after that there's home beef, lamb, chicken and eggs to enjoy, all organic: rustle up a feast on the barbecue on the veranda. Heaven for walkers, families and foodies (two Michelin-starred pubs are close by) and all who find richness in the simple pleasures of life. *Short breaks available. Dogs are welcome everywhere on the farm. Enclosed garden. Plenty of walks direct from the door.*

Rooms	1 cottage for 4 (1 double, 1 twin; 1 bathroom): £495–£850 per week. Dogs £20 per stay. Max. 2.
Meals	Self-catering.
Closed	Never.
🐕	Dog treats, water bowls and advice on walks.

	Kesri Smolas
	Drover's Rest,
	Llan y Coed,
	Hay-on-Wye, HR3 6AG
Tel	+44 (0)1497 831215
Email	holidays@droversrest.co.uk
Web	www.droversrest.co.uk

Entry 88 Map 2

Drover's Rest

Through a tunnel of trees you'll find your meadow-dwelling safari tents – African in looks, but Welsh in spirit. Far enough away from each other to be private but neighbourly enough that you can handily borrow a box of matches for the campfire. Your first tell-tale sign is the chimney of a log-burner popping out of the top of each tent and the rattan sofa with huge cushions on the porch. Beyond the farmhouse-worthy kitchen and living area padded out with sheepskins and cushions, there are two bedrooms, each with cast iron beds, welsh blankets and sheepskin rugs. All tents have their own hot monsoon shower and flushing loo in a fully-heated stable block, just a couple of minutes' walk from the tents and torches are provided for night time trips. The Hayloft barn is yours to share with other glampers and has WiFi, a café, a cocktail bar and its own farm shop. There's also a lounge with bean bags and movie screenings and a dining area for group suppers. Pizzas, curries and BBQs are served up on different days of the week plus there's a BBQ outside each tent and a heavy-duty pot for cooking chillies and stews. *Babies welcome. Walks direct from the door. Dogs allowed in communal chill-out barn while you have dinner. Working farm so farm animals around.*

Rooms	5 safari tents for 4 (1 double, 2 singles): from £99 per night. Dogs £20 per pet per stay. Max. 2 – will come into contact with owners' dog.
Meals	Self-catering.
Closed	November – March.
🐕	Water bowls, doggy treats and advice on walks.

Canopy & Stars
Drover's Rest, Llan y Coed,
Hay-on-Wye, HR3 6AG

Tel	+44 (0)117 204 7830
Email	enquiries@canopyandstars.co.uk
Web	www.canopyandstars.co.uk/droversrest

Entry 89 Map 2

New Inn Brilley

Daphne's individual spirit infuses the whole of New Inn Brilley – you can't miss the stupa draped in prayer flags near the shared shower hut, and there's a barn turned meditation space where you can arrange guided meditation sessions. She acquired The Wagon over the Valley from a kindred spirit called Dale who had fitted it with Gypsy caravan inspired furnishings: a bed with a white linen and lace canopy, a cosy wood-burner and two Edwardian desks with an absolutely magnificent view towards the Black Mountains. Daphne has since added 3 more spaces: Angels, a tabernacle for up to 5 with private deck and handmade furniture shares the compost loo and hot shower with the Wagon. Further along the boardwalk is The Rising Sun, a sun trap for 2 with uninterrupted valley views. Hidden behind the trees is Mother Earth, a roundhouse. Clamber down from the raised double bed into your whisky barrel hot tub and soak up the view. Daphne runs a B&B so she can cook you breakfast if you want. During the day head to the markets in Hay or explore the stunning scenery by bike, horse, canoe or simply by foot. *Many walks and footpaths into the woodland right out of the door.*

Rooms	Wagon for 2 (double): from £75. Cabin for 2 (double): from £95. Tabernacle for 5 (raised double, sofabed, single): from £105. Roundhouse for 6 (raised double, 3 singles, reclining Edwardian chair): from £105. All prices per night. Dogs £20 per pet per stay. Max. 3.
Meals	Self-catering.
Closed	Rarely.

 A big bowl of water for our thirsty friends.

Canopy & Stars
New Inn Brilley, Brilley,
Whitney-on-Wye, Hereford, HR3 6HE
Tel   +44 (0)117 204 7830
Email   enquiries@canopyandstars.co.uk
Web   www.canopyandstars.co.uk/
        newinnbrilley

Entry 90 Map 2

Herefordshire

Wickton Court

At the end of a no-through road, two miles from little Stoke Prior, is a rambling old place steeped in history, a courthouse that dates from the 15th century; ask Sally to show you the wig room! Be welcomed by ducks on the pond, sheep in the field, dogs by the fire, and lovely hosts who make you feel at home. The hallway is flagged, the sitting room panelled, the fireplace huge and often lit; all feels authentic and atmospheric. Visit Hampton Court Castle, antique-browse in Leominster, play golf, walk to the pub. Return to cosseting bedrooms with generous curtains, big bathrooms, wonky floors and ancient beams; one room even has a wood-burner. *Livestock here and on neighbouring land. Have to be very strict on regulations for the sake of everyone concerned!*

Rooms	1 four-poster; 1 twin with separate bathroom: £95. Dogs £5 per dog per night. Max. check before booking.
Meals	Dinner, 2 courses, £25. Cold platter for late arrivals, £12.50. Pubs/restaurants 5 miles.
Closed	Rarely.
	Advice on walks and guided walks, towels, and resident dog playmates!

Sally Kellard
Wickton Court,
Stoke Prior,
Leominster, HR6 0LN

Email   sally@wickton.co.uk
Web   www.facebook.com/WicktonCourt

Entry 91 Map 2

Cover Star Competition

Some of our favourite handsome hounds

Isla is 3 years old and she likes nothing better than chasing a ball along a beach – she will run for miles.

Jim's favourite place is anywhere there's a ball... but the river Dee, Chester is one of his favourite haunts.

This is Merlot at Trewithen Gardens. He loves holidays, runs on the beach and cosy cottages in Cornwall with his best dog-friend Darcy.

Priory Bay Hotel

This lovely old house stands one field up from the sea with woodland paths leading down to the hotel's sandy beach. Medieval monks, Tudor farmers and Georgian gentry have all lived here. The house dates from the 14th century and stands in 60 acres of sprawling grounds. Inside, high ceilings, huge windows and a baby grand wait in the drawing room, but it's all very relaxed with a sitting-room bar and a playroom for children. The odd bag of golf clubs waits for the six-hole course, sunloungers flank the pool in summer, croquet hoops stand on the lawn. Bedrooms have an uncluttered feel: warm colours, tongue-and-groove bathrooms, a sofa if there's room. Some are enormous with timber frames, while luxurious yurts on the estate have claw-foot baths and terraces that look out to sea. As for the food, it's serious stuff, mostly local, some foraged, the fish from the waters around you, the meat from the hills behind. You eat in a stylish brasserie with walls of glass to bring in the view; try Bembridge crab, a tasty steak, Eton Mess with Isle of Wight strawberries and cream. *Minimum stay: 2 nights at weekends. Dogs on leads if livestock in fields please. Dogs welcome in Cluniac (enclosed garden) & Coach House.*

Rooms	16 twin/doubles: £160-£300.
	2 family rooms for 4: £240-£330.
	2 barns for 6: £300-£455 per night.
	2 self-catering houses for 8-10:
	£895-£2,695 per week.
	Dogs £20. Max. 2.
Meals	Lunch from £8.
	Afternoon tea £20.
	Dinner, 3 courses, £25-£35.
Closed	Never.

Advice on walks, 60 acres to roam and private beach to run on.

Andrew Palmer
Priory Bay Hotel,
Priory Road, Seaview, PO34 5BU

Tel	+44 (0)1983 613146
Email	enquiries@priorybay.co.uk
Web	www.priorybay.co.uk

Albion House

This is quite some house, a Regency pile that dates to 1790, with huge rooms, high ceilings and grandeur at every turn. It stands at the top of a hill in the middle of town with fine views over the Royal Harbour. Incredibly, it was left to decay by its last inhabitants, Ramsgate town council, whose headquarters this was until 2008. Now, after a long renovation, interiors shine, mixing contemporary design with the feel of a colonial gentleman's club. There's a fire in reception, watery views through big windows in the restaurant, then a fabulous bar with a grand piano, exotic pot plants, a roaring fire, and sofas everywhere. Classical prints are jammed on the wall, the bar itself came from the town hall. The whole place is a work of art, nothing is here by accident. Downstairs, there's a treatment room, a steam room, a meeting room that doubles as a cinema, then a vaulted cavern for wine tastings. Big bedrooms get smaller as you climb the house, but the best views are at the top. Expect good beds, crisp linen, neutral colours, robes in white marble bathrooms. Don't miss afternoon tea. Brilliant. *Great beach for dog walks just a stone's throw away. Local green to take your dog for a quick walk in the mornings and evenings.*

Rooms	12 twin/doubles, 1 four-poster: £125-£220. 1 suite for 2: £220-£375. Dogs £30 per stay. Max. 2 small.
Meals	Continental breakfast included, full English £10. Lunch from £14. Dinner, 3 courses, £25-£35. Sunday lunch from £16.
Closed	Rarely.
	Dog bed and dog treats.

Ben & Emma Irvine
Albion House,
Albion Place,
Ramsgate, CT11 8HQ
Tel   +44 (0)1843 606630
Email   enquiries@albionhouseramsgate.co.uk
Web   www.albionhouseramsgate.co.uk

Entry 93 Map 4

Kent

The Linen Shed

A weatherboard house with a winding footpath to the front door and a pot-covered veranda out the back: sit here and nibble something delicious and homemade while you contemplate the pretty garden with its gypsy caravan. Vickie, wreathed in smiles, has created a 'vintage' interior: find wooden flooring, reclaimed architectural pieces, big old roll tops, a mahogany loo seat. Bedrooms (two up, one down) are painted in the softest colours, firm mattresses are covered in fine cotton or linen, dressing gowns hang in the smart bathrooms. Food is seriously good here, and adventurous – try a seaside picnic hamper! *Sea near by, woods and walks.*

Leicestershire

Breedon Hall

Through high brick walls find a listed Georgian manor house in an acre of garden, and friendly Charlotte and Charles. Make yourselves at home in the fire-warmed drawing room full of fine furniture and pictures; carpets and curtains are in the richest, warmest reds and golds. Charlotte is a smashing cook and gives you homemade granola, jams and marmalade with local eggs, bacon and sausages; you'd kick yourself if you didn't book dinner. Bedrooms are painted in soft colours, fabrics are thick, beds covered in goose down; bathrooms are immaculate. Borrow a bike and discover the glorious countryside right on the cusp of two counties. *Check availability calendar on owners' website. Secure garden. Both pubs in the village accept dogs, and there are plenty of places for dogs to run.*

Rooms	2 doubles with separate bath/shower; 1 double with separate bath (occasionally shared with family): £85–£110. Dogs £10 per dog per stay. Max. 2.
Meals	Picnic hamper from £20. Pubs/restaurants 300 yds.
Closed	Rarely.
	Home-cooked local sausage. Advice on walks.

Rooms	5 doubles: £75–£150. Dogs £5 per day.
Meals	Supper £25. Dinner, 3 courses, £35. Pub/restaurant 1-minute walk.
Closed	Occasionally.
	Advice on walks.

Vickie Hassan
104 The Street, Boughton-under-Blean, Faversham, ME13 9AP
Tel   +44 (0)1227 752271
Mobile +44 (0)7714 646469
Email   bookings@thelinenshed.com
Web   www.thelinenshed.com

Entry 94 Map 4

Charlotte Meynell
Breedon Hall, Main Street,
Breedon-on-the-Hill, Derby, DE73 8AN
Tel   +44 (0)1332 864935
Mobile +44 (0)7973 105467
Email   charlottemeynell1963@gmail.com
Web   www.breedonhall.co.uk

Entry 95 Map 6

The Barn, Park Farm

On a peaceful road leading to the church, opposite the tiny green (the setting is bucolic) is a farmhouse and an attached barn – solid, Georgian and listed. The garden is a secluded suntrap (with rhubarb, currants and strawberries to share); the interior is aglow with space and light. Floors of shining elm sweep from airy kitchen and dining at one end to wide leather chesterfields and flat-screen TV at the other, as an elegant spiral central stair breaks up the space. Blinds and curtains come in bright stripes and cheerful florals (handmade by owner Siobhan), sturdy beams (sourced from their own oak) soar above, and the hall's crafted coat and boot stand sets the tone: this is no run-of-the-mill renovation but a striking modern space. The bedroom is on the mezzanine – an up-in-the-eaves retreat, cosy and wonderfully romantic, with a superb mattress and a feather duvet (there's non-allergenic bedding if you prefer it). The high-spec, stone-floored shower room is downstairs, plus there are books, puzzles and DVDs, and a warm welcome for your dog. *Minimum stay: 3 nights. Secure garden, lots of walks around. Close to the Lincolnshire Wolds and coast.*

Rooms	1 cottage for 2 (1 double; 1 bathroom): £400-£530 per week. Dogs £10 weekends, £15 week-long stays. Max. 2.
Meals	Self-catering.
Closed	Rarely.
	Blanket and poo bags.

Siobhan Butler
The Barn, Park Farm,
Nocton, LN4 2BG
Tel   +44 (0)1526 320149
Mobile   +44 (0)7786 968448
Email   siobhan.butler@btinternet.com

Entry 96 Map 7

Washingborough Hall

In its day Lincoln was one of the most important cities in England. Its castle holds a copy of Magna Carta and was built by William the Conqueror in 1068; its cathedral dates to 1090 and remains one of the finest in Europe. All of which makes it a great city to visit, and if you want to beat a peaceful retreat into the country at the end of the day, this is the place to stay. It sits two miles east of town in a small village on the river Witham – footpaths by the water lead back into town. As for this Georgian rectory, you'll find smart lawns to the front, then a big welcome within – Edward and Lucy go out of their way to make your stay special. There's a wood-burner in the hall, a breakfast room with garden views, a sitting-room bar for afternoon tea, then a light-filled orangery restaurant. Stylish bedrooms offer unstinting comforts. Rooms at the front are bigger and have the view, all have good beds, bold wallpapers, excellent bathrooms, a sofa if there's room. As for the food, there's posh fish and chips in the bar or sea bass with spring greens in the orangery. *Small woodland within grounds, open countryside within half a mile.*

Rooms	6 doubles, 3 twin/doubles, 2 four-posters: £85-£175. Singles from £75. Dogs £10. Max. 2.
Meals	Lunch from £5.50. Dinner, 3 courses, £25-£35. Sunday lunch from £18.50.
Closed	Never.
	Bowls, biscuits and advice on walks.

Lucy & Edward Herring
Washingborough Hall, Church Hill,
Washingborough, LN4 1BE

Tel	+44 (0)1522 790340
Email	enquiries@washingboroughhall.com
Web	www.washingboroughhall.com

Entry 97 Map 6

London

22 Marville Road

Smart railings help a pink rose climb, orange lilies add a touch of colour, and breakfast is in the pretty back garden on sunny days. Ben, the springer and Tizzie the cocker spaniel, and Christine – music lover, traveller, rower – make you feel at home. Your big light-filled bedroom is high up in the eaves and comes in elegant French grey with comfortable beds, crisp linen, pretty lamps, a smart bathroom and a chaise longue for lounging and reading. The house is friendly with treasures from Christine's travels and gentle music at breakfast; there's a baby grand to play too. Restaurants and shops are a stroll away and the Boat Race down the river. *Children over 10 welcome. Secure small back terrace garden; local parks within walking distance.*

Rooms	1 twin/double: £105. Singles £95. Dogs £15 per night. Max. usually 1 (depends on size).
Meals	Continental breakfast. Pubs/restaurants nearby.
Closed	Rarely.

Pig's ears, dog bed, towels for drying and advice on walks.

Christine Drake
22 Marville Road,
Fulham, SW6 7BD
Tel   +44 (0)20 7381 3205
Email   chris@christine-drake.com
Web   www.londonguestsathome.com

Entry 98 Map 3

Cover Star Competition

Some of our favourite handsome hounds

This is BooBoo and Dave. They love beaches and dog spas!

This is Mungo. He loves nothing more than visiting his favourite holiday destination Blakeney for a week of walking.

Here's Charlie. He loves going for walks along the Dorset coast.

Barsham Barns

Follow the footsteps of Henry VIII to the medieval village of Walsingham, home to the shrine of Our Lady (plus farm shop, two pubs and a rather good restaurant). Return to the luxury of beautiful rooms awash with sunlight and space. Potter Jenny and architect husband have transformed a complex of barns set in a pretty valley that is more Cotswolds than Norfolk – yet the glorious North Norfolk Coast is only five miles away. Find an enticing palate of flint, cobbles, chalk and beams, warm textures and sophisticated furnishings, a hamper full of goodies and romantic country sounds (wagtails and warblers, cockerel and sheep). Living spaces are big and open plan with an inglenook fireplace or groovy wood-burner, the kitchen is perfect for entertaining (you can order a chef), the bathrooms are sleek and the bedrooms delightfully fresh and airy. A shared spa (you can book for exclusive use), a games room, an ornamental herb garden and potager and long lovely views complete the picture. If you've come from the city this is nothing short of heaven. *Two dog-friendly barns. Private garden (unfenced), rural setting, local footpaths. Underfloor heating.*

Rooms	1 barn for 4, 1 barn for 6, 2 barns for 8, 1 barn for 10, 1 barn for 12, 1 barn for 14: £765–£3,815 per week. Short breaks from £455. Dogs £22.40–£72.40 per week (seasonal range).
Meals	Self-catering.
Closed	Never.
	Advice on walks.

Jenny Dale
Barsham Barns, Greenway,
North Barsham, NR22 6AP
Tel   +44 (0)1328 821744
Email   info@barshambarns.co.uk
Web   www.barshambarns.co.uk

The White House

If you don't know Norfolk's six villages called The Burnhams, you're in for a treat. By the creek is Burnham Overy Staithe, where sea, sand, dunes and marshes magically meet… you can walk here over fields from the house. You can walk to Burnham Market too – Georgian, charming, and just a mile away. The White House stands in pretty Burnham Overy, near the windmill and by the parish church. With three traditional cottage-comfy bedrooms upstairs and one down, it's a marvellous place for an outdoorsy family or a bunch of nature-loving friends. Built in 1760, with chunky beams and wonky floors, it is comfortable, cosy and very well-equipped. French windows open to a courtyard garden with pretty seating and a barbecue, and there are two sitting rooms to choose from, one with games, TV and DVD, the other with a wood-burner. As for the kitchen, it's the hub of the house and holds all you need for a feast, including an iPad dock to keep the cook happy. Let the dogs loose on Holkham's glorious sands; visit Holkham Hall, one of England's finest estates. *Neighbouring farmers request dogs on leads. Walks to the creek.*

Rooms	1 house for 8 (1 double – en suite, 1 double, 1 twin, 1 twin/double; 1 bathroom, 1 shower room): £695–£1,418 per week. Dogs £10 per week. Max. 2.
Meals	Self-catering. Restaurants 1 mile.
Closed	Never.

Lovely walks straight from the cottage – perfect for dogs.

Jos & Mary-Anne Otway-Ruthven
The White House,
Wells Road, Burnham Overy,
King's Lynn, PE31 8HU

Tel	+44 (0)1566 782461
Email	stay@hornacott.co.uk
Web	www.norfolkwhitehouse.webs.com

Entry 100 Map 7

Ned's Nest

Deep in the Norfolk countryside, a snug, dog-friendly barn for two. Mark and Jane's imaginative conversion of this black weather-boarded stable has been a labour of love. It's got bags of character – old beams run across the vaulted ceiling, while the double bedroom is in an original stall. A welcome basket of fresh bread, dog biscuits, recently laid eggs and Jane's wonderful truffles is a real treat on arrival. There are only 12 houses in the tiny hamlet of Thurgaton and this lovely bolthole, next to Mark and Jane's redbrick cottage, is surrounded by meadows and woodland. Sit in the peaceful, shingle courtyard and enjoy the silence, or sink into the plump sofa and relax. Interiors are stylish and uncluttered; walls are painted a serene shade of grey and you'll spot interesting furniture and finds throughout, from zinc coat hangers to wire lockers for clothes storage. The well-equipped kitchen makes self-catering a pleasure, and handmade soaps are supplied in the sparkling white shower room. Wonderful walks start from the door and you're only a half-hour drive from the Broads. *Secure gravel garden area with 4-foot fence; close to 4 National Trust parks. Separate utility room with dog crate, spare lead, bowls and holiday tag.*

Rooms	1 barn for 2 (1 double; 1 shower room): £290-£496 per week.
Meals	Self-catering. Pubs 2.3 miles.
Closed	Rarely.

Homemade biscuits, towels, blankets and advice on walks.

Mark & Jane Watts
Ned's Nest,
The Cottage, The Street,
Thurgaton, NR11 7PD
Tel   +44 (0)1263 761676
Email   hello@nedsnest.co.uk
Web   www.nedsnest.co.uk/

Entry 101 Map 7

Beechwood Hotel

Beechwood is charming, an old-school hotel in a sleepy corner of England with a level of service that's hard to match. It sits between Norwich and Cromer in a small medieval wool town where Nelson spent his schooldays. It's hard to beat for its generous prices, its lovely staff and Hugh and Emma, who look after their guests in style. Outside, you find an ivy-clad façade, inside, you get smartly tiled floors, a sitting-room bar, an attractive restaurant for local food and a pretty garden for afternoon tea in summer. There's a small library for the daily papers, then a collection of Agatha Christie novels – she was a frequent visitor in the 1920s and occasionally came to write. Bedrooms have a warm, traditional feel: pretty florals, oak furniture, crisp white linen for Vi-Spring mattresses. Two are small, most have sofas, garden rooms have slipper baths. You get robes and good showers, usually a bath, too. As for the food, most is sourced within ten miles, perhaps Morston mussels, fillet of beef, sticky toffee pudding. Cliff-top walks and sandy beaches wait, as does beautiful Norwich. *Minimum stay: 2 nights. Dinner, B&B at weekends. Dogs are welcome in all public areas of the hotel except the restaurant; lovely big garden.*

Rooms	12 doubles, 2 twins, 3 four-posters: £100-£175. Dogs £12 per night for 1, £15 per night for 2. Max. 2.
Meals	Dinner, 3 courses, £40.
Closed	Rarely.
	Advice on walks.

Hugh & Emma Asher
Beechwood Hotel,
Cromer Road,
North Walsham, NR28 0HD

Tel	+44 (0)1692 403231
Email	info@beechwood-hotel.co.uk
Web	www.beechwood-hotel.co.uk

Entry 102 Map 7

The Old Rectory

Conservation farmland all around; acres of wild heathland busy with woodpeckers and owls; the coast two miles away. Relax in the spacious drawing room of this handsome 17th-century rectory and friendly family home, set in lovely mature gardens (NGS) full of trees and unusual planting. Fiona loves to cook and bakes her bread daily, food is delicious, seasonal and locally sourced, jams are homemade. Comfortable bedrooms have *objets* from diplomatic postings and the spacious suite comes with mahogany furniture and armchairs so you can settle in with a book. Super views, friendly dogs, tennis in the garden and masses of space... If you fancy self-catering then opt for an independent break in the Garden Room: an attractive studio with an airy feel – comfy beds, a wood-burner to snuggle up to, pretty blue crockery, a little kitchen with all you need. Sip your coffee on the sunny terrace by pots brimming with flowers and plan your rambles on the Broads or long sandy beaches. Friends, or children, can stay on the sofabed, and dogs are welcome too. Fiona will bring fresh bread over to you for breakfast! *The garden is not enclosed.*

Rooms	1 suite for 2; 1 double with kitchenette & separate bath/shower: £70–£85. 1 studio for 2 (Garden Room): £235–£420 per week.
Meals	Dinner from £25. Pubs 2 miles.
Closed	Rarely.
	Locally made dog biscuits, wonderful walks, and occasional dog sitting if owners have to leave their dogs for the day. Dog-friendly beaches nearby.

Peter & Fiona Black
The Old Rectory,
Ridlington, NR28 9NZ
Tel +44 (0)1692 650247
Mobile +44 (0)7774 599911
Email ridlingtonoldrectory@gmail.com
Web www.oldrectorynorthnorfolk.co.uk

Entry 103 Map 7

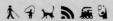

East Cottage, Southlands Farm

You'll fall in love with this rugged county, for its beauty and its space; no crowds, no traffic jams, no rush. Stay in a 19th-century byre and a granary (the original feeding troughs stand outside, spilling flowers in summer), immaculately converted, alongside two others, in an eco-friendly way. Solar panels heat the water, the logs are on the house, electricity comes from renewable sources. Step inside East Cottage to find a light modern space with soaring ceilings, tiles warm underfoot, bright rugs and cushions and a wood-burning stove. The kitchen glows at the other end: hand-built Shaker-style units, granite tops, an old pine dresser with plenty of china, a table for lazy breakfasts; owner Dee delivers a sizzling full English if you want, all local and seasonal. Up the spiral stairs are super bedrooms with buttermilk walls, wooden floors, pastel-striped blankets and exquisite beds; bathrooms are dazzling white, the twin has a wet room, the towels are thick and white. You can walk to a superb pub; or take a sundowner to the patio, and choose a home-cooked supper from the honesty freezer. *Buy home-produced rare breed Dexter beef & pork sausages from the owners' farm shop. North Tyne river walks, a stream to splash in and a public footpath right by the gate.*

Rooms	1 cottage for 4 (1 twin – en suite, 1 double, 1 shower room), 1 cottage for 2 (1 double; 1 bathroom): £360-£800 per week. Dogs £30 per stay. Max. 2.
Meals	Self-catering.
Closed	Never.

Drying room, towels and Bonedrybed dog bed. Advice on walks, and hose pipe area for muddy paws. Birthday cakes on request and 37 acres to explore.

Charles & Dee McGowan
East Cottage,
Southlands Farm, Gunnerton,
Hexham, NE48 4EA

Tel	+44 (0)1434 681464
Email	dee@southlandsfarmcottages.co.uk
Web	www.southlandsfarmcottages.co.uk

Entry 104 Map 9

Brinkburn Northumberland

This is heavenly countryside, and Brinkburn Priory (built in 1135) has an unrivalled position within it. Solitude and peace are yours in a dramatic wooded ravine along the meandering river Coquet – no wonder the monks who built it felt serene. Mark and Emma Fenwick have renovated (beautifully) three lovely old buildings: The Stables, perfect for a big gathering with plenty of outdoor space, Priory Cottage – a cosy bolthole for two; and Bel House with its private south-facing garden. All have superb kitchens and bathrooms, comfortable sofas and chairs by wood-burning stoves, good fabrics and gentle colours. Nothing is other than generous and all has been thought of, even down to bathrobes and good lotions and potions. It's so romantic you may even be inspired to get married here, in a marquee on the terrace in summer, or in the elegant White Room in winter. There are more than 30 acres for you to explore, with woodland walks along the river and lots of wildlife; beaches are peerless and yet you are close to good road and rail links, and the airport. Newbies to Northumberland will fall in love. *Short breaks available. Visit owner's website for availability. Changeover days: Mon & Fri. Woodland walks, beach walks, rivers to jump in.*

Rooms	1 cottage for 2 (1 double, 1 sofabed; 1 bathroom), 1 cottage for 8 (1 double – en suite, 1 double, 1 twin/double, 2 singles; 1 bathroom): £425-£1,690 per week. 1 house for 4 (1 double, 1 twin/double; 1 bathroom): £350-£870 per week. Dogs £20 per stay. Max. 2.
Meals	Self-catering.
Closed	Never.

Towels, bowls, and great dog walking from the door.

Mark Fenwick
Brinkburn Northumberland,
Longframlington,
Morpeth, NE65 8AR

Tel	+44 (0)1665 570870
Email	athome@brinkburnnorthumberland.com
Web	www.brinkburnnorthumberland.com

Entry 105 Map 9

Sky Den

The Sky Den was built by William Hardie Designs with George Clarke during the second series of his *Amazing Spaces* programme. It's composed of three different shapes which blend together the best of outdoors and indoors, taking in everything from the red squirrels in the trees around you to the sweeping river below. The square is the central point and your main living space, with glass doors opening onto a wide balcony with captivating views over the river. Inside, George has created an impressively versatile space, with a functional kitchen in a clutter-phobe's paradise of fold-away furniture (including two single beds) and wet room. Then there's the circle, a simple viewpoint of corrugated iron, where you can have a picnic and brew up a cuppa over the wood-burning stove. Finally the triangle is the loft space of your already lofty suite, accessed by steps from the outside deck. In good weather open the whole roof for an unobstructed view of the Northumberland Dark Skies. You're in the Kielder Water & Forest Park so wildlife lovers and adventure-seeking families will be happy. Bring warm clothes! *Babies welcome. Maps of the area provided. Please note that dogs are not allowed in the centre building unless they are assistance dogs.*

Rooms	Treehouse for 4 (4 singles or 1 double and 2 singles): from £150 per night. Dogs £50 per stay. Max. 1.
Meals	Self-catering.
Closed	Never.
🚶	Food and water bowls, and advice on walks through the forest and along the Lakeside Way.

	Canopy & Stars
	Sky Den,
	Calvert Trust Kielder,
	Falstone, Hexham, NE48 1BS
Tel	+44 (0)117 204 7830
Email	enquiries@canopyandstars.co.uk
Web	www.canopyandstars.co.uk/skyden

Entry 106 Map 9

Battlesteads Hotel

In the land of castles, stone circles and fortified towers is Battlesteads, an old inn given a new lease of life by owners who choose to be 'green'. The boiler burns wood chips from local sustainable forestry, a polytunnel produces the salads, all raw waste is composted; the Slades have won a bevy of awards, from 'Considerate Hotel of the Year' to a Green Tourism gold. Enter a large, cosy, low-beamed and panelled bar with a wood-burning stove and local cask ales. A step further and you find a spacious dining area: leather chairs at dark wood tables and a conservatory dining room that reaches into a sunny walled garden. The menus show a commitment to sourcing locally and the food is flavoursome. The Northumbrian fillet steak with Cumbrian blue cheese is meltingly tender and you must try Dee's award-winning bread and butter pudding! Exemplary is the housekeeping so bedrooms are spotless, spacious, carpeted and comfortable, and there's wheelchair access on the ground floor. Hadrian's Wall is marvellously close. *Large garden, river nearby and Winston the hotel Labrador to play with.*

Rooms	14 doubles, 4 twins: £95–£165.
	3 family rooms for 4: £115–£135.
	1 single: £70–£95.
	Dogs £10 per night.
Meals	Lunch from £9.75.
	Dinner from £10.75.
	Sunday lunch, 3 courses, £15.50.
Closed	Christmas & Boxing Day.

 Blanket, poo bags, towels, dog biscuits and walks from the front door.

Richard & Dee Slade
Battlesteads Hotel,
Wark,
Hexham, NE48 3LS

Tel	+44 (0)1434 230209
Email	info@battlesteads.com
Web	www.battlesteads.com

Entry 107 Map 9

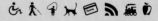

The Waiting Room

Staward Station had trains puffing in and out for over 80 years. It closed in 1950 along with the traditional waiting room now owned by Deb and Steve, who live nearby. You'll be sleeping in the old ticket office, and in fact the original ticket hatch is still in use, opening onto the reading room (although morning cups of tea might be more appreciated than tickets these days). It's also a bit cosier than it used to be, with new double glazing on the replica south-facing windows and with insulation material used by NASA lining the roof. There's still the main entrance from the platform, leading into the sitting room, and if you go through the fully equipped kitchen you'll find another door leading out the back to your private courtyard garden. The old stone railway bridge is just at the end of the platform, and from the top you can see over the tree tops down into Staward Gorge and across to Hadrian's Wall – perfect for planning your walking route through the surrounding countryside. A good one to start with is the John Martin trail, a ten mile off-road walk that you can join just at the bottom of the garden. *Secure area of garden, and advice on woodland walks without stock, and on where leads are required. (Can't accept bitches in season.)*

Rooms	Cabin for 4 (1 double, 1 sofabed): from £72 per night. Max. 2 dogs – please call before booking.
Meals	Self-catering.
Closed	Never.
🐕	Leads, bowls, poo bags, furniture throws, a secure garden and dog-friendly walks away from farm stock.

Canopy & Stars
The Waiting Room, Staward Station, Langley upon Tyne, Hexham, NE47 5NR

Tel	+44 (0)117 204 7830
Email	enquiries@canopyandstars.co.uk
Web	www.canopyandstars.co.uk/ thewaitingroom

Entry 108 Map 6

The Cherry Tree Inn

A short drive from London (and Oxford) is a handsome old pub in Stoke Row, with food, service and bedrooms to match. It is one of three dining pubs in the Henley area run by the same company. Throughout all is fresh, light and airy, with chunky wood tables and pale colours, and floors of stripped wood or stone; of the bars, the biggest is in the middle, warm and cosy with an open fire. You can eat where you like and the food is pub grub done well, with lots on the menu. Sunday lunches see two roasts as well as fish pie or sausages, and always a dish for vegetarians; there are tasty meals for little ones and puddings that sound suitably naughty. You could drop by for a pint of Brakspear and a platter of ham, salami, pork belly and chorizo, or tuck into tandoori chicken breast with all the trimmings, or beer-battered cod. In summer there are hog roasts in the beer garden. Crisp linen, cream walls, big beds, generous breakfasts… it's also a good weekend base for the area, with four ground-floor bedrooms in the wood-clad barn, a stagger away. Your dog can stay too. *Woodland walks, fields; large garden for dogs to play, but not enclosed, River Thames 15-minute drive.*

Rooms	4 doubles: £85–£100.
	Max. 1 large dog or 2 small.
Meals	Lunch from £6.95.
	Sunday lunch from £12.50.
	À la carte dinner £20–£30.
	Not Sunday eve.
Closed	Open all day.

🚶🐕 Advice on walks, bar treats jar, doggie bowls for water. Doggies allowed in some rooms overnight. Freedom to come and go in garden as long as well-behaved.

Lolly & Doug Green
The Cherry Tree Inn,
Stoke Row,
Henley-on-Thames, RG9 5QA
Tel   +44 (0)1491 680430
Email   enquiries@thecherrytreeinn.co.uk
Web   www.thecherrytreeinn.co.uk

Entry 109 Map 3

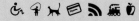

Uplands House

Come to be spoiled at this handsome house, built in 1875 for the Earl of Jersey's farm manager. All is elegant and lavishly furnished; expect large light bedrooms, crisp linen, thick towels and vases of flowers. There are long views from the orangery, where you can have tea and cake; relax here with a book as the scents of the pretty garden waft by. Chat to Poppy while she creates delicious dinner – a convivial occasion enjoyed with your hosts. Breakfast is Graham's domain – try smoked salmon with scrambled eggs and red caviar. You're well placed for exploring – Moreton-in-Marsh and Stratford are close, Oxford just under an hour. *Large garden and sublime walks. Working farm, so owners must be responsible for good behaviour of dogs.*

Rooms	1 double, 1 twin/double, 1 four-poster: £100-£180. Singles £70-£110 (Mon-Thur). Max. 2 dogs.
Meals	Dinner, 2-4 courses, £20-£35. Pub 1.25 miles.
Closed	Rarely.
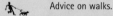	Advice on walks.

Poppy Cooksey & Graham Paul
Uplands House,
Upton, Banbury, OX15 6HJ
Tel   +44 (0)1295 678663
Mobile   +44 (0)7836 535538
Email   poppy@cotswolds-uplands.co.uk
Web   www.cotswolds-uplands.co.uk

Entry 110 Map 3

Cover Star Competition

Some of our favourite handsome hounds

Jack loves woodlands – the wilder the better – failing that any lake, river, stream, pond or puddle will do.

Jarvis loves nothing more than a hop in super long grass and bound into a bog.

Darcy loves the beach: she dodges the waves, climbs the sand dunes and chills on the beach. She collects the sand in her wrinkles!

The Olive Branch

A lovely pub in a sleepy Rutland village, where bridle paths lead out across peaceful fields. It dates to the 17th century and is built of Clipsham stone, as is York Minster. Inside, a warm, informal, rustic chic hits the spot perfectly with open fires, old beams, stone walls and choir stalls in the bar. But there's more here than cool design. This is a place to come and eat great food, the lovely, local seasonal stuff that's cooked with passion by Sean and his brigade, perhaps potted pork and stilton with apple jelly, haunch of venison with a juniper fondant, then a boozy rhubarb trifle. Bedrooms in Beech House across the lane are gorgeous. Three have terraces, one has a freestanding bath, all come with crisp linen, pretty beds, Roberts radios and real coffee. Super breakfasts – smoothies, boiled eggs and soldiers, the full cooked works – are served in a stone-walled barn with flames leaping in the wood-burner. The front garden fills in summer, the sloe gin comes from local berries, and Newark is close for the biggest antiques market in Europe. Picnic hampers can be arranged. A total gem. *Lots of countryside walks nearby.*

Rooms	5 doubles: £115–£195.
	1 family room for 4: £115–£195
	Singles from £97.50.
	Extra beds £30..
	Dogs £10.
Meals	Lunch from £6.25.
	Dinner, 3 courses, £25–£35.
	Sunday lunch from £17.50.
Closed	Rarely.
🚶🐕	Advice on walks.

Ben Jones & Sean Hope
The Olive Branch,
Main Street, Clipsham,
Oakham, LE15 7SH

Tel	+44 (0)1780 410355
Email	info@theolivebranchpub.com
Web	www.theolivebranchpub.com

Entry 111 Map 6

Combermere Abbey Cottages, Combermere Estate

The grounds of the 12th-century Cistercian abbey, a peaceful mile off the road, reveal a clutch of luxurious cottages in the former stable block. They range in style from the traditional and elegant to the contemporary and upbeat. Take a shower in a turret, curl up in a cushioned window seat, peer through mullioned panes, sweep through carriage house doors, dine beneath a gothic screen resurrected from a long-demolished abbey wing. The cottages sleep four to ten, and up to 53 in total; the largest – Beckett, Malbanc and Crossley – are great for groups with heaps of dining space. All come with fresh flowers, welcome packs, local art; most have a private terrace or garden. Kitchens are top-notch and Sarah takes the hard work out of self-catering: there's a shop in the courtyard and you can order a dinner or a luxury hamper in advance. Holistic treatments complete the picture, while dog duvets ensure your best friend gets pampered too. After a round of croquet or tennis, wander the gardens or the estate's organic pastures. And if you want to get married here, you can! *Minimum stay: 3 nights. On site woodland walk and mere.*

Rooms	1 annexe for 10: £1,600–£2,500 per week. 1 cottage for 2–4, 5 cottages for 4, 1 cottage for 5, 1 cottage for 6, 1 cottage for 8: £650–£2,100 per wk. Dogs £10 per night. Max. 1 large or 2 small.
Meals	Self-catering.
Closed	Never.
	Blankets, bowl, treats and advice on walks.

Sarah Callander Beckett
Combermere Abbey Cottages,
Combermere Estate,
Whitchurch, SY13 4AJ

Tel	+44 (0)1948 660345
Email	cottages@combermereabbey.co.uk
Web	www.combermereabbey.co.uk

Offa's Dyke Yurt

The two pod set up, spectacular views from the glass doors and complete privacy make Offa's Dyke Yurt a great place for any kind of escape. You can bring the family down and watch the kids play in your personal play park, or go it alone and lounge in the spacious yurt camp. The main living area is beautifully decorated with rich, glowing woods and soft fabrics and the big double bed is housed in a separate but adjoined mini yurt, giving extra space and privacy. On the same soaring deck is your own gas-powered shower, flushing loo and the wood-store. There's also outdoor furniture, the centrepiece of which, a big wooden chaise longue, is perfect for napping in front of the views of the rolling hills. As the name suggests, the yurt is rather well placed for the Offa's Dyke Path, with some hearty hiking to be done for about 180 miles in both directions and miles of world class mountain biking trails all around. You can also do courses in everything from fruit tree grafting to bench making and woodwork; Jo and Wilf are happy to take you badger spotting in a nearby field after the chickens have settled. *Babies welcome. Best to keep dogs under control as sheep may be in next field. River & plenty of walks. Own garden but dogs could get out.*

Rooms	Yurt for 4 (1 double, 1 sofabed): from £95 per night. Max. 2 dogs – please bring your own bedding and keep them off the furniture.
Meals	Self-catering.
Closed	Never.
	Advice on walks.

Canopy & Stars
Offa's Dyke Yurt,
The Barn Fron Uchaf, Weston Rhyn,
Oswestry, SY10 7NQ
Tel   +44 (0)117 204 7830
Email   enquiries@canopyandstars.co.uk
Web   www.canopyandstars.co.uk/offasdyke

Entry 113 Map 5

Walcot Hall

Lose yourself in the grounds of Walcot Hall – play croquet, go fishing, boating, biking, hiking – and discover quirky treasures galore… There's the Dipping Shed, with stunning views of the Long Mynd, a rough outer shell and a beautifully decorated interior with a high, beamed ceiling, a double room on the mezzanine, and another downstairs. On a grassy hill Buffalo Springfield Yurt – great, fur-covered bed – shares a modern loo in the former hen house and a gas-powered shower in the AA caravan with Lake View Yurt. Both have spectacular views. After The Gold Rush (for the more adventurous) is perched high above two secluded fishermen pools – shares the loo and has a wood-burner, double and sofabed. Also for the hardier and agile, is The Chapel, deep in the arboretum and a 500-yard walk from the nearest parking. It's a delightful airy bolthole, with subtle modern comforts and an organ you can play; curtains shield two separate beds from the fray. Then there's Crazy Horse Yurt with its big brass bed and sheepskins, and Green Glory an authentic showman's caravan… If you like things idiosyncratic you must visit this place! *Babies welcome. Plenty of walking, small pools to swim in, a large arboretum to explore; dog-friendly pubs nearby. Sometimes livestock around estate.*

Rooms	2 cabins for 4 (2 doubles each): from £100. Wagon for 2 (double): from £45. 2 yurts for 3 (double, camp bed): from £65. Yurt for 5 (double, sofabed, camp bed): from £73. All prices per night. Max. 3 dogs.
Meals	Self-catering.
Closed	Rarely.
	Walks, lots of space and many dog-loving staff!

Canopy & Stars
Walcot Hall,
Lydbury, SY7 8AZ

Tel	+44 (0)117 204 7830
Email	enquiries@canopyandstars.co.uk
Web	www.canopyandstars.co.uk/ walcothall

Entry 114 Map 2

Criggin Cottage

Ringed by the gentle hills of the Teme valley, this Shropshire hideout is a converted outbuilding of local stone and wood, with a patio overlooking a sunken garden for summer barbecues and starlit nightcaps. Downstairs is open plan and cottage cosy, with natural fibres, exposed stone walls, old beams and a heated slate floor. Curl up with a book in the sitting area, warmed by the log-burning stove, or gather in the kitchen, whose burr oak units were made by a local carpenter – along with the bedheads and wardrobes of the two bedrooms. These are upstairs – one king, one twin, both fresh and bright, with en suite showers and views worth rising early for. Easy-going, bee-keeping owners Mark and Rita, who live steps away in the main house, greet you with a hamper that includes fresh eggs, homemade jam and their own honey; they can also stock the larder in advance, sparing you a four-mile trip to the nearest shop. Traipse the dales, stroll by the river Teme, and enjoy the silence – broken only by the chirping of songbirds around the feeders or the distant growl of a tractor. *Secure terraces, plenty of walks from door, river to jump in and very quiet roads. Maps provided for short and long walks.*

Rooms	1 cottage for 4 (1 double, 1 twin/double; 2 shower rooms): £495-£695 per week. £400-£500 per week for 2. Short breaks available. Dogs £20 per dog per stay. Max. 2.
Meals	Self-catering.
Closed	Never.

🐕 Homemade treats, towels for drying, advice on walks and outside shower tap with hand-hot regulated water.

Rita Hughes
Criggin Cottage,
Melin-y-Grogue,
Llanfairwaterdine, LD7 1TU
Tel +44 (0)1547 510341
Email rita@criggin.co.uk
Web www.criggin.co.uk

Entry 115 Map 2

Lakeside Retreat

Off-piste drivers will delight in the approach – down a bumpy farm track, over an open field, across a ford and through grassy woodland. You land in a dreamy, bucolic setting with an arboretum and views over two deep water lakes (yes you may swim, yes you may use a little boat) with island, waterfalls, a small summerhouse that revolves, and a stream teeming with wildlife. A veranda and patio with table and chairs face south so you won't miss a thing; writers, artists and those clutching a large drink may take root here on less chilly days. Your wooden cabin is comfortable and very cosy: find one fresh and airy living/dining room with a fully formed kitchen area and plenty of good seating; glass doors open out to the terrace. The main bedroom has a giant bed with a pretty rose-strewn bedspread and a cream rug; the bunk room is fine for adults or children but it's all so romantic you may want to farm them out! Owner Victoria, who lives nearby, leaves you jam from her damsons and raspberries, local apple juice, something baked, and flowers. A gorgeous little watery retreat. *Weekly bookings (Fri-Fri) or 3-night weekends (Fri-Mon). Additional night's stay booked upon request. Children over 5 welcome. Secure 15 acres of garden and woodland.*

Rooms	1 cabin for 4
	(1 double, 1 bunk bed;
	1 bath/shower room):
	£395-£795 per week.
	Dogs £25 per stay. Max. 2.
Meals	Self-catering.
Closed	Never.

Dog treats, blankets and advice on walks.

Victoria Orchard
Lakeside Retreat,
Old Hall Farm, Milson,
Cleobury Mortimer, DY14 0BH
Tel   +44 (0)1299 270780
Email   info@ludlowholidaylet.co.uk
Web   www.ludlowholidaylet.co.uk

Entry 116 Map 2

Millstream Camp

The charmingly ramshackle Millstream Camp is made up of two different spaces for a self-contained escape. The shepherd's hut, beautifully decorated with vintage items from the house, feather down pillows and a huge duvet filled with Welsh sheep's wool, serves as the dog-free sleeping space. The tipi, decked out with old Indian saris, campaign trunks and a lacquered table, is your sitting room. The millstream meanders past – dammed at the mill, on some hot days, to create a bathing pool. Bathing can also take place in a wood-fired tin bath, or under the gas-powered shower, and a private compost loo is just steps away. Food and cooking are an essential part of a Lower Buckton holiday. Carolyn runs cookery courses on site and 'food safaris': tours of local producers with ample opportunity for snacking. Back at the camp, you can use the barbecue, the wood-burner or the campfire to hone your skills. For the less patient, there's a gas hob for a quickly boiled kettle! *Fenced area on site, river swimming, freedom to run in field and walks with resident dog, Copper.*

Rooms	Camp for 2 (1 double): from £90 per night. Max. 1 dog.
Meals	Self-catering.
Closed	November – March.
🚶	Dog bones, old towels, dog walks, plays with Copper and a stream for swimming.

Canopy & Stars
Millstream Camp, Lower Buckton Country House, Buckton, Leintwardine, SY7 0JU
Tel   +44 (0)117 204 7830
Email enquiries@canopyandstars.co.uk
Web   www.canopyandstars.co.uk/ millstreamcamp

Entry 117 Map 2

Lower Buckton Country House

You are spoiled here in house-party style; Carolyn – passionate about Slow Food – and Henry, are born entertainers. Kick off with homemade cake in the drawing room with its oil paintings, antique furniture and old rugs; return for delicious nibbles when the lamps and wood-burner are flickering. Dine well at a huge oak table (home-reared pork, local cheeses, dreamy puddings), then nestle into the best linen and the softest pillows; bedrooms feel wonderfully restful. This is laid-back B&B: paddle in the stream, admire the stunning views, find a quiet spot with a good book. Great fun! *Minimum stay: 2 nights at weekends. More woodland walks and rivers to swim in than you can shake a stick at!*

Hopton House

Karen looks after her guests wonderfully and even runs courses on how to do B&B! Unwind in this fresh and uplifting converted granary with old beams, high ceilings and a sun-filled dining/sitting room overlooking the hills. The bedroom above has its own balcony; those in the barn, one up, one down, each with its own entrance, are as enticing: beautifully dressed beds, silent fridges, good lighting, homemade cakes. Bathrooms have deep baths (and showers) – from one you can lie back and gaze at the stars. Karen's breakfasts promise Ludlow sausages, home-laid eggs, fine jams and homemade marmalade. *Minimum stay: 2 nights. Over 16s welcome. Secure garden; local woods to walk in. Free-range chickens in garden, and resident dogs.*

Rooms	2 doubles; 1 twin/double with separate bath: £100. Dogs £10. Max. 2.	Rooms	1 double: £110–£120. Barn – 2 doubles: £110–£120.
Meals	Dinner, 4 courses, £35. BYO wine. Pub/restaurant 4 miles.	Meals	Restaurant 3 miles.
Closed	Rarely.	Closed	19-27 December.

 Butcher's bones, dog-eared towels and accompanied guided walks from resident dog, Copper the Labrador!

 Throws, dog bowls, towels and advice on walks and places to eat. Downstairs room has direct access to enclosed garden.

Henry & Carolyn Chesshire
Lower Buckton Country House,
Buckton, Leintwardine, SY7 0JU
Tel +44 (0)1547 540532
Mobile +44 (0)7960 273865
Email carolyn@lowerbuckton.co.uk
Web www.lowerbuckton.co.uk

Entry 118 Map 2

Karen Thorne
Hopton House,
Hopton Heath,
Craven Arms, SY7 0QD
Tel +44 (0)1547 530885
Email info@shropshirebreakfast.co.uk
Web www.shropshirebreakfast.co.uk

Entry 119 Map 2

Cover Star Competition

Some of our favourite handsome hounds

This is Basil the Beagle overlooking Bossiney Bay in Cornwall. He loves to walk along the cliffs and look out to sea.

Alfie absolutely loves the lakes.

This is Skye the Labrador. She loves to go to the river Dee in Aberdeenshire to swim and play fetch. She is a little water baby.

Shropshire

Clun Farm House

A relaxed country feel here, with heavenly hills all around. Friendly hosts Susan and Anthony are enthusiastic collectors of country artefacts and have filled their listed 15th-century farmhouse with eye-catching things; the cowboy's saddle by the old range echoes Susan's roots. Bedrooms have aged and oiled floorboards, fun florals and bold walls; there is space for children in the extra bunk room; bathrooms are small and simple. Walk Offa's Dyke and the Shropshire Way; return to rescue hens wandering the garden, a warm smile and a glass of wine by the cosy wood-burner – before supper at one of the local pubs. Good value. *Horses welcome. Fenced farmyard, miles of off-road walks and river for a dip.*

Rooms	1 double with extra bunk-bedroom; 1 twin/double with separate shower: £80. Dogs £10 per dog per night. Max. 3 in one group.
Meals	Packed lunch £4. Pubs/restaurants nearby.
Closed	Occasionally.
	Advice on walks and maps.

Anthony & Susan Whitfield
Clun Farm House, High Street, Clun, Craven Arms, SY7 8JB

Tel	+44 (0)1588 640432
Mobile	+44 (0)7885 261391
Email	anthonyswhitfield0158@btinternet.com
Web	www.clunfarmhouse.co.uk

Entry 120 Map 2

The Hunters Rest Inn

Astride Clutton Hill with fine views over the Cam valley the inn began life in the 1750s as a hunting lodge. Later it became a smallholding and tavern. It's a big place, rambling around a large central bar, part wood, part stone, its bar topped with copper. There's plenty of jostling space so get ready to order from the Butcombe, Otter and guest ales and the Original Broad Oak and Pheasant Plucker ciders. Get cosy amongst the old oak and pine settles, the red carpeting and the tables to fit all sizes, the quirky wine-label wallpaper, the horse and country paraphernalia, the fires crackling away. Food is hale and hearty: shepherd's pie, pickled beetroot, crusty bread, wild mushroom risotto. Children are well looked after and there's a play area in the garden. The fun continues upstairs with rooms that range from traditional four-poster with antiques to contemporary chic. All are distinctive, all have views, several look south to the Mendips; others have private terraces. Stylish bathrooms have bold tiles, roll top baths and thick towels. A most enjoyable 'sprack and spry' hideaway. *Lots of walks from your own private entrance, big pub garden and dog-friendly log fires!*

Rooms	4 doubles, 1 twin: £95-£130.
	Singles £67.50-£77.50.
	Dogs £10 per stay.
Meals	Lunch & dinner £8.25-£17.95.
Closed	Rarely.

Black pudding treats, great walks – and towels if needed.

Paul Thomas
The Hunters Rest Inn,
King Lane, Clutton Hill,
Clutton, BS39 5QL
Tel   +44 (0)1761 452303
Email   info@huntersrest.co.uk
Web   www.huntersrest.co.uk

Entry 121 Map 2

Streamcombe Farm Shepherd's Hut

A peaceful spot in the woods just south of Exmoor: a break from city life. Karen and Ian have started a cookery school (where you can learn game or fish cookery during your stay). The area is a dark sky reserve completely unspoilt by light pollution and the woods near the hut shelter a herd of wild deer among other forest creatures. You can see them all on the 2 mile hike over the hills to Dulverton, where you'll find some lovely pubs and shops. The shepherd's hut itself was built in the late 19th century and retains its original oak panelling and floors. It has been redecorated in the simple plain colours of Shaker style and positioned near the house but shielded by the barn, set up to catch the morning sun on the front door. The hut is off grid, lit with candles and heated by the big wood-burner. The shower, sink and organic chemical loo are all housed in the barn a few yards away. As the presence of an on-site cookery school suggests, the food available is superb. You can book BYO evening meals or have breakfast and lunch hampers delivered to the hut, so you can eat surrounded by the sounds of the country. *Free-range chickens and sheep everywhere: leads at all times please. Exmoor is a dog-walker's paradise.*

Rooms	Shepherd's hut for 2 (1 double): from £95 per night. Max. 2 dogs.
Meals	Self-catering.
Closed	November – March.
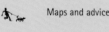	Maps and advice on local walks.

Canopy & Stars
Streamcombe Farm Shepherd's Hut,
Streamcombe Lane, Dulverton, TA22 9SA

Tel   +44 (0)117 204 7830
Email   enquiries@canopyandstars.co.uk
Web   www.canopyandstars.co.uk/
          streamcombe

Entry 122 Map 2

Cider Barn

Set back from the lane is a newly converted and refurbished barn. Step in to find fine old proportions, heated oak floors and heaps of character. Louise's stunning living quarters spread under the beams and bedrooms lie privately below on the ground floor. One opens to the courtyard, and all are airy and peaceful with modern fabrics and cream walls. There's a sunny guest sitting room leading onto the garden, and delightful Louise, a great cook, serves breakfast at a long table by the wood-burner. You can walk through fields to the river or hills, stroll to the pub for supper – and alternative therapies can be arranged locally. *Rivers to jump in, fairly secure garden. Sheep in field – leads needed.*

Park Farmhouse

'Artisan Baker' says the sign on the lane… you're in for a treat here. Buy bread and pastries on Saturdays, learn how to bake them on Sundays, tuck into Friday pizza, enjoy the most delicious croissants (all French butter and flour) for breakfast. Frank is bonkers about bread! He and Carolyn like you to feel part of the family. Their Georgian farmhouse has classic elegance with a French rustic twist: furniture painted in soft tones (Carolyn's creations), original oak parquet floor in the pretty bread-shop room, big comfy sitting room with wood-burner, airy bedrooms with pots of roses. Supper with your hosts too, or walk across fields to the pub. *Babes in arms & children over 10 welcome. On a working farm but with a secure garden. Many footpaths and bridleways – one footpath goes past the front door.*

Rooms	1 double, 1 twin/double: £75-£85. Singles £50-£65. Dogs £7 per night. Max. 1 (more possible if they sleep in car: arrange with owner).
Meals	Pub 1 mile.
Closed	Rarely.

Towels for drying, pig's ears and advice on walks.

Louise Bancroft
Cider Barn,
Runnington,
Wellington, TA21 0QW
Tel   +44 (0)1823 665533
Email   louisegaddon@btinternet.com
Web   www.runningtonciderbarn.co.uk

Entry 123 Map 2

Rooms	1 double; 1 double with separate bath: £60-£80. Singles £50.
Meals	Supper from £10. Pubs/restaurants 15-minute walk.
Closed	Rarely.

Homemade biscuits, pig's ears, blankets, towels for drying and advice on walks.

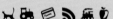

Carolyn & Frank Heuff
Park Farmhouse,
Bickenhall,
Taunton, TA3 6TZ
Tel   +44 (0)1823 480878
Email   breadbedandbreakfast@gmail.com
Web   www.breadbedandbreakfast.co.uk

Entry 124 Map 2

The Westleton Crown

This is one of England's oldest coaching inns, with 800 years of continuous service under its belt. It stands in a village two miles inland from the sea at Dunwich, with Westleton Heath running east towards Minsmere Bird Sanctuary. Inside, stripped floors, smouldering fires, exposed brickwork and ancient beams sweep you back two hundred years. Weave about and find nooks and crannies in which to hide, flames flickering in open fires, a huge map on the wall for walkers. You can eat wherever you want, there's a conservatory breakfast room with fine local photography, then a colourful terraced garden for barbecues in summer. Fish comes straight off the boats at Lowestoft, local butchers provide local meat, so you eat well, perhaps wild rabbit and ham hock, spiced sea bass with curried cockles, coconut panna cotta with roasted pineapple. Bedrooms are scattered about (Will and Kate loved theirs!), some in the main house, others in converted stables. Expect limed whites, comfy beds, crisp linen, flat-screen TVs. Pretty bathrooms come courtesy of Fired Earth, some with claw-foot baths. Aldeburgh and Southwold are close. *Minimum stay: 2 nights at weekends. All year round dog-friendly beach just 3 miles away.*

Rooms	26 doubles, 2 twins: £95-£180.
	3 suites for 2: £185-£215.
	2 family rooms for 4: £160-£180.
	1 single: £90-£100.
	Dogs £7.50.
Meals	Lunch & bar meals from £5.50.
	Dinner from £11.95.
	Sunday lunch from £14.95.
Closed	Never.

Dog treats, water bowls, doggie breakfast, blanket, map with local walks, dog wash and towels.

Gareth Clarke
The Westleton Crown,
The Street, Westleton,
Saxmundham, IP17 3AD

Tel	+44 (0)1728 648777
Email	info@westletoncrown.co.uk
Web	www.westletoncrown.co.uk

Entry 125 Map 4

The Ship

Once a great port, Dunwich is now a tiny (but famous) village, gradually sinking into the sea. Its well-loved smugglers' inn, almost on the beach, overlooks the salt marsh and sea and pulls in wind-blown walkers and birdwatchers from the Minsmere Reserve. In the old-fashioned bar – nautical bric-a-brac, flagged floors, simple furnishings and a stove that belts out the heat – you can tuck into legendary hake and chips washed down with a pint of Adnams. There's also a more modern dining room where hearty food combines with traditional dishes: glorious big platefuls of ham, egg and chips, Blythburgh pork belly and ham hock terrine, and lamb cutlets served with an individual shepherd's pie. Up the fine Victorian staircase are spruced up bedrooms – simple, uncluttered – with period features, cord carpets, brass beds, old pine, little shower rooms. Rooms at the front have glorious salt marsh views, two new rooms overlook the garden, courtyard rooms are cosy with pine, and the family room under the eaves is fabulous: single beds, a big futon-style bean bag, and a flat-screen for the kids. *Special midweek rates off season. Huge garden. Great walks on heaths, in forests and on the all-year-round dog-friendly Dunwich beach.*

Rooms	12 doubles, 1 twin: £112–£135.
	3 family rooms for 4: £130–£135.
	Dogs £5.
Meals	Lunch from £6.95.
	Bar meals from £9.75.
	Dinner from £9.95.
	Sunday lunch £11.95.
Closed	Never.
	Dog biscuits, water bowls and maps with local walks.

Matt Goodwin
The Ship,
St James's Street, Dunwich,
Saxmundham, IP17 3DT

Tel   +44 (0)1728 648219
Email info@shipatdunwich.co.uk
Web   www.shipatdunwich.co.uk

Entry 126 Map 4

Twee Gebroeders

Twee Gebroeders is a fabulous 1897 Dutch Skûtsje type sailing barge, now enjoying a pampered retirement in a quiet corner of Suffolk. In the hands of Gill and Tim, she has undergone an extensive yet subtle modernisation. The original feel of the boat has been maintained in the glowing Iroko panelling and the colouring in the fabrics. Modern touches, such as the shining red Aga at the heart of the boat, the hot shower, flushing loo and entertainment systems, simply enhance the experience of floating in a piece of classic maritime splendour. The boat is normally stationary, but river day trips can be arranged, and Gill and Tim will throw one in if you stay for a week. Crab fishing equipment is provided – if you find you aren't catching, keep the barking to a minimum and the seals and cormorants will appear to show you how it's done. Should you decide to send a landing party ashore, there are villages aplenty to raid for provisions, the Minsmere RSPB reserve to visit, and many miles of the Stour/Orwell path for you and your dog to tread. *Plenty of local walks and areas to run off lead and river for cooling down.*

Rooms	Boat for 4 (1 double, 2 singles): £135 per night. Max. 1 dog – well behaved pets only.
Meals	Self-catering.
Closed	Never.
	Dog biscuits and advice on walks.

Canopy & Stars
Twee Gebroeders,
Pin Mill, Ipswich, IP13 0RD
Tel   +44 (0)117 204 7830
Email   enquiries@canopyandstars.co.uk
Web   www.canopyandstars.co.uk/
        tweegebroeders

Entry 127 Map 4

The Crown & Castle

Orford is unbeatable, a sleepy Suffolk village blissfully marooned at the end of the road. River, beach and forest wait, as does the Crown & Castle, a fabulous English hostelry where the art of hospitality is practised with great flair. The inn stands in the shadow of Orford's 12th-century castle. The feel is warm and airy with stripped floorboards, open fires, eclectic art and candles at night. Rooms come with Vi-Spring beds, super bathrooms, lovely fabrics, the odd armchair. Four in the main house have watery views, the suite is stunning, the garden rooms big and light, the courtyard rooms (the latest addition) utterly sublime. All have crisp white linen, TVs, DVDs and digital radios. Wellington boots wait at the back door, so pull on a pair and explore Rendlesham Forest or hop on a boat and chug over to Orfordness. Ambrosial food awaits your return, perhaps seared squid with coriander and garlic, slow-cooked pork belly with a shellfish broth, crushed pistachio meringue with a chocolate ice cream sundae. A great place to wash up for a few lazy days. Sutton Hoo is close. Very dog-friendly. *Minimum stay: 2 nights at weekends. Children over 8 welcome. Lots of walking both by the river and in the forest.*

Rooms	18 doubles, 2 twins: £115–£195.
	1 suite for 2: £240–£270.
	Dogs £10 for up to 2 dogs per room per night. Max. 2.
Meals	Lunch from £8.50.
	À la carte dinner around £35.
Closed	Rarely.

Homemade treats, towels, walks, and a bookable "doggie table" in the restaurant.

David & Ruth Watson
The Crown & Castle,
Orford,
Woodbridge, IP12 2LJ

Tel	+44 (0)1394 450205
Email	info@crownandcastle.co.uk
Web	www.crownandcastle.co.uk

Entry 128 Map 4

Kesgrave Hall

This Georgian mansion sits in 38 acres of woodland and was built for an MP in 1812. It served as home to US airmen during WWII, becoming a prep school shortly after. Refurbished in 2008, it was an instant hit with locals, who love the style, the food and the informal vibe, and despite its country-house good looks, it is almost a restaurant with rooms, the emphasis firmly on the food. Find Wellington boots in the entrance hall, high ceilings in the huge sitting room, stripped boards in the humming bistro and doors that open onto a terrace in summer. Excellent bedrooms have lots of style. One is huge and comes with a faux leopard-skin sofa and freestanding bath. The others might not be quite as wild, but they're lovely nonetheless, some in the eaves, others in beautifully refurbished outbuildings. Expect warm colours, crisp linen, good lighting and fancy bathrooms. Back downstairs tasty bistro food flies from the kitchen, perhaps goat's cheese panna cotta, cottage pie with red cabbage, pear tart with rosemary and vanilla ice cream. Suffolk's magical coast waits. *Woods to roam in, lawns to run on. Beach and rivers about 20 minutes away.*

Rooms	10 doubles, 7 twin/doubles: £130–£230. 6 suites for 2: £275–£300. Dogs £10.
Meals	Breakfast £10–£16. Lunch & dinner, 3 courses, £25–£30.
Closed	Never.
	Blankets, towels, walks, bowls and doggy dinners.

Oliver Richards
Kesgrave Hall,
Hall Road,
Kesgrave, Ipswich, IP5 2PU

Tel	+44 (0)1473 333741
Email	reception@kesgravehall.com
Web	www.milsomhotels.com

Entry 129 Map 4

Suffolk

Poplar Farm House

Only a few miles from Ipswich but down a green lane, this rambling farmhouse has a pretty, whitewashed porch and higgledy-piggledy roof. All light, elegant and spacious with wonderful flowers, art, sumptuous soft furnishings (made by Sally) and quirky sculptures; expect comfy beds, laundered linen and smart bathrooms. Sally is relaxed and friendly and will give you eggs from her handsome hens, homemade bread, veg from the garden on an artistically laid table. Play tennis, swim, steam in the sauna or book one of Sally's arts and crafts courses, then wander in the woods beyond with beautiful dogs Shale and Rune. Great value. *Woodland and large garden; 5-minute walk to a park, 20 minutes to the river.*

Rooms	2 doubles, 1 twin sharing 2 bath/shower rooms: £70. Yurt – 1 double: £70. Dogs £5 per night. Max. 2.
Meals	Dinner, 3 courses, £15–£25. Packed lunch £7. Pub 1 mile.
Closed	Rarely.

Towels for drying wet dogs, pooper scoop bags and a bedtime biscuit.

Sally Sparrow
Poplar Farm House, Poplar Lane,
Sproughton, Ipswich, IP8 3HL
Tel   +44 (0)1473 601211
Mobile +44 (0)7950 767226
Email   sparrowsally@aol.com
Web   www.poplarfarmhousesuffolkbb.eu

Entry 130 Map 4

Cover Star Competition

Some of our favourite handsome hounds

Here is Freeo, a Rhodesian ridgeback. His favourite place is snoozing in front of a log fire, with his teddy.

Introducing Monty, who is so very easily pleased – if he has a stick to play with he is content absolutely anywhere!

Jack loves to run, anywhere! Mountains, fields, canals, beaches, you name it, he loves it. He's full of beans and full of fun.

The Inn @ West End

Wine importer Gerry Price pulls the punters in from all over Surrey: the wine shop glows with 500 lines. Inside is just as good. Stylish bar areas are light and modern with wooden floors and Shaker colours, and the atmosphere is warm and friendly... quiz nights, film club, barbecues in the garden. There are local beers, hand-pumped Fuller's and Young's and that wine list is most enticing, with a nod to Portuguese shores. Tuck in to lunch or dinner by the open fire, or in the more traditional dining room. Seasonal menus announce fresh modern food, perhaps courgette and feta risotto or twice-cooked pork belly with sage jus; in autumn there's pheasant, woodcock and teal. A pastry chef oversees the crumbles and tortes, the cheeses are farmhouse best, there are good-value set lunches, popular wine dinners, even a summer wood oven. As for dogs, they're welcome in the bar – and in a couple of the rooms in the stable block behind (replete with clock tower). Enjoy modern oak beds with Hypnos mattresses, excellent Wifi, swish wet rooms, even gun cupboards and safes. Breakfast is the final treat. *Close to woodland and parks; outside space for doggy ablutions. 2 rooms suitable for dogs.*

Rooms	12 doubles: £125–£150. Dogs £10 per dog per night.
Meals	Lunch & dinner £5.25–£32.50. Sunday lunch £24.95. Not 25 & 26 December.
Closed	Rarely.
🐕	Water bowls, doggy biscuits, a cosy spot near the open log fire and advice on local walks. Attention and affection too – a warm welcome to dogs and their owners!

Gerry & Ann Price
The Inn @ West End,
42 Guildford Road, West End,
Woking, GU24 9PW

Tel	+44 (0)1276 858652
Email	greatfood@the-inn.co.uk
Web	www.the-inn.co.uk

Strand House

As you follow the Royal Military Canal down to miles of sandy beach, bear in mind that 600 years ago, you'd have been swimming in the sea. This is reclaimed land and Strand House, built in 1425, originally stood on Winchelsea Harbour. Outside, you find wandering wisteria, colourful flowerbeds and a woodland walk that leads up to the village. Inside, medieval interiors have low ceilings, timber frames and mind-your-head beams. There are reds and yellows, sofas galore, a wood-burner in the sitting room, an honesty bar from which to help yourself. It's a home-spun affair: Hugh cooks breakfast, Mary conjures up tasty meals at weekends. Attractive bedrooms are warm and colourful. One has an ancient four-poster, some have wonky floors, all have comfy beds and compact shower rooms. Airy rooms in the cottage have more space, and the suite, with its balcony and views across the fields, is a treat. The house, once a work house, was painted by Turner and Millais. Local restaurants wait: Webb's Fish Café, The Globe in Rye, a Michelin star at the Curlew in Odium. Dogs are very welcome. *Minimum stay: 2 nights at weekends & in high season. 3 dog-friendly rooms available. Canal towpath to walk along just in front of the hotel.*

Rooms	6 doubles,
	1 twin/double: £80–£150.
	1 suite for 4: £180.
	5 triples: £80–£150.
	Singles from £60.
	Dogs £7.50 per night.
Meals	Dinner, 3 courses, £34.50,
	Fridays & Saturdays, on request.
Closed	Rarely.

Homemade biscuits, drying towels and drying room. Lots of local walks and places to eat too.

Mary Sullivan & Hugh Davie
Strand House,
Tanyards Lane,
Winchelsea, Rye, TN36 4JT
Tel   +44 (0)1797 226276
Email   info@thestrandhouse.co.uk
Web   www.thestrandhouse.co.uk

The Ship Inn

The 16th-century smuggler's warehouse stands by the quay at the bottom of cobbled Mermaid Street. Climb the church tower for stunning coast and marsh views, then retreat to the laid-back warmth of the Ship's rustic bars. Cosy nooks, ancient timbers, blazing fires and a quirky delicious décor characterise this place; there are battered leather sofas, simple café-style chairs, old pine tables and good paintings and prints. Quaff a pint of Harvey's Sussex or local farm cider, leaf through the daily papers, play one of the board games – there are heaps. Lunch and dinner menus are short and imaginative and make good use of local ingredients, so tuck into confit duck with grilled aubergine and saffron yoghurt, roast sea bream with buttered samphire, warm salad of squid, fennel and chorizo, and fresh Rye Bay fish. The relaxed funky feel extends to bright and beachy bedrooms upstairs: find painted wooden floors, jazzy wall coverings, comfortable beds, splashes of colour. Quirky extras include Roberts radios, sticks of rock, and rubber ducks in simple bathrooms. And they love dogs. *Brilliant beach walks; maps and advice on walks also given.*

Rooms	10 doubles: £80–£125. Dogs £10 per dog per night. Max. 2 per room.
Meals	Lunch & dinner £11.75–£18.50.
Closed	Rarely.
	Sausages for breakfast.

Karen Northcote
The Ship Inn,
The Strand,
Rye, TN31 7DB

Tel	+44 (0)1797 222233
Email	mayistay@theshipinnrye.co.uk
Web	www.theshipinnrye.co.uk

Entry 133 Map 4

The Nook

All is fresh and spacious in this couple's hideaway near Hastings – a restful base for gentle walks or tough hikes through AONB countryside and trips to Battle Abbey, Scotney Castle, Sissinghurst and the Sussex coast. Spliced onto the owners' late 18th-century house, off the main road by the village church, this modern wing has a private entrance through a vine-ringed, plant-filled courtyard which begs you to sit out in the peace on fine days. Spread yourselves out in a spacious, pale-hued sitting room with cheery wood-burner, big red and white checked sofas and matching curtains, plus a large pine dining table and dresser. A separate modern kitchen will please cooks and has all the essentials. Upstairs, find a good-sized double bedroom in aqua blue and white with a touch of turquoise in the bathroom; gaze over trees and church. Ever-smiling Sue and family fill your generous welcome hamper with local treats: eggs, milk, cheese, beer. And if biodynamic wine tickles your fancy, Sedlescombe Organic Vineyard is within a mile – as are a good pub, the village green and shop. *Short breaks available. The Nook has no garden, but opens straight onto a footpath across the fields.*

Rooms	1 cottage for 2 (1 double): £400–£550 per week.
Meals	Self-catering.
Closed	Rarely.
	Dog towels, bowls, biscuits and maps for walks.

Sue Langer
The Nook,
Castlemans,
Sedlescombe, Battle, TN33 0QP
Mobile   +44 (0)7940 855277
Email   sue@castlemanscottages.co.uk
Web   www.castlemanscottages.co.uk

Entry 134 Map 4

The Big Green Bus

A mixture of upcycled furniture, bright retro splashes of colour and original bus features (tickets, please!) the Big Green Bus narrowly escaped destruction before it was rescued by owner Adam. Now enjoying a leisurely retirement in an East Sussex field – apart from a starring role in *George Clarke's Amazing Spaces* on Channel 4 – it has oak flooring, painted walls, and a beautifully custom-made kitchen and shower room. All thoroughly modern, it sports chrome LED lights, Farrow & Ball paint, even charging sockets for your iPhone. The log-burner downstairs keeps the whole bus toasty and a boiler ensures you have hot water – a shower on the side of the bus means you can enjoy it outside too! Everyone knows the best views are from the top deck – up here, thick carpet, and 2 bunks and 2 comfy doubles in individual sleeping pods are cosy at night. Lounge around on lime green sofas or just enjoy the rural setting within an hour of London – you have plenty of space around the bus itself including a wood-fired hot tub. Bring the gang – it's great for groups. *Babies welcome. Woodland walks. Dogs not allowed on the top deck.*

Rooms	Bus for 6 (2 doubles, 2 bunks): from £160 per night. Dogs £20 per pet per stay. Max. 2.
Meals	Self-catering.
Closed	Never.
	Advice on walks.

Canopy & Stars
The Big Green Bus,
Broomham Lane,
Lewes, BN8 6JQ

Tel	+44 (0)117 204 7830
Email	enquiries@canopyandstars.co.uk
Web	www.canopyandstars.co.uk/biggreenbus

Entry 135 Map 4

Merrion Farm

Local and sustainable are the two principles at the heart of Merrion Farm. Withyfield Cottage is half rustic log cabin, half comfortable cottage; an incredible straw bale structure it was designed by Ben Law, builder and permaculture expert whose project was voted the most popular ever to feature on Channel 4's *Grand Designs*. Throughout, modern comfort blends seamlessly with rustic design. It's a graceful work of art: exposed timber beams sweep down from the high, arched ceiling and sink into the worktops and floor, framing the open-plan kitchen and living room. One of the bedrooms has its own bathroom, two are on the ground floor; all are simply decorated, letting the breathtaking quality of the workmanship shine through. From the veranda, you can see the very woodlands where the timber to clad the exterior was cut and then replenished. A 10-minute walk away and sharing the woods with badgers, woodpeckers and barn owls, you'll find Withywood Shepherd's Hut, a private hideaway for up to 4. Further afield is the Sussex landscape, criss-crossed with walking trails taking in places of history and beauty. *Babies welcome. Heaps of lovely walks, private garden — and lots of good smells for dogs!*

Rooms	Cottage for 6 (1 double, 4 singles): from £121 per night. Shepherd's hut for 4 (1 double, 2 pull-out singles): from £100 per night. Max. 1 dog.
Meals	Self-catering.
Closed	Never.
	Towels, advice on walking and walks from the door. Dog sitting and dog kennel (if you want to go out without your dog).

Canopy & Stars
Merrion Farm, Partridge Green, Horsham, RH13 8EH

Tel	+44 (0)117 204 7830
Email	enquiries@canopyandstars.co.uk
Web	www.canopyandstars.co.uk/merrionfarm

Entry 136 Map 3

Rubens Barn

Pheasant strut, shy deer bounce by – sure signs that you're immersed in the Goodwood Estate. This little flint barn is tucked into one of the most unspoilt woody corners of Sussex. Rush hour here, on a leafy lane, consists of the occasional tractor, car or combine. Renovated and decorated to the highest order – in duck-egg blue with hints of gold – this is one stylish retreat. Downstairs, a luxurious bedroom with a huge bed, silk throws, velvet cushions and a shower room with slate tiles, heated rails and fluffy bathrobes. In the living room, cream sofas, fresh flowers, a Shaker kitchen. Upstairs, a big twin bedroom, a roll top bath, soft lights and white towels. A welcome pack of fruit, ham, cheese, coffee and croissants is provided by the lovely owners who live in the main house – as are binoculars so you can spy on the wildlife! Sit out on the neat little patio through the French windows, enjoy a game of tennis, borrow the barbecue. Or set off for East Dean – it has two wonderful pubs. Sussex at its best, hidden well away yet never far from civilisation: historic Chichester is close by. *Minimum stay: 2 nights. Short breaks available. Secure garden, surrounded by walks through forests and farmland. Area of Outstanding Natural Beauty in the South Downs National Park.*

Rooms	1 barn for 4 (1 double, 1 twin, sofabed): £500-£850 per week. Dogs £30 per dog per stay. Max. 2.
Meals	Self-catering.
Closed	Rarely.
	Advice on walks and dog-friendly pubs nearby.

Rob & Rachel Hill
Rubens Barn,
Droke Lane,
East Dean, PO18 0JJ
Tel   +44 (0)1243 818187
Email   info@rubensbarn.co.uk
Web   www.rubensbarn.co.uk

Entry 137 Map 3

The Cat

Owner Andrew swapped grand Gravetye Manor for the buzzy, pubby atmosphere of The Cat in 2009; he hasn't looked back. The 16th-century building, a fine medieval hall house with a Victorian extension, has been comfortably modernised without losing its character. Inside are beamed ceilings and panelling, planked floors, splendid inglenooks, and an airy room that leads to a garden at the back, furnished with teak and posh brollies. Harvey's Ale and some top-notch pub food, passionately put together from fresh local ingredients by chef Max Leonard, attract a solid, old-fashioned crowd: retired locals, foodies and walkers. Tuck into rare roast beef and horseradish sandwiches, Rye Bay sea bass with brown shrimp and caper butter, South Downs lamb chops with dauphinoise (and leave room for treacle tart!). The setting is idyllic, in a pretty village opposite a 12th-century church – best viewed from two of four bright and comfortable bedrooms. Crisp linen on big beds, rich fabrics, fawn carpets, fresh bathrooms and antique touches illustrate the style. A sweet retreat in a charming village backwater. *Lots of walks in the area.*

Rooms	4 doubles: £110–£150.
	Singles £90–£110.
	Extra bed/sofabed available £20 per person per night.
	Dogs £10. Max. 2.
Meals	Bar meals from £6.
	Lunch & dinner from £12.
	Sunday lunch, 3 courses, £26.
Closed	Open all day.
	Poop bags, dog biscuits and towels for drying.

Andrew Russell
The Cat,
Queen's Square, West Hoathly,
East Grinstead, RH19 4PP
Tel   +44 (0)1342 810369
Email   thecatinn@googlemail.com
Web   www.catinn.co.uk

Entry 138 Map 3

1 The Mews

"I'm not a fan of dogs, but I'm happy to host pet birds, oh and mice, I do so love MICE!" purrs Kitty, the glamorous owner of The Mews as she sashays down the hallway bedecked in her trademark fur onesie and diamanté choker. Best to arrive at night when she's sure to be up and about – during the day, she tends to laze atop the piano or squashed into a hat box; it's all quite laissez-faire so don't be surprised either if she joins you in bed. Unlike most B&Bs, the guests provide the host with breakfast and she'll certainly let you know when she's ready, possibly by caterwauling or scratching at your door. Sleep well.

The Flint Barns

An extraordinarily beautiful setting in the stunning South Downs with views all the way to the sea, a pioneering English vineyard (discover the story and take a tour) and this perfect flint barn – an unusual place to stay in huge comfort and style with a homely feel thanks to cheery Ade. More poshtel than hostel, find chunky doors, reclaimed oak floors, view-filled windows, bedrooms with luxurious mattresses, crisp white cotton, good lighting and shower rooms worthy of Babington House. A fabulous sitting room has plenty of seating for all, a roaring wood-burner and books; breakfast (and supper if you want it) is fresh, local, lovingly cooked, and served in the lofty dining room at long tables. Spill out into the pretty courtyard for summer barbecues, walk straight onto the South Downs Way. Lovely. *Minimum stay: 2 nights. Direct access to South Downs Way, Friston Forest close by; beach walks.*

Rooms	2 doubles both with en suite compost loo. Payment in Go Cat preferred payable twice a day.
Meals	Dropped at the door each morning.
Closed	Maybe.

 "A treat! For a dog! Not a cat in hell's chance!"

Rooms	3 doubles: £110.
	1 family room for 3: £140–£180.
	Bunk rooms (1 for 2, 1 for 4, 1 for 5, 3 for 8): £80–£280.
	Dogs £5 per night. Max. 2 per booking.
Meals	Dinner, 2 courses, £20. Pubs 2–3 miles.
Closed	Mid-Jan to mid-Feb; end of Sept to end of Oct.

 Treats, poo bags and advice on walks.

Kitty La Blanche
1 The Mews,
Mousehole, CAT 9LV
Tel   Quicker to stand in the garden and shout.
Web www.herekittykitty.co.uk

Entry 139 Map 99

Adrian Lamb
The Flint Barns,
Rathfinny Wine Estate,
Alfriston, Polegate, BN26 5TU
Tel   +44 (0)1323 874030
Email flintbarns@rathfinnyestate.com
Web www.flintbarns.com

Entry 140 Map 4

Lambcote Barn

At the end of a short farm road, a cluster of buildings ringed by fields. Farmhouse, barn and outbuildings face inwards, and stand on historic ground. Lambcote Barn, all yours, is flanked by a neatly trimmed lawn that runs to rougher ground; roses edge up the old stone walls and a walnut tree laden with nuts sits square on the grass. Relaxed families will love this place, and the dog can come too (an ancestor established the Kennel Club in 1873). Inside: a bright sitting room with beams, painted stone walls and sofas flanking a log-burner that belts out the heat. The dining room/kitchen is one, functional but due for updating, while the bedrooms and bathrooms, all charming, are upstairs. Find a double with ancient beams and deep windows; a sweet single; a twin with its own sitting area, entrance and stairs. Visit Warwick Castle, Oxford, or a National Trust house and garden: the area is stuffed with them! Walk the Centenary Way; amble across the fields to Ettington; bring the horses if you have them – the horse trials at Blenheim are close. Charlie the farmer's wife lives locally and is very happy to advise. *Short breaks available. Logs provided. Large garden, surrounded by beautiful open countryside and many wonderful long walks. Occasionally horses or sheep in adjacent fields.*

Rooms	1 barn for 5 (1 double – en suite, 1 twin, 1 single; 1 bathroom, 1 wc): £500-£700 per week. Max. 1 large dog or 2 small ones.
Meals	Self-catering. Meals available on request. Restaurants 1 mile.
Closed	Rarely.

Plenty of lovely soft towels for drying, and a comfortable bed in front of the fire.

Charlie Coldicott
Lambcote Barn,
Halford Road, Ettington,
Stratford-upon-Avon CV37 7PJ
Mobile   +44 (0)7774 776682
Email   grovefarmbb@btconnect.com

Entry 141 Map 3

The Fuzzy Duck

Nestled in the rolling folds of the Cotswold countryside, close to Stratford-upon-Avon, is this 18th-century coaching inn, polished to perfection by Tania, Adrian and their team. Beautiful fireplaces and gleaming tables, fine china and big sprays of wild flowers tell a tale of comfort and luxury, while the smiling staff are rightly proud of this gem of a pub. You dine like kings and queens in the sparkling bar, or in the clever conversion at the back, overlooking grounds that are part-orchard, part-walled-garden. Try Cotswold chicken breast with slow-cooked chorizo and white bean stew, or a splendid ploughman's with warm Scotch quail's egg. For pudding, try the zingy lemon posset, or treacle tart with orange scented milk ice. If you over-indulge, borrow wellies in your size for a bracing walk then back to your beautiful bed above the bar; rooms are sound-proofed and two have double loft beds (up very vertical ladders) for families. Best of all, the generous team has provided indulgent treats: lovely slippers; a nightcap tipple – come prepared to be spoiled. Bliss. *Secure outside garden; lots of walks on the doorstep. Some livestock nearby.*

Rooms	2 doubles: £110–£140.
	2 family rooms for 4: £180–£200.
Meals	Starters from £4.50.
	Mains from £9.95.
Closed	Never.

Dog biscuits, pig's ears, water, dog beds, blankets and advice on walks.

The Manager
The Fuzzy Duck,
Ilmington Road, Armscote,
Stratford-upon-Avon, CV37 8DD

Tel	+44 (0)1608 682 635
Email	info@fuzzyduckarmscote.com
Web	www.fuzzyduckarmscote.com/

The Wagon

The unusual craftsmanship and design that have gone into The Wagon reflect, perhaps, the county's history and mysticism. Using the natural forms of Sussex oak, forester and furniture maker James Noble conjures wonders out of wood. The Wagon is one of them. A carefully crafted living space, it has a comfy bedroom, a mini kitchen with all you need and a seating area, cleverly contrived using a few well placed hinges. Perfect seclusion means that you can swing in the hammock, laze by the lake and shower with only the trees for company – naturists will swoon! During the day, explore some of Britain's most famous archaeological sites, take tea in attractive market towns and walk in miles of rolling countryside. At night, light the barbecue or fire up the clay pizza oven, open the wine and let yourself sink into the comfort of a slower life. There's a lovely walk from Marlborough to Avebury that crosses the Ridgeway – only a few hours each way so you can arrive back in Marlborough for dinner or linger in Avebury for lunch. The Kennet & Avon canal has gentler walks, or cycles, along the tow path. *Babies welcome. Lake and river to jump in.*

Rooms	Wagon for 4 (1 double, 2 bunks): from £98 per night. Max. 2 dogs.
Meals	Self-catering.
Closed	December – March.
	Maps and advice on walks – and towels if required.

Canopy & Stars
The Wagon,
Pewsey, Puckshipton, SN9 6HG
Tel   +44 (0)117 204 7830
Email   enquiries@canopyandstars.co.uk
Web   www.canopyandstars.co.uk/
           thewagon

Entry 143 Map 3

The Garden Cottage

You'll love the Woodford Valley and this thatched cottage at the edge of the village. It has long views, stacks of character and traditionally decorated rooms: a ground floor twin with roll top bathroom and two cosy doubles upstairs that share a bathroom. Fabrics are flowered, headboards upholstered, mattresses top quality. Or choose to snuggle up by the wood-burner in a charming shepherd's hut and sleep out under the stars – one has a king-sized bed. Breakfast in the handsome kitchen, or pretty garden, on Annie's homemade soda bread and good things local. Sit out by the roses, honeysuckle and an ancient mulberry; head off to Avebury and Stonehenge. *Cash or cheque accepted. Arrivals before 4pm. Shepherd's huts perfect for dog owners. Walks of 20 minutes or 2 hours. River and fields on doorstep.*

Rooms	Cottage: 2 doubles sharing bath (let to same party only); 1 twin with separate bath: £90. 2 shepherd's huts for 2: £90. Dogs: voluntary contribution. Max. 2 small breed.
Meals	Pub 0.5 miles.
Closed	Occasionally.

 Blankets, towels, advice on walks and free range of garden.

Annie Arkwright
The Garden Cottage,
Upper Woodford,
Salisbury, SP4 6PA
Tel +44 (0)1722 782447
Email annie747@btinternet.com

Bridges Court

You're in the heart of the village with its small shop, friendly pub and the Melvilles' lovely 18th-century farmhouse. They haven't lived here long but it's so homely you'd never tell. Dogs wander, horses whinny, there's a beautiful garden with a Kiftsgate rose and a swimming pool for sunny days. On the second floor, off a corridor filled with paintings, are three florally inspired bedrooms: comfortable, bright and spacious with views to the village green. Breakfast leisurely on all things local at the long table in a dining room filled with silver and china. And there's a pleasant guests' sitting room to relax in. *Enclosed walled garden and lots of walks in beautiful countryside. Close to the Badminton estate & Westonbirt Arboretum where dogs are welcome.*

Rooms	1 double, 1 twin; 1 double with separate bath: £90. Singles £65. Discount for 3 nights or more, excluding Badminton w/e..
Meals	Pub in village.
Closed	Rarely.

 Dog treats, water bowls, towels for drying, advice on walks – and dog bed if required.

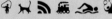

Fiona Melville
Bridges Court, Bridges Court,
Luckington, SN14 6NT
Tel +44 (0)1666 840215
Mobile +44 (0)7711 816839
Email fionamelville2003@yahoo.co.uk
Web www.bridgescourt.co.uk

Long Cover Cottage

Stealing its name from the backdrop of ancient undisturbed woodland, the cottage and its surrounds make a natural family home – for both frazzled humans and local badgers. Winding your way up the long peaceful track to this converted stable, you catch glorious glimpses of the Teme and Kyre valleys; the setting is spectacular. On arrival, you're greeted by the delightful Ellie, whose grounds and beautifully tended English country garden you share. Generous windows flood rooms with light that bounces off polished elm floorboards; a wood-burner and Aga keep things cosy, the kitchen is handcrafted, the views are long and bucolic. Upstairs, bedrooms are brass-bedded and floral, tucked under the eaves in that cottagey way. You get a handy loo and basin up here, and a sparkling bathroom with a roll top tub downstairs. Lucky children have seven acres to romp in, and a secret treehouse with hammocks and a barbecue for midnight feasts. Resting on the borders of three counties, this is prime walking country. Bustling Ledbury and Ludlow, England's Slow Food capital, are just a drive away. *7 acres of specially fenced land for carefree scampers and no roads for miles.*.

Rooms	1 cottage for 6 (2 doubles, 1 twin; 1 bath & shower room, 1 separate wc): £900 per week.
Meals	Self-catering.
Closed	Never.
	Towels, dog bowl and doggie treats.

Ellie Van Straaten
Long Cover Cottage, Vine Lane,
Kyre, Tenbury Wells, WR15 8RL

Tel	+44 (0)1885 410208
Mobile	+44 (0)7725 972486
Email	ellie_vanstraaten@yahoo.co.uk
Web	www.a-country-break.co.uk

Entry 146 Map 2

The Coach House

Head for the hills…and the dancing daffodils. In the grounds of a 16th-century timber-framed house, the perfect retreat à deux. Way up a simple track, your stone-walled, stone-tiled hideaway was built almost entirely from reclaimed materials. Inside is open plan and easy. Recline on your leather chesterfield, toes directed at a wood-burner stacked with logs from the woods. The kitchen, of hand-crafted oak, has a double Belfast sink and a sweep of wood floor, the well-dressed bed is to the side, and the shower room is a step away. Follow the brook through this ancient orchid-dotted woodland, rest awhile at the owner's little treehouse (with hammocks), then come home to your own little patch and magnificent views across open pastures to the Teme and Kyre valleys. Venture further to foodie Ludlow, book-lined Hay-on-Wye and the grand industrial heritage that is Ironbridge. Take to the slow life on the steam railway, stride out on the Mortimer Trail, meander through Herefordshire villages. Buzzards soar overhead, rabbits scamper in the fields that surround you. *7 acres of specially fenced land for carefree scampers and no roads for miles.*

Rooms	1 house for 2 (1 double): £700 per week.
Meals	Self-catering.
Closed	Never.
	Towels, water bowls and doggie treats.

Ellie Van Straaten
The Coach House, Vine Lane,
Kyre, Tenbury Wells, WR15 8RL

Tel	+44 (0)1885 410208
Mobile	+44 (0)7725 972486
Email	ellie_vanstraaten@yahoo.co.uk
Web	www.a-country-break.co.uk

Entry 147 Map 2

The Traddock

A northern outpost of country-house charm, beautiful inside and out. It's a family affair and those looking for a friendly base from which to explore the Dales will find it here. You enter through a wonderful drawing room – crackling fire, pretty art, the daily papers, cavernous sofas. Follow your nose and find polished wood in the dining room, panelled walls in the breakfast room, then William Morris wallpaper in the sitting room bar, where you can sip a pint of Skipton ale while playing a game of Scrabble. Bedrooms are just the ticket, some coolly contemporary, others deliciously traditional with family antiques and the odd claw-foot bath. Those on the second floor are cosy in the eaves, all have fresh fruit, homemade shortbread and Dales views. Elsewhere, a white-washed sitting room that opens onto the garden and a rug-strewn restaurant for fabulous local food, perhaps Whitby crab, slow-roasted pork, raspberry and white chocolate soufflé. Spectacular walks start at the front door, there are cycle tracks and some extraordinary caves – one is bigger than St Paul's. Brilliant. *Minimum stay: 2 nights at weekends, March – November. Walks from the door in the Yorkshire Dales National Park.*

Rooms	8 doubles, 1 twin/double, 2 family rooms for 4: £95–£165. 1 single: £85–£100. Dogs £5 per dog per day. Max. 2 per room (some of the smaller rooms can only take 1).
Meals	Lunch from £9.50. Dinner, 3 courses, around £30.
Closed	Never.
	Towels for drying and advice on walks.

Paul Reynolds
The Traddock,
Austwick,
Settle, LA2 8BY

Tel	+44 (0)15242 51224
Email	info@thetraddock.co.uk
Web	www.thetraddock.co.uk

Entry 148 Map 6

The Burgoyne Hotel

Reeth is one of those English throwbacks, a beautiful village in the Dales that's hardly changed in 200 years. It was mentioned in the Domesday Book, has the finest grouse moors in the land and its sweeping views over Swaledale stretch for miles. The Burgoyne looks out over it all – afternoon tea in the garden on a sunny day is hard to beat. Inside, an elegant past lives on: a smart drawing room with a crackling fire where you gather for drinks before dinner; a restaurant in racing green where you feast on delicious Yorkshire food; country-house bedrooms full of comfort, with warm colours, good beds, white linen, a sofa if there's room. You'll find pine shutters, cushioned window seats, a four-poster in the old snooker room; all but one has the view. The food is old-school, but utterly delicious, perhaps pheasant and venison terrine, Dover sole with brown shrimps, lemon tart with raspberry sorbet. Best of all are Julia and Mo, who run the place with unstinting kindness. There are maps for walkers, fishing can be arranged, a market passes on Fridays. Richmond is close, too. A delight. *The hotel has 2 black labs and can give details of walks and pubs that are dog-friendly in the Dales.*

Rooms	4 doubles, 1 twin, 1 four-poster; 2 doubles, both with separate bathrooms: £130-£190. 1 suite for 2: £210. Extra bed for children under 13: £25. Dogs £10 per night. Max. 2.
Meals	Dinner, 2-4 courses, £27-£40.
Closed	Mid-week in January (Mon-Thur).

 Towels for drying and advice on great walks. Dogs are allowed in the sitting rooms.

Julia & Mo Usman
The Burgoyne Hotel,
Reeth,
Richmond, DL11 6SN
Tel   +44 (0)1748 884292
Email   enquiries@theburgoyne.co.uk
Web   www.theburgoyne.co.uk

Entry 149 Map 6

The Mollycroft

The Mollycroft is a 1940s showman's living van, restored to gleaming glory and as eccentric as the people who once toured in it. Inside, a combination of dark wood and bright yellow and green décor creates a lively but homely feel. There are sofas in both the living room and the bunk room, which doubles as the kitchen, so you have plenty of space for lazy loafing in this tumbling, spacious wagon. You're far from the '40s in comfort: gas hobs and fridge in the kitchen, mains power and WiFi bring things up-to-date. Next to The Mollycroft is a fire pit complete with cooking gear; the compost loo and outdoor shower are both a walk away (you're still camping, after all). With no other guests around, it's ideal for families or groups looking for peace, though the 3ft high deck makes it unsuitable for toddlers. The grounds hold rare bamboo gardens, a lake, and your host Greville has converted a chapel to display his modern art collection. The Yorkshire Dales are stunning and close. Don't miss the enormous Sunday market at Catterick racecourse — or the races, or course. *Babies welcome. Secure garden, woodland and lakes. Dogs must be kept on lead.*

Rooms	Wagon for 4 (1 double, 2 bunks): from £89 per night. Max. 2 dogs.
Meals	Self-catering.
Closed	Never.

A lake for dog swimming, lovely walks on site, and a contained 2-acre bamboo garden for comfort and safety.

Canopy & Stars
The Mollycroft,
Tunstall, DL10 7PJ

Tel	+44 (0)117 204 7830
Email	enquiries@canopyandstars.co.uk
Web	www.canopyandstars.co.uk/ mollycroft

Entry 150 Map 6

Dalesend Cottages

Imagine staying on a sheep-dotted, beck-babbled, early 18th-century estate – 'the secret jewel of Lower Wensleydale.' Emma and Charles, lovers of animals, art and Yorkshire, have created four stunning apartments in the listed stable block. With an open-plan, fresh and contemporary layout they are perfect for peace lovers who seek comfort and style. Head Lad is on the ground floor – delighted to accept one small, well-behaved dog – and the rest are on the first; you'll pass fellow guests on the landing. All are spacious but the Hayloft is twice the size of the rest; in fact, it's a wow of a space, with pendants hanging from high rafters and a half-wall separating the freestanding bath and heavenly bed from the sofas and sleek kitchen. But all ooze luxury: drenching showers and toasty floors, wood-burners and WiFi, books and magazines, soothing colours and impeccable linen. And individual touches: we loved the old saddles in the Tack Room and the reindeer cushions in the Groom's Rooms. All this and hands-on hosts, shared seating on an outdoor deck, barbecue, laundry, and a pub you can stroll to. *Min. stay: 3 nights on weekdays, 7 in high season. Beautiful 25-acre park bordered by a stream on the doorstep. Detailed maps of local walks. Dogs welcome in Head Lad.*

Rooms	3 apartments for 2 (1 double; 1 bathroom): £395-£645 per week. 1 hayloft for 2 (1 double; 1 bathroom): £450-£695 per week. Dogs £5 per night.
Meals	Self-catering.
Closed	Rarely.

Meaty rolls from Pedigree, and a handy guide of dog-friendly pubs and restaurants.

	Emma & Charles Ropner Dalesend Cottages, Patrick Brompton, Bedale, DL8 1JL
Email	dalesendcottages@yahoo.co.uk
Web	www.dalesendcottages.co.uk

Entry 151 Map 6

Bewerley Hall Cottage

Pretty pretty pretty! Once the home of Bewerley Hall's head gardener, this couple's hideaway is comfy, cute and at the tail of a terrace of stone cottages. Step in to a sitting room that envelops you in cheering warmth: a wood-burner in the inglenook; two squishy red sofas dotted with cushions; a bookcase brimming with books, an iPod dock, guides and maps. For muddy wellies there's a boot room, and next to this, a cottagey kitchen. Upstairs is a double with excellent linen and lovely views over cherry trees and the village green, and a bathroom with slipper bath and local lotions. On sunny days, follow the sun front or back, dine out and soak up the views over Bewerley Park, the river and town beyond. Walk from the door, along the river Nidd or to How Stean limestone gorge; you're in beautiful Nidderdale and the Yorkshire Dales are a few miles away. Explore by foot, bike or horse – a mountain bike centre and stables are nearby – and well-behaved dogs are welcome downstairs. For a more sedate ramble, stroll to charming Pateley Bridge (5 minutes) and pick up your dinner – there's a deli, butchers and a good pub. *Minimum stay: 4 nights on weekdays. 3 nights at weekends. Great walks from the door, dog-friendly pubs along the way!*

Rooms	1 cottage for 2 (1 double): £650 per week. Dogs £20 per stay. Max. 2.
Meals	Self-catering.
Closed	Never.
	Doggie treats upon arrival.

Denise & Nigel McConnell
Bewerley Hall Cottage,
9 The GreenBewerley,
Pateley Bridge, HG3 5HU

Tel	+44 (0)1765 658565
Email	denise.mcconnell@btinternet.com
Web	www.cottageinbewerley.com

Entry 152 Map 6

Lodge Cottages

There is a danger that, once inside, you might never leave this cottage; it is ridiculously romantic, from its low beams to its sheepskin rugs. Tucked next to Rick and Sue's house in a quiet one-street village of handsome Georgian buildings, its charming roses-and-hollyhocks covered brick and cobble exterior does not disappoint. Inside it's all cosy country comfort but with a clever contemporary eye. Step straight into the low-beamed sitting room (tall folk beware) with its soft colours, bright gingham armchair, traditional Yorkshire range and table-for-two. At one end, there's colourful pottery in the smart kitchen – Rick is a professional chef and it shows. For lazy suppers, Rick can prepare meals to re-heat or you can slip next door to the pub. Upstairs to a dove-grey bedroom with exposed brickwork, ruby-red splashes of colour and soft rugs on painted floorboards. Good-size bathroom, too. Ripon Cathedral and Harrogate's spa town are nearby or take bracing walks on the North York Moors or cycle in the Yorkshire Dales. Come back to relax in your tiny, courtyard garden. Chocolate-box perfect. *Minimum stay: 3 nights at weekends & in high season. Plenty of wonderful walks locally, and dog-friendly pub right next door!*

Rooms	1 cottage for 2 (1 double; 1 bathroom): £450–£600 per week.
Meals	Dinner, 3 courses, £25. Pub next door.
Closed	Never.
	Advice on walks, and a lovely nature reserve just 2 minutes from the cottages.

Sue & Rick Hodgson
Lodge Cottages,
1 Lodge Cottage,
Main Street, Staveley, HG5 9NJ

Tel	+44 (0)1423 340700
Email	info@lodgecottages.co.uk
Web	www.lodgecottages.co.uk

Entry 153 Map 6

The Hayloft at Flamborough Rigg

On and on the road goes, deeper into the woods until the single track stops at an 1820s farmhouse surrounded by open fields. The gravelled drive crunches nicely under the tyres and the kitchen sports a hamper of local goodies (and, on occasion, home-brewed elderflower champagne!). Philip and Caroline love making guests feel at home and you may freely roam their super big garden with orchard, vegetable patch, loungers and barbecue. You can head off for a long walk over the rolling North Yorkshire Moors and come back to deep comfort. Snuggle up with a book in front of the wood-burner, watch a DVD, play a round of cards at the chunky table. There are quirky touches like old Singer sewing machines as table bases, a shelf of vintage china in the well-thought out kitchen/diner, and modern art on the walls. The bedrooms feel light and fresh with local oak furniture and cheerful cushions. Jump in the car for a trip to the coast or wander round the charming market town of Helmsley. The Hayloft feels as though it's in the middle of nowhere and yet moors, dales and the sea are wonderfully close. *Short breaks available. Large fully enclosed garden.*

Rooms	1 barn for 4 (1 double, 1 twin): £295–£650 per week. Max. 2 dogs.
Meals	Self-catering.
Closed	Rarely.
	A guide to local dog-friendly pubs and beaches.

Philip & Caroline Jackson
The Hayloft at Flamborough Rigg,
Middlehead Road, Stape,
Pickering, YO18 8HR

Tel   +44 (0)1751 475263
Email   enquiries@flamboroughriggcottage.co.uk
Web   www.thehayloftatflamboroughrigg.co.uk

Entry 154 Map 6

Little Garth

In the gentle foothills of the North York Moors, four miles from the market town of Kirkbymoorside, lies Normanby, an ancient settlement blessed with a Norman church and a trout stream. And, tucked behind the village street, through the picket gate, this immaculate little cottage. Having swapped a farmhouse in the Lakes for Little Garth, Pippa has poured love into its revival. Now all is light, warm and cosy inside, with plenty of pretty things to catch the eye: old paintings, quirky pots, cheerful rugs on polished flagged floors. Fresh flowers glow on old pine tops, cotton-covered armchairs are deep and comfortable, and a super, bright, light kitchen with all the kit opens to a very private rose and honeysuckle garden. After a day's roaming the sheep-speckled moors, bliss to snuggle down here. Light the candles, throw another log on the fire, pop the cork, or stroll to the pub for a drink. For eating out, Pippa recommends The Sun Inn at Normanby, a short walk. Return to sweetly floral bedrooms with gleaming white woodwork and generously clad beds. A lovely, very comfy hideaway. *Secure garden.*

Rooms	1 house for 5 (1 double, 1 twin, 1 single; 1 bath/shower room, 1 separate wc): £320–£700 per week. Max. 2 dogs.
Meals	Self-catering.
Closed	Never.
🏃🐕	Dog bowl.

Pippa Galloway
Little Garth,
Normanby, Sinnington,
York, YO62 6RH

Tel	+44 (0)1904 431876
Email	p.galloway@talk21.com
Web	www.holidaycottage-normanby.co.uk

Entry 155 Map 6

Yorkshire

Stow House

Past ancient stone walls and fields of lambs you reach sleepy Aysgarth and this dignified rectory. Step inside to find – Shoreditch pizzazz! Sarah and Phil have swapped the world of London advertising for a dream house in the Dales; she does cocktails, he does breakfasts and their take on Victoriana is inspiring. Floors, banisters and sash windows have been restored, stairs carpeted in plush red, sofas covered in zinging velvet. Bathrooms are wow, bedrooms are soothing and the papier mâché hare's head above the bar says it all. A stroll down the hill are the Aysgarth Falls, beloved of Turner, Ruskin and Wordsworth. *Minimum stay: 2 nights at weekends. Magnificent walks and big garden. Owners to keep dogs on a lead when walking through livestock.*

Rooms	6 doubles, 1 family room for 3: £110–£175. Extra bed/sofabed available £10–£20 per person per night. Max. 1 dog per room.
Meals	Pubs/restaurants 5-minute walk.
Closed	January & occasionally.

 Raw beef bones from the butcher, great dog walks, and towels.

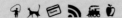

Sarah & Phil Bucknall
Stow House,
Aysgarth,
Leyburn, DL8 3SR
Tel   +44 (0)1969 663635
Email   info@stowhouse.co.uk
Web   www.stowhouse.co.uk

Entry 156 Map 6

Dale Farm

Huge skies as you drive along the open road to Dale Farm… the sea is just over the brow. Nifty inside too: bedrooms and bathrooms sparkle in whites and beach blues; mattresses are luxurious and handmade (the double is snugly in the attic); lots of books in the sitting room. Paul is a keen cook so breakfast is a varied feast: home-grown tomatoes, salmon from a local smokehouse, full English, and more! Peaceful woodland surrounds you; the logs fuel the biomass boiler and fires. Ramble and find Paul's metal sculptures and a fire-pit in the woods, croquet on the lawn, a beach down the road with a café… lovely. *Short breaks available for the cabins at £60 per night. 3 acres of land, other dogs to play with and 5 minutes from 5-mile long dog-friendly beach.*

Rooms	1 double, 1 twin: £90. 1 triple with separate bathroom: £90. 3 cabins for 2 (bathroom & wc in house, 50yds): £350 per week. Max. 1 dog.
Meals	Pubs/restaurants 2 miles.
Closed	Rarely.

 Advice on dog-friendly places and walks. Poo bin!

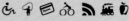

Elizabeth Halliday
Dale Farm, Bartindale Road,
Hunmanby, Filey, YO14 0JD
Tel   +44 (0)1723 890175
Mobile   +44 (0)7751 674706
Email   elizabethhalliday1@gmail.com
Web   www.dalefarmholidays.co.uk

Entry 157 Map 7

Pubs-for-a-pint

When you're away on a break with your dog it's handy to have a list of dog-friendly pubs to visit for a pint or a snack. Here is a small selection of pubs in England that welcome dogs in at least one area of the pub – most likely to be by the fire, at the bar or in the garden. Most pubs, though – even the dog-friendly ones – draw the line at allowing dogs in dining rooms, but if you want to check the details beforehand just give them a call.

We've visited each of these pubs and written about them ourselves. They're here because we like them. (We've not inspected any bedrooms they may have.) They are all taken from our hugely popular *Pubs & Inns of England & Wales* guide. Now in its twelfth edition, this guide brings you a huge variety of pubs from the charming to the rustic and the real-aled to the Michelin-starred. Visit www.sawdays.co.uk/bookshop to buy the guide.

Here is an explanation of the symbols you'll find at the foot of each Pub's entry. They apply to bar areas.

   ♿   Wheelchair access to both bar and wcs.

   🏃   Children of all ages welcome in parts of pub (highchairs not necessarily available).

   💳   Credit cards accepted, most commonly Visa and MasterCard.

   🍺   Pub serves four or more hand pumped ales.

   🍷   Pub serves eight or more wines by the glass.

   📶   Wireless internet access available in the bar.

Berkshire

The Little Angel

Winning a mention in 'The Haunted Pub Guide', the not-so-little Little Angel is one of the oldest pubs in Berkshire. Enter a huge bar to find sofas on one side, vintage oars on the walls, new dark oak on the floors, and a log-burner lit on cool days. This handsome sash-windowed pub stands alongside a famous rowing club (hence the oars) and the oldest part dates from the 1600s. If you bring your dog you can eat in the bar, or at snazzy high-backed chairs in the big-but-intimate 'barn'. There's a modern conservatory too, and a smart garden overlooking the cricket pitch. Trendy, friendly staff ferry the likes of fillet of lamb with fondant potato and baby vegetables to a contented Henley crowd, along with seasonal "superfood salad", burgers with skinny fries, rippled cookies and cream cheesecake. Stroll to the river and catch a boat down the Thames. *Secure patio garden, woodland, riverside & field close to pub. Few livestock fields, so good free running space for dogs.*

Buckinghamshire

Swan Inn

A 13th-century beauty in the heart of a sprawling New Town; across roundabouts, through housing estates, to arrive at 'Milton Keynes Village'. Spruced up in a stylish gastropub style, keeping its beams, fireplaces and layout, the Swan has cool colours and scatter cushions, chic chairs in the snug and a glowing open fire in the bar. In the cosy dining room – wooden floors, chunky tables, open-to-view kitchen – a selection of sharing platters are on the menu alongside gammon, egg and chunky chips, or opt for a vegetarian treat of couscous-stuffed Romano pepper with goat's cheese. Some produce comes from local allotments (in return for a pint or two), while imaginative evening meals might include dishes such as gilt pork hock, Toulouse sausage and white bean cassoulet. In summer you can eat on the sun terrace or in the pretty orchard garden. *Secure garden. Dogs welcome in the bar area. Dogs to be kept on leads please.*

Meals	Starters £5-£11.50. Mains £10.95-£21.50.		Meals	Lunch & dinner £7-£16. Sunday roast £13.95.
Closed	2 January, Monday after regatta.		Closed	Open all day.

 Biscuits, advice on walks, doggie bowls – and freedom of the pub (except the conservatory!).

 Advice on walks.

Lolly & Doug Green		Wanida Sae-lau	
	The Little Angel,		Swan Inn, Broughton Road,
	Remenham Lane,		Milton Keynes Village,
	Henley-on-Thames, RG9 2LS		Milton Keynes, MK10 9AH
Tel	+44 (0)1491 680430	Tel	+44 (0)1908 665240
Email	info@thecherrytreeinn.com	Email	info@theswan-mkvillage.co.uk
Web	www.thelittleangel.co.uk	Web	www.theswan-mkvillage.co.uk

Entry 158 Map 3

Entry 159 Map 3

The Old Queens Head

Run by the small and intimate Little Gems group, this pub by the green oozes character and charm: dating from 1666, its old beams and timbers blend perfectly with a stylish and contemporary décor in both the rambling bar and the dining rooms. Find rug-strewn flags, polished boards, classic fabrics, lovely old oak, innovative seasonal menus and chalkboard specials. Choices range from 'small plates' – confit duck leg, ham hock and apricot terrine with toasted rye bread and a ginger and plum salsa – to big dishes of slow-cooked shin of beef with saffron risotto, bone marrow crust and gremolata jus. For those who have room left, there's a tempting selection of puddings, classic raspberry Bakewell tart with clotted cream for one. To top it all, a parasol-strewn stone terrace, glorious summer garden, and walking in the ancient beech woodlands of Common and Penn Woods. *Dogs welcome in bar area and garden. Log fire for dogs to sit by and get cosy after their walks.*

The Royal Oak

The old whitewashed cottage stands in a hamlet on the edge of the common – hard to believe that Marlow is just a mile away. It's one of a thriving small group of dining pubs (the Alford Arms, Herts, and the Swan Inn and Old Queens Head, Bucks). Beyond the terrace is a stylish open-plan bar, cheerful with terracotta walls, rug-strewn boards, cushioned pews and crackling log fires. Order a pint of local Rebellion and check out the daily chalkboard or printed menu. Innovative pub grub comes in the form of 'small plates' such as Wobbly Bottom goat's cheese with basil quinoa and walnuts, and main meals – slow-cooked beef cheek bourguignon or pan-roast venison loin; all is fresh and delicious. Indulge in a marshmallow parfait with banana, chocolate and honeycomb. The sprawling gardens are perfect for summer. *Just down the road from beautiful Marlow Common. Dogs welcome in the bar.*

Meals	Lunch, bar meals & dinner £11.75–£22.75.		Meals	Lunch & dinner £11.75–£19.75.
Closed	Open all day.		Closed	Open all day.
	Doggie biscuit jar on the bar. Advice on walks in the nearby beech woodlands of Common and Penn Woods.			A huge garden to run around in. Dog biscuits on the bar, fresh water bowls outside and a large OS map by the front door. Lovely circular walk on iFootpath.

The Manager
The Old Queens Head,
Hammersley Lane, Penn,
High Wycombe, HP10 8EY
Tel   +44 (0)1494 813371
Email   info@oldqueensheadpenn.co.uk
Web   www.oldqueensheadpenn.co.uk

Entry 160 Map 3

David & Becky Salisbury
The Royal Oak,
Frieth Road, Bovingdon Green,
Marlow, SL7 2JF
Tel   +44 (0)1628 488611
Email   info@royaloakmarlow.co.uk
Web   www.royaloakmarlow.co.uk

Entry 161 Map 3

Blackwood Arms

This unassuming pub could be in the middle of the woods; indeed, it is near Burnham Beeches. There's a nose bag by the trees for horses, a dismounting block for riders and a dreamy garden bright with doves, pheasants and blackbirds that reaches down to a field of horses. Inside it is cottagey, quirky, full of character: plain boards, dark settles, hops on beams, old horsebrasses, stacked logs, and a basket of rugs for hardy drinkers. English Chancellors have patronised the Blackwood over the years (Profumo too) and *My Week with Marilyn* was filmed here. Children are welcomed and so are dogs: Sunday lunch is like Crufts! Ales, ciders, gins, wines by the glass, it's all waiting for you along with game from local shoots, tasty seafood grills, juicy burgers, nursery puds and a Moroccan chef; the 'bourek' parcels are gorgeous. *Woodland walks, secure garden, 2 local ponds and spare leads.*

The Jolly Cricketers

When the Jolly Cricketers came on the market, Seer Green residents Chris and Amanda couldn't resist. Now pretty plants clamber up the brickwork outside, while behind the bar, optics have been replaced by sweet shop jars filled with roasted nuts, olives and lollipops – a picture of individuality matched by a freehouse ale selection that shows off the best of local breweries. Ornate fireplaces, oddment-cluttered shelves and pine tables create an unpretentious backdrop for cider-braised ham, crispy poached egg, pineapple chutney and triple-cooked chips; or succulent beef rump, tongue and cheek with potato purée. Coffee mornings, book clubs and pub quizzes contribute to a community spirit but do nothing to dilute this pub's new-found dining status. *Secure garden. Dogs welcome in main bar on a lead.*

Meals	Starters from £5.25.
	Mains from £7.50.

 Homemade treats, blankets, local woodland walks map and Sunday meat treats.

Meals	Lunch from £6.50.
	Bar meals from £10.50.
	Dinner from £12.50.
Closed	Open all day.

 Homemade dog biscuits with money raised going to Search Dogs Bucks charity. Water bowls and great walks from the doorstep in the Chiltern countryside.

Sean Arnett
Blackwood Arms, Common Lane,
Littleworth Common,
Burnham, Slough, SL1 8PP
Tel   +44 (0)1753 645672
Email   info@theblackwoodarms.net
Web   www.theblackwoodarms.net

Entry 162 Map 3

Amanda Baker & Chris Lillitou
The Jolly Cricketers,
24 Chalfont Road, Seer Green,
Beaconsfield, HP9 2YG
Tel   +44 (0)1494 676308
Email   amanda@thejollycricketers.co.uk
Web   www.thejollycricketers.co.uk

Entry 163 Map 3

Buckinghamshire Pub

The Swan Inn

Swap the bland and everyday for the picture-book perfection of Denham village and the stylish Swan. Georgian, double-fronted, swathed in wisteria, the building is now in the capable hands of the Little Gems pub group. It's inviting and charming with rug-strewn boards, chunky tables, cushioned settles, a log fire and a fabulous terrace for outdoor meals. Food is modern British; choose from the 'small plates' list – a honey roast ham hock with baby gem and pea salad, soft boiled quail's egg with homemade salad cream. If you've nothing to rush for, enjoy pan-fried pork tenderloin with cider braised savoy cabbage and caramelised nectarine jus, accompanied by a pint of Rebellion IPA or one of 20 wines by the glass. The owners have thought of everything, and the gardens are big enough for the kids to go wild in. *Spacious and secure enclosed garden; beautiful village setting for walks. Dogs welcome in the bar area.*

Meals	Lunch, bar meals & dinner £11.75–£19.50.
Closed	Open all day.
	Advice on walks.

The Manager
The Swan Inn,
Village Road, Denham,
Uxbridge UB9 5BH
Tel   +44 (0)1895 832085
Email   info@swaninndenham.co.uk
Web   www.swaninndenham.co.uk

Entry 164 Map 3

Cheshire   Pub

The Church Inn

Tim Bird and Mary McLaughlin's mini-pub empire continues to thrive and grow with the addition of the 18th-century Church Inn. Sister pub to the Bull's Head, also in Mobberley, it has been fully restored and refurbished, retaining the small intimate dining rooms, all featuring wood and tiled floors, exposed brick and beams, soft lamplight, and glowing candles. On a wild winter's day it's hard to leave, with four craft ales on tap and decent wines to quaff and some great food: sautéed lambs' kidneys followed by grilled hake with tarragon and white wine sauce, then a sticky date bread and butter pud. Or try lighter dishes like smoked haddock tart or a sirloin steak sandwich with roast tomatoes and chips. Summer terraces give views of the church or across rolling fields. A village gem. *Secure terrace and garden. Own pub walk, lots more nearby; you can walk to sister pub in the village, the Bull's Head.*

Meals	Lunch & dinner £15–£24.95.
Closed	Open all day.
	Dog bowls, dog biscuits and Doggie Beer too. A great pub walk, and extensive gardens and terrace to play in.

Simon Umpleby
The Church Inn,
Church Lane, Mobberley,
Knutsford, WA16 7RD
Tel   +44 (0)1565 873178
Email   info@churchinnmobberley.co.uk
Web   www.churchinnmobberley.co.uk

Entry 165 Map 6

The Bull's Head

You feel the warmth as soon as you walk through the door. Candles glow on the tables of this pretty village pub, fires crackle, and the staff couldn't be nicer. Under a low-beamed ceiling, seven hand pumps dispense the finest local ales from Storm, Wincle and Redwillow as well as the inimitable Mobberley Wobbly – ale is king! Add in a Highland extravaganza of over 80 whiskies and other tempting brews and you have the makings of a celebration. Chef Steve cooks 'pub classics from the heart' with full English flavours; the steak and ale pie is a fully encased masterpiece in itself, and the Irish whisky sticky toffee pudding too indulgent for words. With outside tables for sunny days, this is as good as it gets for a village pub. *A garden for dogs and the Whisky Snug. Beautiful Mobberley walk.*

Meals	Bar meals £2.85–£12.
	Lunch £3.95–£19.95.
	Sunday roast £13.95.
Closed	Open all day.

 Biscuits on the bar, water bowls and Doggie Beer. A good pub walk between The Bull's Head and The Church Inn.

Barry Lawlor
The Bull's Head,
Mill Lane, Mobberley,
Knutsford, WA16 7HX
Tel   +44 (0)1565 873395
Email   info@thebullsheadpub.co.uk
Web   www.thebullsheadpub.co.uk

Entry 166 Map 6

The Three Greyhounds Inn

The bright, many-bottled bar winks and glows as you enter, while host James has a welcome for all. Fat purple cushions soften wooden benches around a huge dual-facing fireplace; reach for the 'Brandy Bible' and settle in. The clever layout makes the space cosy and intimate, with snugs around every corner – four with firesides – and nooks and crannies aplenty. James is proud of the atmosphere, and rightly so. Families nibble and natter with relish, while walkers and couples take their time over delicious smoked haddock and leek tart or pan-fried lamb's kidneys. During annual Cheshire Game Week you can tuck into dishes such as pheasant breast with sautéed white pudding and red leg partridge croquette…. Deep in the Cheshire countryside, this well-restored pub is conveniently close to the M6. *A secure garden and great walk around Shakerley Mere next to the pub.*

Meals	Lunch from £10.50.
	Bar meals from £5.95.
	Dinner from £10.50.
	Not Christmas Day.
Closed	Please check before you visit.

 Dog biscuits, dogs' dinner menu, Doggie Beer and water bowls. Shakerley Mere bird nature reserve walks, and a play in enclosed extensive gardens.

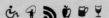

James Griffiths
The Three Greyhounds Inn,
Holmes Chapel Road, Allostock,
Knutsford, WA16 9JY
Tel   +44 (0)1565 723455
Email   info@thethreegreyhoundsinn.co.uk
Web   www.thethreegreyhoundsinn.co.uk

Entry 167 Map 6

Derbyshire Pub

The Devonshire Arms

Straddling Yorkshire and Derbyshire, the handsome 'Dev', sits back off a leafy lane, surrounded by rolling fields. A smart pale grey makeover draws you in, though there's seating by the front door if you fancy a Kelham Island pint in the sunshine. Inside: a light, contemporary space full of interest and quirk – original art on the walls, squashy leather sofas, a pair of thrones... In the stone-floored snug, a wood stove adds cheer on a chill day. The airy dining area has artfully mismatched furniture, some vintage, a couple of church pews and one long canteen-like table big enough for a full family. The short, rustic menu includes the likes of braised ox cheek, shoulder of Derbyshire lamb, ham hock fritter and a tasty monster of a hot pork and apple sandwich; wash it down with a glass of wine from nearby Renishaw Hall, the Sitwell family seat.

Meals	Starters from £5. Mains from £10.
Closed	Mondays.
	Advice on walks, fresh water in a clean bowl and a dog chew.

Jill Swift
The Devonshire Arms,
Lightwood Lane, Middle Handley,
Sheffield, S21 5RN
Tel   +44 (0)1246 434800
Email   enquiries@devonshirearmsmiddlehandley.com
Web   www.devonshirearmsmiddlehandley.com

Entry 168 Map 6

Hertfordshire Pub

The Alford Arms

It isn't easy to find, so come armed with precise directions! In a hamlet enfolded by acres of National Trust common land, David and Becky Salisbury's gastropub is worth any number of missed turns. Inside are two interlinked rooms, bright and airy, with soft colours, scrubbed pine tables, wooden and tile floors. Food is taken seriously and ingredients are as organic, free-range and delicious as can be. Try warm confit rabbit and wild mushroom tart, baked smoked haddock and prawn pancake, pan-roasted Buckinghamshire venison haunch with sticky red cabbage, whole baked sea bass and homemade ice cream. Wine drinkers have the choice of 22 by the glass; service is informed and friendly. Arrive early on a warm day to take your pick of the teak tables on the sun-trapping front terrace. *Path into Ashridge Forest opposite, with thousands of acres of beautiful ancient beech woods. Dogs welcome in the bar.*

Meals	Lunch, bar meals & dinner £11.75–£19.75.
Closed	Open all day.
	Dog biscuits on the bar, fresh water bowls outside and a large OS map by the front door. Lovely circular walk on iFootpath.

David & Becky Salisbury
The Alford Arms,
Frithsden,
Hemel Hempstead, HP1 3DD
Tel   +44 (0)1442 864480
Email   info@alfordarmsfrithsden.co.uk
Web   www.alfordarmsfrithsden.co.uk

Entry 169 Map 3

Truscott Arms

A place of note, its pared back lofty interiors home to wine tastings, art exhibitions, events and summer parties as well as to seriously good food. It is independently owned, dynamically run, and a Swiss-born designer was behind the restoration. The result is a light, airy, friendly space with a zinc-topped bar down one side, a Moorish tiled floor, and the subtlest, palest paintwork. Find yourself a velvet bar stool and order a craft beer (Camden Hells Lager? why not!) or sail upstairs to ceiling roses and elegant parquet. Head chef is Irish Aidan McGee (ex Launceston Place, with a passion for sustainability) and his menus are a wonder: Trealy Farm Scotch quail's egg with salsa verde; 35-day aged rib-eye with girolle mushrooms; Kentish Well Pudding with russet apples and brandy ice cream – it doesn't get much better. *Perfect for your drink after a good walk down Little Venice canal way! Max. 1 dog per person.*

Meals	Breakfast available. Bar snacks from £8. Set evening menu, 2-3 courses, £32-£37.

 Water bowls.

♿ 🐦 📶 🚂 🍷 ☕ 🍷

Andrew & Mary Jane Fishwick
Truscott Arms,
55 Shirland Road,
Maida Vale, W9 2JD
Tel   +44 (0)20 7266 9198
Email   maryjane@thetruscottarms.com
Web   www.thetruscottarms.com

Entry 170 Map 3

The Sheppey Inn

A funky country pub, one of the best in the west. Its exterior gives no hint of the wonders within – part cider house, part cool hotel. Low beamed ceilings in the bar, high white walls in the barn. There are cute booths, David Hockney prints, 50s retro furniture, the odd guitar waiting to be played. Music matters here: fantastic jazz, blues and funk bubbles away nicely, while a small stage hosts the odd travelling band. Local ales, scrumptious ciders, Belgian beers and lovely wines all wait, as does super food. Try French onion soup, a splendid fish stew or Somerset beef with Yorkshire pudding and red wine gravy. In summer, life decants onto a small terrace that hangs above a tiny river; otters pass, fields stretch out beyond. Glastonbury and the Somerset Levels wait. Out of this world. *Walks, rivers and an otter to scent.*

Meals	Lunch from £5.95. Dinner from £8.95. Sunday lunch from £10.50.
Closed	3pm-5pm Tues-Fri.

 Dog treats and dog beer.

🐦 📶 ☕ 🍷

Mark Hey & Liz Chamberlain
The Sheppey Inn,
Lower Godney,
Glastonbury BA5 1RZ
Tel   +44 (0)1458 831594
Web   www.thesheppey.co.uk

Entry 171 Map 2

Staffordshire	Pub

The Duncombe Arms

The bar is sleek and stylishly laid out, with rustic nooks to settle into, the music plays discreetly and the food is absolutely beautiful. Diners include many regulars and returning Londoners, even though this is Derbyshire. James is passionate about making the Duncombe excel, and excel it does: the staff are on the ball and there's a top team in the kitchen, headed by Matt Wadsley. Platefuls of flavoursome food, modern British with touches of rusticity, are delivered to inviting tables in dining areas cosy, lofty, private, airy or al fresco; take your pick. Our sea bass with crushed new potatoes and slow-cooked cherry tomatoes was faultless. There are wines from Bibendum, 13 top malts, Duncombe Ale on tap, and in summer you can spill into a huge garden with views across the Dove Valley. *Lovely walks around the Peak District. If guests come for a meal and bring their dog they should give the pub a call first if possible.*

Sussex	Pub

The Crown

Just a short stroll up from the beach and the contemporary Jerwood Gallery, this old corner boozer oozes artful charm and hipster-cool. Décor is shabby-chic, the mood is laid-back, and the craft beer list is curated by an expert palate. Taken over by Tess and Andrew in 2014, the Crown celebrates fantastic local produce. Menus bristle with local artisan producers; there's coffee from Rye Bay, ice cream from Bodiam, and mugs from Gopsall Pottery in Winchelsea. Sit back and enjoy a pint of Old Dairy Red Top, lunch on local-ale rarebit with chutney, or go the whole hog and tuck into beach-landed skate with caper, lemon and parsley butter. Community spirit rings throughout and everyone is welcome, including the kids and the dog. Anything goes, from live music, weekly quizzes and pub games to Sunday morning storytelling and monthly craft groups. *Near to the bottom of the East Hill country park, and close to the beach.*

Meals	Starters £5–£8. Mains £12–£20. Sunday lunch, 3 courses, £21.95.	Meals	Starters £4–£9. Mains £10–£16. Puddings £3–£7.
Closed	Open all day.	Closed	Open all day.
	Dog bowls with fresh water.		Locally made dog biscuits, water bowls – and a friendly welcome!

James Oddy
The Duncombe Arms,
Ellastone,
Ashbourne, DE6 2GZ
Tel   +44 (0)1335 324275
Email   hello@duncombearms.co.uk
Web   www.duncombearms.co.uk

Tess Eaton & Andrew Swan
The Crown,
64–66 All Saints Street,
Hastings TN34 3BN
Tel   +44 (0)1424 465100
Email   hello@thecrownhastings.co.uk
Web   www.thecrownhastings.co.uk

The Vine Tree

With a fine store of ales and over 40 wines by the glass this former watermill is a watering hole in every sense. It may be hidden away but the faithful return for the food and the beer. On Sundays, memorable roast sirloin of beef from the neighbour's farm is served with all the trimmings. There's plenty of fresh fish, too, local game in season, sautéed scallops with wild mushroom risotto, and a very pretty niçoise salad. Cheeses are local and delicious. Service is young and friendly and surroundings are inviting: deep red walls, candlelight and beams, a wood-burning stove. Tables in the minuscule upstairs room are super-cosy; in summer, relax and gaze on the big immaculate terrace. This Vine Tree has a rich harvest for guests (and their dogs) to reap, and the walking is lovely. *Westonbirt Arboretum nearby, plenty of walks as the pub is in the middle of the countryside.*

The Barbury Inn

Ancient and mysterious chalk downland scenery all around with horses both real and carved onto hillsides. This late 18th-century inn sits beside the road to Avebury and has been given a kind makeover with a plush-rustic mix of exposed brick, scrubbed pine and painted furniture, rattan chairs and pews – it's all super-civilised. Take your pick from St Austell or Prescott ale or peruse the extensive wine list. Chef Roger Hawkshaw believes in letting the produce do the talking, seasonal menus feature his own salted beef and tongue, terrines, pickles and sauces, and bread. There's fillet of Loch Duart salmon, olive mustard potatoes, roasted peppers and basil pesto too, as well as pub classics and great desserts. After a blast along The Ridgeway, a mile away, this is the perfect post-walk treat. *Walks to Ridgeway from the door and Avebury which is also near.*

Meals	Lunch from £8.95. Dinner from £13.95. Bar meals from £4.95.		Meals	Lunch & dinner £10.75–£19.75.
Closed	3pm-6pm Mon-Sat, 5pm-11pm Sun.		Closed	Open all day.

 Scrumptious lovely biscuits, organic treats, towels and a brush. Dogs also get their own champagne buckets full of fresh water.

 Scrumptious lovely biscuits, organic treats, towels and a brush. Dogs also get their own champagne buckets full of fresh water.

Charles Walker & Tiggi Wood
The Vine Tree,
Foxley Road, Norton,
Malmesbury, SN16 0JP
Tel   +44 (0)1666 837654
Email   tiggi@thevinetree.co.uk
Web   www.thevinetree.co.uk

Entry 174 Map 3

Charles Walker & Tiggi Wood
The Barbury Inn,
Broad Hinton,
Swindon, SN4 9PF
Tel   +44 (0)1793 731510
Email   info@thebarburyinn.co.uk
Web   www.thebarburyinn.co.uk

Entry 175 Map 3

Fox & Hounds

Beech trees and high ridges: make time for a walk with views over the vale, then land at the 17th-century thatched pub on the green. Inside are two areas: one bright and conservatory-like, with a great view, the other older and cosier, its fireplace flanked by small red leather sofas. There are warming ales from Palmers and Butcombe, and Hop Back's inimitable Summer Lightning, and a well-presented wine card that tells you exactly what you'll get. No-nonsense New Zealander Murray cooks in an eclectic, untypical gastro style. Tuck into a chorizo, bean and red pepper casserole in red wine with belly pork, or a sweet onion, ricotta and parmesan tart, and follow with melting chocolate fondant and mascarpone cream; no need to feel sinful. Then stay till the pub closes. *Secure garden; woodland walks.*

The Royal Oak

In a distractingly pretty village is a handsome stone pub, once neglected, now revived, and loved by all who visit. Jill and Abbi (Italophiles both) are introducing Italy to North Yorkshire. No surprise that families are given a big welcome, and fish and chips join arms with the 'menu al giorno' (there's Yorkshire rarebit, gammon and pineapple, sticky toffee pudding and Sunday roasts, too). Plates of Tuscan deliciousness are ferried from the kitchen to the dining bar, which is shambolic in the nicest way. Tartan wool carpets, standing timbers, scrubbed tables, old mirrors, fresh flowers, tons of books, a wall of old keys, an eclectic mix of music on the stereo – seems like they've been here for years! There's a games room with bar billiards, a patio at the back and cosy fires. Cask ales, wines, local craft beers, espresso… marvellous. *Wonderful walks in the village and the Howardian Hills. Outside patio area if guests prefer to eat out with their dogs.*

| Meals | Lunch & dinner £9-£17. |
| Closed | 3pm-5.30pm. |

 Water bowl, homemade doggie treats and advice on walks.

Meals	Starters from £4.50.
	Mains from £9.50.
Closed	Mon & Tue all day.

Always water, dog biscuits, towels and advice on walks. Dogs are welcome in the pub if well-behaved. Some owners buy them an ice cream!

Murray Seator
Fox & Hounds,
The Green, East Knoyle,
Salisbury, SP3 6BN
Tel   +44 (0)1747 830573
Email   fox.hounds@virgin.net
Web   www.foxandhounds-eastknoyle.co.uk

Entry 176 Map 3

Jill & Abbi Greetham
The Royal Oak, Church Street,
Nunnington, York YO62 5US
Tel   +44 (0)1439 748271
Mobile   +44 (0)7715 869270
Email   info@nunningtonroyaloak.co.uk
Web   www.nunningtonroyaloak.co.uk

Entry 177 Map 6

Wales

The Black Lion Inn

The lion roars again thanks to the hard work of owners Mari and Leigh who have transformed this once derelict late 18th-century country inn into an award-winning local champion. Contemporary slate tiles wrap round a modern bar, lime rendered walls host modern pictures – one a fabulous collage of the menu's provenance. French windows open to a paved patio with views across the car park to fields, one of which will soon grow vegetables and herbs for the kitchen. Ales from local Welsh breweries and interesting wines set you up for modern British dishes made with locally grown, foraged and reared produce. Try fresh-as-can-be seared scallops with black pudding, pancetta and pea purée, or braised shoulder of local lamb with a root vegetable rösti. Upstairs are two hugely comfortable rooms with open rafters, thick carpets and handmade oak furniture: the mattresses are top of the range, the bathrooms gleam with white tiles, mosaic inlay and sleek chrome. You are beside a road but thick walls and small windows ensure blissful calm, while eco-energy keeps you snug. Glorious Anglesey awaits. *Plenty of local beaches and lovely walks; large car park.*

Rooms	1 double: £115.
	1 family room for 4: £140.
	Singles £90.
Meals	Lunch & dinner £6-£19.
Closed	From November to Easter,
	closed Mon-Tues.

Dog biscuits and advice on walks.

Leigh & Mari Faulkner
The Black Lion Inn,
Llanfaethlu,
Holyhead, LL65 4NL
Tel   +44 (0)1407 730718
Email   info@blacklionanglesey.co.uk
Web   www.blacklionanglesey.com

Entry 178 Map 5

Wonderfully Wild

The safari tent lodges at Wonderfully Wild are classic safari style with plenty of added Welshness, including slate hearths from local quarries and warm woollen rugs in the spacious living areas, not to mention the mountain views of Snowdonia from the outside decks. Derw, at one end of the field (and closest to the car park), is Welsh for Oak, and then there's Castan (Conker), Onnen (Ash) and Jacmor (Sycamore) at the far end. As well as the private showers, toilets and fully equipped kitchens in each one, owners Victoria and Robin have toured the auctions to fill the lodges with quality upcycled furniture. You're surrounded by 200 acres of fields, woodland and streams – in fact the nearest stream to splash in borders the field where you'll be staying. The Telor Cycle Route borders another side of the field and is a great way to explore this beautiful corner of Anglesey. It's a short drive to a choice of beaches, or just 40 minutes' walk will take you to the lovely seaside town of Beaumaris – perfect for a day out, with comfy beds and a big chest of board games to come back to in the evening. *Babies welcome. Fields to walk in, stream to play in; safe environment.*

Rooms	4 safari tents for 6 (1 double, 1 double cupboard bed, 2 singles): from £100 per night. Dogs £20 per stay. Max. 1.
Meals	Self-catering.
Closed	November – March.
	Advice on dog-friendly pubs, beaches and days out.

Canopy & Stars
Wonderfully Wild,
Cichle Farm, Beaumaris, LL58 8PS
Tel +44 (0)117 204 7830
Email enquiries@canopyandstars.co.uk
Web www.canopyandstars.co.uk/ wonderfullywild

Entry 179 Map 5

Tŷ Cerrig Woodland Retreats

Deeply rural but only half an hour's drive from Cardiff, you can choose between the cabin (Bwncath) and a shepherd's hut (Gwdihŵ), among the saplings of Andrew and Charlotte's Christmas Tree farm. They also keep bees and make great Welsh cakes! Gwdihŵ is comfortably snug with a wood-burning stove, sheep's wool insulation, a goose feather duvet on the fold-down bed, an impressively well-equipped kitchen, a hot shower and flushing loo. There are even bunk beds for two little ones to sleep in – or for a siesta. Bwncath is about 100 metres away, but the meadow in between is the only thing you need share. It, too, is wool-insulated for warm nights and has big French windows to fling open onto the wooden deck when the sun comes up. It's a place for simply spending time together: over a lazy breakfast at the farmhouse table, playing board games on the leather sofa and chairs by the wood-burner, or outside with barbecues and drinks around the fire pit. You and your dog can walk for miles in the lovely Vale of Glamorgan; head for the coast for a change of scene and a swim if the mood takes you. This is a lovely place to be. *Babies welcome. Over 25 acres of woodland to run around in and right next to forestry commission. Close to dog-friendly beaches and pubs.*

Rooms	Cabin for 4 (1 double, 2 singles, 1 travel cot available): from £95 per night. Shepherd's hut for 4 (1 double, 2 child's bunks, 1 moses basket available): from £85 per night. Max. 1 dog in shepherd's hut, 2 in cabin.
Meals	Self-catering.
Closed	Never.
	Towels, and advice on walks and local dog-friendly pubs.

Canopy & Stars
Tŷ Cerrig Woodland Retreats,
Maerdy Newydd,
Bonvilston, CF5 6TR

Tel   +44 (0)117 204 7830
Email   enquiries@canopyandstars.co.uk
Web   www.canopyandstars.co.uk/tycerrig

Entry 180 Map 2

The Log House Studio

You may well be greeted by the ever-exuberant Charlie Brown, terrier and proprietor of Cwm Farm. Well, technically that's Tim, who lives with Charlie in the cottage across the field, and whose paintings festoon the walls of this raised, Swedish-style log cabin built from local timber. Step inside and you'll find an open-plan space, complete with artists' easel and desk, a comfortable double bed and a wood-burner to keep things cosy whatever the weather throws at you. Everything you might need for coffee brewing or sausage frying is also on hand and Charlie will be delighted to assist. The mezzanine level, reached by wooden ladder, provides space either for extra guests or just to read a book. The private compost loo and wonderfully hot, gas-powered shower are reachable down a few steps. Although secluded, you'll never feel too alone here; there are cows and sheep in the fields, and from time to time you'll hear the odd barking from the kennels next door too. The surrounding countryside offers plenty of walks, some of Wales' best mountain biking trails, and a whole selection of ruined castles to explore. *Babies & children over 10 welcome. The fields are mostly fenced from livestock next door. Resident dog Charlie Brown welcomes friends.*

Rooms	Cabin for 4 (1 double, 1 sofabed): from £100 per night. Dogs £10 per pet per stay. Max. 2.
Meals	Self-catering.
Closed	Never.
	Advice on walks.

Canopy & Stars
The Log House Studio, Cwm Farm,
Capel Isaac, Llandeilo, SA19 7UE

Tel	+44 (0)117 204 7830
Email	enquiries@canopyandstars.co.uk
Web	www.canopyandstars.co.uk/ loghouse

Entry 181 Map 2

The Dolaucothi Arms

David and Esther's cute little inn sits in a village deep in rural Carmarthenshire. It's an absolute gem, a testament to beautiful simplicity, with lovely interiors that see no need to abandon their period charm for contemporary design. Instead, you find beautiful Georgian windows, original tiles in the bar, then varnished floorboards in the airy restaurant. It's a little like walking onto the pages of a Jane Austen novel, a touch of old-world charm. Pick up a pint of local ale, sink into a chesterfield sofa and roast away in front of the wood-burner; in summer you decant into the pretty garden for a pint in the sun. Excellent food awaits you – homemade soups and pies, lamb from the Dolaucothi estate, the best local steaks, sticky toffee pudding. Circular walks help you atone, there's a river at the bottom of the garden, then National Trust goldmines to visit in the village. Bedrooms upstairs are a steal with smart colours, woollen throws and sparkling bathrooms; some have garden views, all get decanters of port. Breakfast is a treat. Aberglasney Gardens are within easy reach. Don't miss Sunday lunch. *Large garden, please be aware of the chickens. Easy to follow walks from the door. Dogs welcome in 1 dining area and the lounge bar.*

Rooms	2 doubles: £75–£80. Singles £55. Extra bed/sofabed available £20 per person per night. Dogs £10 per stay. Max. 2.
Meals	Lunch from £5. Dinner, 3 courses, £20. Sunday lunch from £9.
Closed	26 December to 2 January.

Dog treats in your room.

David Joy & Esther Hubert
The Dolaucothi Arms,
Pumpsaint,
Llanwrda, SA19 8UW
Tel   +44 (0)1558 650237
Email   info@thedolaucothiarms.co.uk
Web   www.thedolaucothiarms.co.uk

Entry 182 Map 2

Ty Mawr Country Hotel

Pretty rooms, attractive prices and delicious food make this welcoming country house hard to resist. It sits in a very peaceful spot. You drive over hills, drop into the village, then wash up at this 16th-century stone house that comes in soft yellow. Outside, a sun-trapping terrace laps against a trim lawn, which in turn drops into a passing river. Gentle eccentricities abound: croquet hoops take odd diversions, logs are piled high like giant beehives, a seat has been chiselled into a tree trunk. Inside, original stone walls and low beamed ceilings give a warm country feel. There are fires everywhere – one in the attractive sitting room that overlooks the garden, another in the dining room that burns on both sides. Excellent bedrooms are all big. You get big beds, warm colours, crisp linen, good bathrooms. Some have sofas, all are dog-friendly, three overlook the garden. Back downstairs, the bar doubles as reception, while Welsh art on the walls is for sale. Steve's cooking is the final treat, perhaps Cardigan Bay scallops, organic Welsh beef, calvados and cinnamon rice pudding. Top stuff. *Children over 10 welcome. Dogs welcome in sitting room, bar and bedrooms (just not in the breakfast room or restaurant).*

Rooms	4 doubles, 2 twin/doubles: £115-£130. Singles £75. Dinner, B&B £80-£88 per person.
Meals	Dinner £25-£30.
Closed	Rarely.
	Advice on lots of walks.

Annabel & Steve Thomas
Ty Mawr Country Hotel,
Brechfa, SA32 7RA
Tel +44 (0)1267 202332
Email info@wales-country-hotel.co.uk
Web www.wales-country-hotel.co.uk

Entry 183 Map 2

Troedyrhiw Holiday Cottages

Come for the wide wooded valley, the Preseli Hills on show in the distance, and plenty of animals for children to befriend. You're down a rural track with other holiday makers; pygmy goats, Shetland ponies, kune kune pigs and chickens litter the fields around you and the owners (who will greet you) live on site should you need them. All the sitting rooms have wood-burners (logs are on the house), local art on the walls and comfy sofas and chairs; kitchens and bathrooms are modern (if slightly small) but fine for holiday needs. Bedrooms are spotless and bright – you'll sleep well, away from traffic noise. Each cottage has its own small garden or tranche of decking, plus barbecue and furniture so you can spill out for summertime meals and games. Fields lead down to the wide stream, perfect for welly (or barefoot in summer) splashing, and woodland walks. You're just a mile away from the nearest pub and shops and there are wide safe beaches for picnics and swimming; also walking, birdwatching, rugged mountain biking. Shopaholics will enjoy Cardigan, an appealing Welsh estuary town. *Short breaks available. Woodland walks, streams to jump in, hills to walk up and coast path to explore.*

Rooms	1 cottage for 2, 2 cottages for 4, 1 cottage for 6, 1 cottage for 8: £420–£1,505 per week. Dogs £20. Max. 2.
Meals	Self-catering.
Closed	Never.
	Advice on walks and dog-friendly beaches.

Rob & Michelle Silcox
Troedyrhiw Holiday Cottages,
Penparc, Cardigan, SA43 2AE
Tel   +44 (0)1239 811564
Email   info@troedyrhiw.com
Web   www.troedyrhiw.com

Entry 184 Map 1

Painted Wagon

Tucked out of sight of the smallholding's other buildings, this tranquil wagon has been a labour of love for owners Ann and Terry. They've transformed the space into a Gypsy-inspired wagon to share with others. The handcrafted features and wood-burner are homely and you'll find towels and extra blankets in the trunk at the foot of the double bed. Outside there's a barbecue and fire pit for extra warmth while you enjoy the outdoors – no light pollution makes this a great spot for stargazing! Your private camp is completed by a small hut alongside the wagon, containing a hot shower and compost loo. Although it's off-grid, there are cool boxes to keep your milk cool for the morning. Discover special places to sit in the woodlands, filled with old oaks and willows. Terry has also crafted a hobbit house out of a fallen tree root ball, where you can go owl spotting in the evenings! There's lots to do outside of the farm, including browsing the independent shops and cafés of pretty Georgian harbour town Aberaeron, or visiting the great beaches in Newquay for watersports, boat trips and dolphin watching. *Woodland and fields to play in, but please respect the livestock.*

Rooms	Wagon for 2 (1 double): from £70 per night. Max. 2 dogs.
Meals	Self-catering.
Closed	November – March.
	Towels and good walks.

Canopy & Stars
Painted Wagon, The Cabin,
Glantren Lane, Llanybydder, SA40 9SA

Tel	+44 (0)117 204 7830
Email	enquiries@canopyandstars.co.uk
Web	www.canopyandstars.co.uk/ paintedwagon

Entry 185 Map 2

One Cat Onnen Den

In the wild meadows of a quiet valley live one cat, two owners, Jessie and Lyndon, and four grass-roofed dens; lovingly crafted by Lyndon. Onnen Den, pitched at the top, overlooking the pond and the other huts, is dog-friendly. The grassy exteriors aren't the only thing Nordic here – the dens are simple and cosy inside and the flexible layout make them a perfect fit for families and couples. There is a double bed and a single bed which you can also use as a sofa in the day. Tucked underneath the single is another bed which can be pulled out. As night falls, you can sit around the campfire enjoying the stars, moon and sounds of country life. Once a home for saddlebacks, The Pig Shed is now a warm communal barn, a two-minute walk away from the dens, with a kitchen and a big dining table where you can get to know your fellow glampers. Take some afternoon coffee and cake to the picnic tables just outside, then watch the sun set with a local beer. The hot showers and flushing loo are next door. With beaches and mountains both nearby, it's a perfect base for fishing, walking, horse riding and surfing. *Babies welcome. Numerous walks from doorstep and nearby; beaches are close. Surrounded by working farmland so dogs must be kept on leads on site.*

Rooms	Cabin for 4 (1 double, 2 singles): from £55 per night. Dogs £20 per pet per stay. Max. 2 small or 1 large.
Meals	Self-catering.
Closed	Never.
🐕	Water bowl and advice on walks.

Canopy & Stars
One Cat Onnen Den,
One Cat Farm, Bronfre Fach,
Ciliau Aeron, Lampeter, SA48 7PT

Tel   +44 (0)117 204 7830
Email enquiries@canopyandstars.co.uk
Web   www.canopyandstars.co.uk/onnenden

Entry 186 Map 2

Locke's Cottage

It's difficult to know what to call the charming building sitting on the side of the Hoffnant valley – downstairs, thick stone walls give away this former barn's agricultural past, while the timber upper level with an oak tree 'growing' through the centre has a distinctly cabin-like feel. In wonderfully thrifty style, many of the materials used in this unusual creation are recycled; floors and window sills have been cleverly fashioned from scaffold boards used during the renovation, the double-ended bath sits on a cradle handmade from reclaimed wood and the pan rack in the large downstairs kitchen was once an old meat spit retrieved from somewhere in the grounds. Big windows along the front look down over the valley, and double doors lead from the upstairs living area onto an open balcony. You're so close to the sea that you can hear waves breaking. You have direct access onto the coastal path: follow the headland round to beautifully sandy West Wales beaches. Owners Kathryn and Geoff recommend the beach at Llangrannog for a great pub and unbeatable homemade ice cream from the beachside café. *Babies welcome. 2 beaches within 1.5 miles, with welcoming pubs. Huge network of tracks, paths and hills to explore.*

Rooms	Cottage for 5 (1 double, 2 sofabeds): from £95 per night. Dogs £10 per pet per stay. Max. 2.
Meals	Self-catering.
Closed	Never.
	Towels for drying and advice on walks.

Canopy & Stars
Locke's Cottage,
Brynhoffnant, SA44 6EF

Tel   +44 (0)117 204 7830
Email   enquiries@canopyandstars.co.uk
Web   www.canopyandstars.co.uk/
            lockescottage

Entry 187 Map 2

Penbontbren

You're lost in lovely hills, yet only three miles from the sea. Not that you're going to stray far. These gorgeous suites don't just have wonderful prices, they're heaped with comforts, too – this is a great spot to come and do nothing at all. Richard and Huw have thought it all through. You get crockery and cutlery, kettles and fridges, then you're encouraged to bring your own wine or to buy provisions from the farm shop for lunch. As for the suites, expect big beds, super bathrooms, sofas and armchairs in pretty sitting areas, then doors onto semi-private terraces – perfect for lunch in summer. You get iPod docks, flat-screen TVs, robes and White Company lotions, too. The new garden room is a little smaller than the others, but has a big terrace to compensate. Breakfast is served in the main house – the full Welsh works. Beautiful hills, sandy beaches, Cardigan and magical St Davids all wait. Good local restaurants are on hand: lobster from the sea, lamb from the hills. Don't miss The Shed in Porthgain for excellent fish and chips. A great place to unwind with discounts for longer stays. *Minimum stay: 2 nights in high season. Large gardens and country walks. No dogs on croquet lawns because that's where the bees are kept.*

Rooms	5 suites for 2, 1 garden room: £99–£120. 1 cottage for 7: £700–£1,150 per week Singles £80–£95.. Dogs free for guests via Sawday's. Max. 2 small or 1 large.
Meals	Restaurants within 3 miles.
Closed	Christmas.
	Dogs truly welcome! Lovely gardens and lots of advice on beaches, local pubs and days out.

Richard Morgan-Price & Huw Thomas
Penbontbren,
Glynarthen,
Llandysul, SA44 6PE,
Tel +44 (0)1239 810248
Email contact@penbontbren.com
Web www.penbontbren.com

Entry 188 Map 2

Pwll y Garth

The road twists and turns until you arrive at a small 19th-century slate house in a wild, magical setting. Step inside to oak floors, thick lime-plaster walls and beamed ceilings. This is not a place for luxury seekers, this is a modest, simple retreat without a TV or a dishwasher. Complete and utter tranquillity. There's a dining room with a wooden table and chairs, a dresser with glasses and crockery. The basic kitchen is off here; find local goodies, a Rayburn to cook on and deep slate windowsills. The cosy living room has a bookcase, Moroccan rugs, armchairs, a sofa and a wood-burner to belt out the heat – and enough wood to last a couple of days. Upstairs is a tiled bathroom, with Ecover smellies, and two simple bedrooms (one twin, one double) both with sloped ceilings and incredible views. Beds are draped with Welsh woollen throws. The delightful owners, who live close by, are the custodians of Ty Mawr, a 16th-century traditional Welsh house; Wil is passionate and can tell you its history. You're minutes from the A5 that takes you straight through Snowdonia but bring a torch, it's dark here at night. *River to jump in and endless amazing walks – many away from livestock (though sheep / ponies often in fields immediately next to cottage).*

Rooms	1 cottage for 4 (1 double, 1 twin; 1 bathroom): £450-£550 per week. Max. 2 dogs.
Meals	Self-catering.
Closed	During freezing weather.
	Advice on walks, a dog bowl and a warm welcome.

Liz Green
Pwll y Garth,
Penmachno,
Betws-y-Coed, LL25 0HJ
Tel   +44 (0)1690 760296
Email   info@pwllygarth.co.uk
Web   www.pwllygarth.co.uk

Entry 189 Map 5

Cover Star Competition

Some of our favourite handsome hounds

My name is Flint and I love my walks. I always have a woofly time in the beautiful English countryside.

Max's favourite place is the beach of Mawgan Porth, Cornwall, where he's pictured here.

Dandy loves to run and sniff out new places. She likes pub gardens where the tables aren't too close together!

Flintshire

Plas Penucha

Swing back in time with polished parquet, tidy beams, a huge Elizabethan panelled lounge with books, leather sofas and open fire – a cosy spot for Nest's dogs and for tea in winter. Plas Penucha – 'the big house on the highest point in the parish' – has been in the family for 500 years. Airy, old-fashioned bedrooms have long views across the garden to Offa's Dyke and one has a shower in the corner. The L-shaped dining room has a genuine Arts & Crafts interior; outside, rhododendrons and a rock garden flourish. There are views to the Clywdian Hills and beyond is St Asaph, with the smallest medieval cathedral in the country. *Quiet rural setting for walks.*

Rooms	1 double, 1 twin: £76. Singles £38. Max. 3 dogs.
Meals	Dinner £19. Packed lunch £5. Pub/restaurant 2-3 miles.
Closed	Rarely.
	Towels for drying, advice for walks and space for exercise.

Nest Price
Plas Penucha,
Pen y Cefn Road,
Caerwys, Mold, CH7 5BH

Tel	+44 (0)1352 720210
Email	nest@plaspenucha.co.uk
Web	www.plaspenucha.co.uk

Entry 190 Map 5

Y Felin

Such a stunning drive through the Snowdonia National Park, down a long track to this remote water mill with the Dysynni river babbling past the front door. Inside is a symphony of local oak, slate and stone in a modern hi-tech interior with white walls and plenty of games and books; heat comes from an air-source pump and wood for the burner from the farm: you'll be cosy on the chilliest days. Cooks will be thrilled with the river view from the kitchen window – and the bread-maker. All has been beautifully considered. All three bedrooms are on the ground floor, the master with its own wood-burner and windows on three sides, the smaller double bright and sweet. The bunk room is suitable for children and teenagers; the big bathrooms are fabulous. An honesty freezer is filled with local produce if you can't be bothered to shop, and there's a fire pit outside with wooden seats for flame-gazers. The owners can point you towards rugged mountain walking and bike rides, farm tours, fell running and sheep dog trials. Long sandy beaches are near, and the air is superb. *Secure garden and 2,000 acres beyond to roam. Dogs must be kept on leads near sheep.*

Rooms	1 cottage for 8 (1 double, 1 twin/double, 1 bunkroom for 4, sofabed; 1 bathroom, 1 shower room): £640-£850 per week. Short breaks 3-4 nights £320-£460.
Meals	Self-catering.
Closed	Rarely.
	Advice on walks, lots of private space and a river on the front doorstep.

Sarah Watkins
Y Felin,
Maes y Pandy Farm,
Tal y Llyn, LL36 9AQ
Mobile   +44 (0)7952 712104
Email   distinctlywales@btinternet.com
Web   www.distinctlywales.com

Entry 191 Map 5

Bryn Adda

High up on private land, down the driveway, through the natural garden, and there it is, Bryn Adda – a rambling L-shaped stone building that dates from the 16th century. It's a fine house in anyone's book. Landscaped gardens drop away in all directions and you can walk to Dolgellau. Find a warren of little stairways and landings in the old part, larger rooms in the new and a low-ceilinged farmhouse kitchen right in the middle, with Belfast sinks and a big old Aga. You get a dining room for 18, two sitting rooms opening to terraces – one big and sunny, with a dog-dozy fire and an old-fashioned charm, the other with nut-brown sofas and gleaming parquet floor. There's a bedroom on the ground floor and seven more above, all comfy, all delightful, with various modern takes on traditional design. Bathrooms are new with a retro feel; antiques, pictures and books abound. Play hide-and-seek in the rhododendrons, table tennis in the barns, surf at Barmouth, hike in the forest, fish on their own stretch of river. Return to a blissful sauna – and toast your good fortune! *Short breaks & discounts for reduced occupancy available. Secure garden including woodland, within even bigger wild space. Please keep dogs on lead near sheep.*

Rooms	1 house for 16 (4 doubles, 3 twins/doubles, 1 bunk room; 6 bathrooms): £1,200-£3,200 per week.
Meals	Self-catering.
Closed	Rarely.
🚶	Advice on walks and 7 acres of garden to play in.

Sarah Watkins
Bryn Adda,
Dolgellau, LL40 1YA
Mobile   +44 (0)7952 712104
Email   distinctlywales@btinternet.com

Hen Dy, Nanhoron

In the heart of the Llyn peninsula, an immaculate house in gardens people travel to see. The 5,000 acre estate has been in David's family for centuries; open to guests until 6pm, ablaze with rhododendrons and azaleas in spring, it has views down to lake, pastures, woodland and sea. As for Hen Dy, it's the oldest house on the estate and was the gardener's bothy and laundry, with a bell tower that once announced mealtimes. Find a large, sunny sitting room with books, games, soft sofas and Sky TV; in winter, estate logs crackle. The kitchen is to star in (superb equipment, gleaming red Aga), the dining room seats eight. Up stairs – or lift – to big bedrooms that feed off a wide landing, three of which overlook the gardens (one with topiary, statues and gazebo). Red fabrics add pizzazz to the master bedroom, whose dressing room is now a charming double (access being via the shared bathroom). For ball games and barbecues you have your own patch. Just the ticket for garden lovers, comfort-seekers and aspiring country landowners... Dogs will be in heaven too – you're surrounded by some of most gorgeous countryside in Gwynedd. *Woodland for walks and ponds to jump in. Occasionally cattle in park so keep dogs out of there when asked.*

Rooms	1 house for 7 (1 twin – en suite, 1 double, 1 twin/double, 1 single; 1 bath/shower room, 1 shower room): £750–£1,350 per week. Max. 4 dogs.
Meals	Self-catering.
Closed	Rarely.

Biscuits, special dog bowls and mat, dog towels and wonderful, safe, traffic-free dog walks on the estate.

Bettina Harden
Hen Dy, Nanhoron,
Pwllheli, LL53 8DL
Tel   +44 (0)1758 730610
Email   bettina.harden@nanhoron.com
Web   www.nanhoronestate.co.uk

Entry 193 Map 5

Plas Dinas Country House

The family home of Lord Snowdon dates to the 1600s and stands in 15 rural acres with an avenue of oak sweeping you up to the house. Princess Margaret often stayed and much of what fills the house belongs to the family: striking chandeliers, oils by the score, gilt-framed mirrors – an Aladdin's cave of beautiful things. There's a baby grand piano in the drawing room, where you find a roaring fire and an honesty bar, but potter about and find masses of memorabilia framed on the walls (make sure you visit the private dining room). Bedrooms – some with views across fields to the sea – mix a graceful past with modern design. You get four-posters, period colours, bold wallpapers, a sofa if there's room. A cute room in the eaves has mountain views, all have hot-water bottles, Apple TVs and excellent bathrooms, some with showers, others with freestanding baths. Good food waits in the restaurant, perhaps fishcakes with lime and ginger, lamb shank with a rosemary jus, chocolate tart with white chocolate ice cream. Snowdon is close, as you'd expect, so bring walking boots and mountain bikes. *Minimum stay: 2 nights on bank holiday weekends. 15 acres of grounds. 3 dog-friendly rooms: Buckley, Mount and South.*

Rooms	5 doubles,
	5 twin/doubles: £99–£249.
	Dogs £10 per night. Max. 2.
Meals	Dinner, 3 courses, £25–£35.
Closed	Christmas.

🐕 Advice on dog-friendly dining, dog biscuits, dog towel, poop bags and suggestions for walks.

Neil Baines & Marco Soares
Plas Dinas Country House,
Bontnewydd, Caernarfon, LL54 7YF
Tel   +44 (0)1286 830214
Email   info@plasdinas.co.uk
Web   www.plasdinas.co.uk

Little Oasis Pandy

Emma and Paul fell for the wooded land where they have created their Little Oasis while in search of an escape from London. They replaced the existing campsite with the two lovely wagons, Josie and Rosy, but kept eccentric former owner Bill's network of streams and mini watermills, adding friendly sheep and curious chickens who make hide and seek tricky as well as laying fresh eggs. From the moment you arrive, when you gleefully raid your welcome hamper for marshmallows and wine for you and pig's ears for your furry friend, you'll find Little Oasis Pandy an amazing place to unwind. Josie the Blue Wagon sits at the bottom of the meadow and Rosy the Red Wagon has settled at the top. They both have a 5ft pull-out double bed, as well as space for two roll-out mattresses for kids to sleep on the floor plus the opportunity for up to 6 more campers. There is ample storage under the main bed, perfect for stashing picnic blankets, spare clothes and for kids to hide in. Each wagon has a private compost loo, camp kitchen and outdoor seating, and there are shared showers about 100 metres away in the barn. *Babies welcome. Lovely walks and lots of dog-friendly pubs, cafés and restaurants nearby. Dogs on lead as free-ranging chickens and sheep in adjacent fields.*

Rooms	2 wagons for 4 (1 double, 2 roll mats): from £83 per night. Dogs £10 per pet per stay. Max. 2.
Meals	Self-catering.
Closed	October – April.

Pig's ears, and advice on walks and dog-friendly pubs and restaurants.

Canopy & Stars
Little Oasis Pandy, Ty Newydd Farm, Pandy, Abergavenny, NP7 8DW
Tel   +44 (0)117 204 7830
Email enquiries@canopyandstars.co.uk
Web   www.canopyandstars.co.uk/
       littleoasispandy

Entry 195 Map 2

The Bell at Skenfrith

The position here is magical: an ancient stone bridge, a river snaking through the valley, glorious hills rising beyond, cows grazing in lush fields. It's a perfect spot, not least because providence blessed it with this chic little inn. Inside, you find a locals' bar for the odd game of rugby, sofas in front of a wood-burner in the sitting room, then an airy restaurant for some very good food. In summer, doors fly open and life spills onto a stone terrace with views of hill and wood – a fine spot for lunch in the sun. Elegant country-house bedrooms brim with light. Some are beamed, most are big, you'll find padded bedheads, Farrow & Ball colours, perhaps a walnut bed or a claw-foot bath in your room. Those at the front have river views, those at the back look onto the hills, some have sofas, all have robes in excellent bathrooms. Seven circular walks start at the front door with maps to show you the way. Delicious food awaits your return, perhaps Welsh rarebit with a poached egg, braised beef brisket with dauphinoise potatoes, apple doughnuts with toffee sauce and mulled cider. *Minimum stay: 2 nights at weekends. Secure garden; circular walks from the door. Beware of sheep and cows.*

Rooms	5 doubles, 3 twin/doubles, 3 four-posters: £130–£220. Singles from £75. Dinner, B&B from £85 per person. Dogs £20 per dog per night. Max. 2.
Meals	Lunch from £5.95. Sunday lunch from £12.95. Dinner, 3 courses, around £35.
Closed	Rarely.
	Dog parlour and towels. Dog treats for well-behaved dogs.

Richard Ireton & Sarah Hudson
The Bell at Skenfrith,
Skenfrith,
Abergavenny, NP7 8UH
Tel   +44 (0)1600 750235
Email   enquiries@skenfrith.co.uk
Web   www.skenfrith.co.uk

Entry 196 Map 2

The Humble Hideaway

Kate Humble and husband Ludo stepped in to save Upper Meend Farm when it was nearly sold off in pieces. They and their team have preserved it carefully, keeping sheep and cattle as well as doing their best to help all the local wildlife flourish. Screened from curious animals with a chunky log fence, you'll find your two huts, fire pit and bench seating under the trees in a large wooded area. It's an off-grid, cosy space that suits its woodland haven perfectly. The first hut is the bedroom, containing the big double bed with custom made mattress stuffed with wool from the farm's own sheep – even your dog can sleep in comfort in a custom built kennel. The second hut was once the property of Great Western Railways, and has been ingeniously converted into your kitchen and shower room. A double compost loo about five metres away from the huts completes your private, hidden camp. Around the farm you'll find plenty to do: join one of the crafty courses and learn anything from woodcraft to sheep shearing, walk in the woods and hills, or head down to Kingstone Brewery for a tour and a dark ale. *Babies welcome. Plenty of fabulous woodland & riverside walking. Working farm so dogs must be kept on leads. Please check with farmers to find out which fields are suitable for walking through.*

Rooms	Shepherd's hut for 2 (1 double, extra space for 2 in own tent): from £80 per night. Dogs £15 per pet per stay. Max. 2.
Meals	Self-catering.
Closed	November – March.
	Specially made dog kennel and advice on walks.

Canopy & Stars
The Humble Hideaway, Upper Meend
Farm, Lydart, Monmouth NP25 4RP
Tel   +44 (0)117 204 7830
Email   enquiries@canopyandstars.co.uk
Web   www.canopyandstars.co.uk/
         thehumblehideaway

Entry 197 Map 2

The Piggery

A neat-as-a-pin refurbishment of an 18th-century Welsh farmhouse bang in the middle of a proper working farm. You're surrounded by a sweet garden (mostly edible) and sheep, cows, chickens, the most beautiful pigs and inspiring views. If you're keen you can join farmer Tim for a morning and learn the ropes. Or try your hand at bee keeping, orchard planting, smallholding or foraging. This is Wordsworth and Turner country, with delicious landscapes accessible by foot, canoe, car or bike. Return to a perfect home-from-home with slate floors, jolly rugs, good art, a roaring wood-burner (logs on the house), comfy vintage chairs and sofa, books, games, and a cook's dream of a blue-panelled kitchen where local cook Katherine Marland can come and give you a private lesson – but lazy bones can order tasty home-cooked food to be delivered. Sleep peacefully: pristine bedrooms have soft Welsh blankets and thick blinds at the windows with a bit of a hare theme going on; wallow in a deep bath – solace for walk-weary limbs. In summer spill out to the garden for perfect barbecues and long convivial evenings watching the sun slither down. *Secure garden. Plenty of lovely woodland and riverside walks. Working farm so dogs must be kept on leads.*

Rooms	1 cottage for 4 (1 double, 1 twin; 1 bathroom): £450-£650 per week. Short breaks available £100-£130 per night. Minimum stay: 3-5 nights. Dogs £5 per dog per night. Max. 2.
Meals	Self-catering.
Closed	Never.
	Advice on walks.

Ludo Graham
The Piggery, Upper Meend Farm,
Lydart, Monmouth, NP25 4RP

Tel	+44 (0)1600 714595
Email	info@humblebynature.com
Web	www.humblebynature.com/ accommodation

Entry 198 Map 2

CANOPY&STARS

Cwtch Camping

The Welsh camping experience has been given a thoroughly contemporary spin by Beth, creator of the Cwtch (meaning a hug, or a snug place, in Welsh). The three handcrafted timber pods are a short walk through the trees from where you park your car, or a scenic cycle from local stations. Light pours through French windows, chunky brocante finds distinguish the interiors and a real double bed is bliss after a day in the fresh air. The cabins share a kitchen, shower and loo, but are privately sited with their own deck and picnic table. Local eggs, fresh bread and organic milk are among the goodies in your welcome hamper and Beth can supply extras for your private barbecue if you ask in advance. The Cwtch stands firm in all seasons in the midst of Pembrokeshire's natural beauty: follow the riverbank walk to a nature reserve teeming with bird life – and a family of otters – or take a boat trip to the island of Skomer. Camping has never been cosier!

Babies welcome. Many dog-friendly pubs, restaurants and cafés nearby. Advice on dog-friendly beaches given.

Rooms	2 pods for 2 (1 double): from £80 per night. Pod for 4 (2 doubles): from £80 per night. Max. 2 dogs.
Meals	Self-catering.
Closed	November – March.

Dog biscuits, towels, walking advice and 3 acres of woodland where dogs can run around off the lead.

Canopy & Stars
Cwtch Camping, Rosemarket,
Milford Haven, SA73 1LH
Tel   +44 (0)117 204 7830
Email enquiries@canopyandstars.co.uk
Web   www.canopyandstars.co.uk/
       cwtchcamping

Entry 199 Map 1

The Sleepout

The good solid bones of this little cabin were affectionately crafted by botanist Rachel and tree surgeon Mike, whose warm welcomes feel totally relaxed and unscripted. Down a rough track and through wonderful wilderness, you'll find The Sleepout; a cosy cabin where a wooden ladder leads from the small sitting area up to a sleeping den. We love the magic of climbing up to the little nook and, other than a bunch of sweet peas, a welcome basket and a pile of logs for the wood-burner, there are no knick-knacks to crowd up the sleeping space; just a bed, pale wool throws, and the stars. Who wouldn't want to spend time up there? There's space for a couple of your little lambs to kip too if they bring their own sleeping bags. Rachel and Mike provide delicious Welsh cakes for you to snack on and the camp kitchen with a few pots and pans, a fire bowl, gas burner and pizza oven is perfect for heating up your morning café au lait or preparing light suppers. The private hot shower is only 60 paces away, and the compost loo with a cool rally car door is even closer. *Babies & children over 4 welcome. Keep dogs on lead on site as livestock around.*

Rooms	Cabin for 4 (1 double, 2 platforms): from £95 per night. Dogs £10 per stay. Max. 1.
Meals	Self-catering.
Closed	Never.
	Maps of local walks and advice on dog-friendly pubs.

	Canopy & Stars The Sleepout, Sunnylea, Meifod, SY22 6YA
Tel	+44 (0)117 204 7830
Email	enquiries@canopyandstars.co.uk
Web	www.canopyandstars.co.uk/sleepout

Entry 200 Map 5

Beudy Banc

Three lovely spaces surrounded by some of the best biking trails and beaches, miles of quiet country lanes, wooded bridleways and ancient drovers' roads. Caban Cader's floorboards were reclaimed and the walls are festooned with collected treasures. There's a living area with a double sofabed, a dining area and kitchen and the sleeping loft above has a double bed and little window seat. There's also a small bathroom. Outside, you can build a fire and relax on the deck. Cylindrical Caban Crwn has a ladder which leads up to the mezzanine bed and the lounge area (with a single day bed) off to your left. The compact compost loo and shower unit are through the hidden door in front of you. Outside you can set the fire pit or relax on the deck after a hard day. Caban Coch, artfully crafted by its owner from an old hay trailer, has a wood-burning stove together with a kitchen/dining area with a full-sized cooker, sink and storage. The sleeping area and the wet room with the shower are just off the main space and here you'll find the king-sized sleeping platform, low slung for resting your tired limbs. *Babies welcome. Nearby stream; marked walking routes on the farm.*

Rooms	Cabin for 2 (1 double): from £75. Cabin for 3 (1 double, 1 single): from £70. Cabin for 4 (1 double, 1 sofabed): from £80. All prices per night. Dogs £10 per stay. Max. 1.
Meals	Self-catering.
Closed	Never.
🐕	Water bowl and tether. Maps and routes for walks around the farm and local footpaths and bridleways.

Canopy & Stars
Beudy Banc,
Machynlleth, SY20 8NP

Tel   +44 (0)117 204 7830
Email   enquiries@canopyandstars.co.uk
Web   www.canopyandstars.co.uk/
         beudybanc

Entry 201 Map 5

The Felin Fach Griffin

It's quirky, homespun, and thrives on a mix of relaxed informality and colourful style. The low-ceilinged bar resembles the sitting room of a small hip country house, with timber frames, cool tunes and comfy sofas in front of a smouldering fire. Painted stone walls come in blocks of colour, there's live music on Sunday nights, and you dine informally in the white-walled restaurant, with stock pots simmering on an Aga. The food is excellent, perhaps dressed Portland crab, rump of Welsh beef, treacle tart with bergamot sorbet; much of what you eat comes from a half-acre kitchen garden, with meat and game from the hills around you. Bedrooms above have style and substance: comfy beds wrapped in crisp linen, good bathrooms with fluffy towels, Roberts radios, a smattering of books, but no TV unless you ask. Breakfast is served in the dining room; wallow with the papers, make your own toast, scoff the full Welsh. A main road passes outside, but quietly at night, while lanes lead into the hills, so walk, ride, bike, canoe. Hay is close for books galore. Don't miss excellent off-season deals. *Large garden with plenty of space to run around and local rivers for swimming. Stunning walks in the Brecon Beacons.*

Rooms	2 doubles, 2 twin/doubles, 2 four-posters: £125–£160. 1 family room for 3: £165. Dinner, B&B £90 per person.
Meals	Lunch from £7. Dinner, 3 courses, about £30. Sunday lunch from £20.
Closed	Christmas. 4 days in January.
🐕	Doggie biscuits, blanket, towels, advice on walks, black bags, dog bowls – and very friendly staff.

Charles & Edmund Inkin
The Felin Fach Griffin,
Felin Fach,
Brecon, LD3 0UB

Tel   +44 (0)1874 620111
Email   enquiries@felinfachgriffin.co.uk
Web   www.felinfachgriffin.co.uk

Entry 202 Map 2

Baddegai

You leave the road, bump down the track, then there you are. It's a lovely spot, deeply rural, with sheep grazing the fields and a stream that rolls past the house. Outside, you find an 18th-century stone barn. Inside, a stylish conversion has kept all the lovely old bits while adding contemporary comfort and style. You'll find painted stone walls, lots of beams, maps and books, pretty fabrics. There's a wood-burner in the low-ceilinged dining room, then another in the airy sitting room, where doors open onto a dining terrace for views of field and mountain. Uncluttered bedrooms – all en suite – keep things simple: white walls to soak up the light, comfy beds, small sofas and good views; one has a Juliet balcony. Back downstairs, a well-equipped kitchen opens onto the terrace for breakfast in the sun. There's safe storage for bikes, badminton and croquet on the lawn. Perfect for friends, family, children and dogs. Brecon, a cute Welsh town, is five miles north for good shops. Pen-y-Fan, the highest peak in the Brecon Beacons, waits down the track. Hereford for the Mappa Mundi, Hay-on-Wye for books galore, Cardiff is close. *Minimum stay: 3 nights, 7 in high season. Enclosed garden with kennel and dog run; 3 acres of paddocks to exercise dogs.*

Rooms	1 cottage for 8 (4 twin/doubles, all en suite): £860–£1,260 per week. Short breaks available: £690–£800. Dogs £10 per dog per stay. Max. 4.
Meals	Self-catering.
Closed	Never.

Lots of information on walks in the area and dog-friendly pubs. Dog bowl, throws for the furniture, 2 wood-burning stoves to sleep by and a utility room for drying dogs off.

Annabel & Steve Thomas
Baddegai,
Libanus,
Brecon, LD3 8NF
Mobile   +44 (0)7880 613347
Email   info@breconbeaconscottagebreaks.co.uk
Web   www.breconbeaconscottagebreaks.co.uk

Entry 203 Map 2

Danyfan Carriage

Danyfan Carriage is the latest project of Emma & Stevie, who fled London for the country life a few years ago. They found a perfect spot to make their home, and also the perfect place for a little glamping. The railway wagon, as far as they know, is an early 20th-century artefact. In converting it they have kept as much of the original work as possible, adding only what will complement the period feel, with a grand wicker-headboarded bed and a burnished walnut wardrobe. The whole site is completely off-grid, with a cleverly designed (piping hot!) gas shower and washing up area, plus a separate compost loo, just steps from the carriage. Being off-grid doesn't have to mean hardship: the wood-burner keeps you beautifully warm and the bed is a wonder of mountainous soft pillows. Lanterns and torches give a soft light, and the gas hobs make cooking easy. Your corner of the garden is sheltered, with mountain views and a rushing stream. Walks through the Brecon Beacons National Park stretch out from the door and wildlife and nature surround you. *Large garden, owners' dog (lives next door) to play with, and wonderful walks up in the mountains. Livestock in neighbouring fields.*

Rooms	Train carriage for 2 (1 double): from £80 per night. Max. 1 dog.	
Meals	Self-catering.	
Closed	January.	
	Biscuits, dog leads, bowls and advice on walks.	

Canopy & Stars
Danyfan Carriage,
Danyfan, Cwmgwdi,
Brecon, LD3 8LG
Tel   +44 (0)117 204 7830
Email   enquiries@canopyandstars.co.uk
Web   www.canopyandstars.co.uk/danyfan

Entry 204 Map 2

Ty'r Chanter

Warmth, colour, children and activity: this house is huge fun. Tiggy welcomes you like family; help collect eggs, feed the lambs, drop your shoes by the fire. The farmhouse and barn are stylishly relaxed; deep sofas, tartan throws, heaps of books, long convivial table; views to the Brecon Beacons and Black Mountains are inspiring. Bedrooms are soft, simple sanctuaries with Jo Malone bathroom treats. The children's room zings with murals; toys, kids' sitting room, sandpit – it's child heaven. Walk, fish, canoe, book-browse in Hay or stroll the estate. Homemade cakes and whisky to help yourself to: fine hospitality and Tiggy is wonderful. *River to swim and large field to run around in. But lots of livestock around – and mind the chickens!*

The Old Store House

Unbend here with books, chattering birds, and charming, generous Peter. He asks only that you feel at home. Downstairs are a sunny, ramshackle, conservatory overlooking the garden, chickens, ducks and canal, and an equally ramshackle sitting room with a wood-burner, sofas and a piano – no TV. Bedrooms are large and generously cosy, with more books, soft goose down, armchairs and bathrooms with views. Breakfast, at any time you wish, on local bacon and sausages, perhaps with chickens clucking at your feet. Unconventional and amiably chaotic. We love it and have awarded Peter prizes. Walk into the hills from the back door. *Children over 6 welcome. Canal at the bottom of the garden, 30 miles of fenced-in tow path for instant walks. Dogs need to be on a lead in the garden if inclined to eat chickens!*

Rooms	3 doubles: £95. 1 twin with separate bath/shower (children's room, price per child): £20. Singles £55.	Rooms	3 doubles, 1 twin: £80. Singles £40.
		Meals	Packed lunch £4. Pubs/restaurants 0.75 miles.
Meals	Packed lunch £8. Pub 1 mile.	Closed	Rarely.
Closed	Christmas.		
	Sausages for breakfast, towels, dog bowls and walks.		Blankets, towels, dog sitting, walk advice – and dog food if you've forgotten to bring some.

Tiggy Pettifer
Ty'r Chanter,
Gliffaes, Crickhowell, NP8 1RL
Tel   +44 (0)1874 731144
Mobile   +44 (0)7802 387004
Email   tiggy@tyrchanter.com
Web   www.tyrchanter.com

Peter Evans
The Old Store House,
Llanfrynach, Brecon, LD3 7LJ
Tel   +44 (0)1874 665499
Email   oldstorehouse@btconnect.com
Web   www.theoldstorehouse.co.uk

Entry 205 Map 2

Entry 206 Map 2

Cover Star Competition

Some of our favourite handsome hounds

3-year-old Holly is an English Springer Spaniel. She loves springing in the heather.

My name is Alfie and I love the beach, especially dog-friendly Dunwich where I can swim and run for miles and miles.

Toby's favourite place on earth is the beach. He's 9 now but still behaves like a puppy running straight into the sea. He just loves it!

Powys

B&B

Hafod Y Garreg

A unique opportunity to stay in the oldest house in Wales — a fascinating, 1402 cruck-framed hall house, built for Henry IV as a hunting lodge. Informal Annie and John have filled it with a charming mix of Venetian mirrors, Indian rugs, pewter plates, rich fabrics and oak pieces. Dine by candlelight in the romantic dining room — all sorts of delicious dishes; tuck into a big breakfast in the sweet conservatory. Bedrooms are luxuriously comfortable with embroidered linen, quirky lamps, nifty bathrooms. Reach this relaxed retreat by a bumpy track up across gated fields crowded with chickens, cats... a peaceful, special place. *Hens here — so dogs to be on a lead in yard.*

Rooms	2 doubles: £92. Singles £90. Max. 2 dogs.
Meals	Dinner, 3 courses, £27. BYO. Pubs/restaurants 2.5 miles.
Closed	Christmas.
	Great walks from the house.

Annie & John McKay
Hafod Y Garreg,
Erwood,
Builth Wells, LD2 3TQ

Tel	+44 (0)1982 560400
Email	john-annie@hafod-y.wanadoo.co.uk
Web	www.hafodygarreg.co.uk

Entry 207 Map 2

Fairyhill

This lovely country house on the Gower sits in 24 acres of beautiful silence with a sun-trapping terrace at the back for lunch in summer. Potter about and find a walled garden, a stream-fed lake, free-range ducks and an ancient orchard. Inside, country-house interiors come fully loaded: smart fabrics, warm colours, deep sofas, the daily papers. There's an open fire in the bar, a grand piano in the sitting room, then delicious food in the restaurant, most locally sourced. Stylish bedrooms hit the spot. Most are big and fancy, a couple are small, but sweet. Some have painted beams, others a sofa or a wall of golden paper. Sparkling bathrooms, some with separate showers, have deep baths, white robes and fancy oils; if that's not enough, there's a treatment room, too. Outside, the Gower waits — wild heathland, rugged coastline, some of the best beaches in the land — so explore by day, then return for a good meal, perhaps scallops with cauliflower and chorizo, Gower lamb with gratin potatoes, baked honey and amaretto cheesecake. The wine list is one of the best in Wales, so don't expect to go thirsty. *Children over 8 welcome. 24 acres of woodland for walks; small lake. Ducks in walled garden so leads advised. Dogs permitted in rooms with you but not in the public rooms.*

Rooms	3 doubles, 5 twin/doubles: £200-£300. Singles from £180. Extra beds £75 per person. Dinner, B&B from £125 per person. Dogs £10 per night.
Meals	Lunch from £10. Afternoon tea £20. Dinner £35-£45. Sunday lunch £27.50.
Closed	First 3 weeks in January. Mon & Tue, November – March.
	Advice on walks.

Andrew Hetherington &
Paul Davies
Fairyhill, Reynoldston,
Gower Peninsula SA3 1BS,
Tel   +44 (0)1792 390139
Email   postbox@fairyhill.net
Web   www.fairyhill.net

Entry 208 Map 2

Scotland

Barley Bothy

Barley Bothy stands in a secluded corner of a field that owners Jane and James use to grow barley for malting whisky. They also breed sheep and grow strawberries — you'll get a taste of their homemade strawberry jam in your welcome hamper, along with fresh strawberries in season and other Scottish treats. The exterior is traditional, corrugated tin, and a veranda down its length has an outside bike wash and storage for wet boots when you come back from countryside walks, perhaps up Bennachie, along the Moray coast or somewhere on the famous Malt Whisky Trail. The open-plan interior is actually an upcycled chicken shed! Wool insulation, a log-burning range cooker and a vintage wood-burner have been added though to keep you warm even in Aberdeenshire winters. The two fun and cosy king-size cupboard beds have stargazing windows, as does the bathroom, which comes with a luxurious roll-top bath as well as a curiously ornate, vintage loo. Windows on three sides of the living space have views of barley fields, distant wind turbines, and down to the burn behind the bothy — take a sketch pad or a good novel. *Stream by Bothy and walks from the door. Fabulous dog-friendly beaches, Sandend and Cullen. Dogs to be kept on leads on the farm.*

Rooms	Bothy for 4 (2 double cupboard beds): from £85 per night. Dogs £5 per pet per stay. Max. 3.
Meals	Self-catering.
Closed	Never.
🐕	Doggie sleepover pack! Includes gravy bones, towel, blanket to put on the sofa, dog bed, dog bowls and lead for use during their stay. (Must keep off the beds!)

Canopy & Stars
Barley Bothy, Newton of Begshill,
Drumblade, Huntly, AB54 6BJ

Tel	+44 (0)117 204 7830
Email	enquiries@canopyandstars.co.uk
Web	www.canopyandstars.co.uk/ barleybothy

Entry 209 Map 9

The Old House

An extremely comfortable home for a family holiday, or a secret hideaway for two. You feel miles from anywhere (and the night skies are gloriously unpolluted), yet the train from London chugs into the local village. The former sporting lodge has been renovated from top to toe with sensitivity and along green lines with solar panels and a micro hydro powerhouse. On the ground floor is a golden yellow sitting room with a wood-burning stove and a railway-sleeper mantelpiece, and the four-poster bedroom is next door – along with a utility room and a Belfast sink for washing the day's catch; the 'wet room' is so large the whole family could scrub up at once. Upstairs are two light and pleasingly simple twin rooms with valley views. Leave the car behind – delightful Erica or John can pick you up from the village station – and hike to your heart's content. You are spoilt for choice – walk up the hill on the other side of the river for magical woodlands, or climb 2,500 feet up Ben Udlaidh for views to the islands. The pretty garden slopes towards the river, you can relax on the decking and help yourself to home-grown veg. *Well-behaved dogs welcome. Secure garden, river to jump in, woodland walks. Working farm – sheep, be careful!*

Rooms	1 house for 6 (1 four-poster – en suite, 2 twins; 2 bath/shower rooms): £550–£1,020 per week. Prices based on 2 people. Additional guests £75 per week each. Dogs £15 per pet per week.
Meals	Self-catering.
Closed	Rarely.

 Biscuits, water and blankets. Expert advice on wild, carefree walks and a special welcome from terrier Boris the Arbuthnott.

John & Erica Kerr
The Old House,
Arichastlich,
Glen Orchy, PA33 1BD
Tel   +44 (0)1838 200399
Email   glenorchyb8074@gmail.com
Web   www.glen-orchy.co.uk

Entry 210 Map 8

Tiroran House

The setting is magnificent – 17 acres of gardens rolling down to Loch Scridian. Otters and dolphins pass through, buzzards and eagles glide above, red deer visit the garden. As for this 1850 shooting lodge, you'll be hard pressed to find a more comfortable island base, so it's no surprise to discover it was recently voted 'Best Country House Hotel in Scotland' for the second year in a row. There are fires in the drawing rooms, fresh flowers everywhere, games to be played, books to be read. Airy bedrooms hit the spot: crisp linen, beautiful fabrics, the odd chaise longue; some have watery views, all have silence guaranteed. You eat in a smart dining room with much of the delicious food from the island or waters around it, perhaps mussel and oyster broth, saddle of lamb with carrot purée, chocolate tort with vanilla ice cream. You're bang in the middle of Mull with lots to do: Tobermory, the prettiest town in the Hebrides; Calgary and its magical beach; day trips to Iona and its famous monastery; cruises to Staffa and Fingal's Cave. Come back for afternoon tea – it's as good as the Ritz. *Private beach, woodland walks: dog paradise!*

Rooms	5 doubles,
	5 twin/doubles: £175-£220.
Meals	Dinner, 4 courses, £48.
Closed	Rarely.
	Dog biscuit.

Laurence & Katie Mackay
Tiroran House,
Tiroran,
Isle of Mull, PA69 6ES
Tel   +44 (0)1681 705232
Email info@tiroran.com
Web   www.tiroran.com

Entry 211 Map 8 + 10

Lochinch Castle Cottages

On an isthmus hugged by freshwater lochs is one of Scotland's finest gardens with the dreamy ruins of Castle Kennedy at one end and Lochinch Castle, the family home of the Stairs (they've been here for generations) at the other. With 75 acres to roam, all ages will be happy here; walks ramble off in all directions. Explore land sculptures built in the 1730s; spot geese, herons, maybe an osprey, red squirrels and otters too. There are mesmerising displays of rhododendrons, azaleas and embothrium, and the ancient Monkey Puzzle Avenue is a treat. Find three charming properties. Chauffeur's, on the top floor of a two-storey Victorian carriage house, has pretty French château style turrets, an open fire, long views, a large kitchen and three beautifully restful bedrooms. Balker Lodge, originally a gate house, is a cleverly revived bolthole for two. Ice House is a single-storey cottage with two pretty bedrooms, a log-burner in the sitting room and a pristine kitchen. All have their own private outside space, splendid welcome baskets with delicious cakes, and you get the run of the gardens. Why not take a guided tour with head gardener, John, who's worked here for 25 years! *Short breaks available.*

Rooms	1 house for 2: £345–£530.
	1 cottage for 4: £400–£625.
	1 apartment for 6: £450–£715.
	Dogs £15 per dog. Max. 2.
	All prices per week.
Meals	Continental breakfast £24–£48.
	Cooked breakfast £26–£54.
	Dinner £24–£60.
Closed	Never.

Dog basket, acres of gardens, beautiful countryside and advice on great walks.

Emily Stair
Lochinch Castle Cottages, Lochinch
Castle, Stranraer, DG9 8RT

Tel	+44 (0)1776 702024
Email	housekeeping@lochinchcastle.com
Web	www.castlekennedygardens.com/
	holiday-cottages/

Entry 212 Map 5

Trigony House Hotel

A small, welcoming, family-run hotel with good food, nicely priced rooms and a lovely garden, where you may spot red squirrels. The house dates to 1700, a shooting lodge for the local castle. Inside, you find Japanese oak panelling in the hall, a wood-burner in the pretty sitting room and an open fire in the dining room, where doors open onto the terrace for dinner in summer. Adam cooks lovely rustic fare, perhaps goat's cheese tart, loin of roe venison, chocolate brownie cheesecake with chocolate ice cream; there's a small, organic kitchen garden that provides much for the table in summer. Bedrooms vary in size, but not style – all have pretty fabrics, summer colours and good bathrooms. Some are dog-friendly, one has a conservatory/sitting room that opens onto a private lawn, there's a film library downstairs for your TV. After a full cooked breakfast, head west for the Southern Upland Way or the spectacular country between Moniaive and the Galloway Forest. Don't miss Drumlanrig Castle up the road for its gardens, walking trails and excellent mountain bike tracks. *Beautiful walks. Well-behaved dogs welcome in the lounge and bar area.*

Rooms	4 doubles, 4 twin/doubles: £85-£130. 1 suite for 2: £155. Dinner, B&B from £82.50 per person. Dogs £9 per dog per night.
Meals	Lunch from £5. Dinner, £25-£35.
Closed	24-26 December.
🐕	Poo bag, map of local dog-friendly walks, bag of treats and dog blanket/bed.

Adam & Jan Moore
Trigony House Hotel,
Closeburn,
Thornhill, DG3 5EZ
Tel   +44 (0)1848 331211
Email   trigonyhotel@gmail.com
Web   www.trigonyhotel.co.uk

Entry 213 Map 9

Cover Star Competition

Some of our favourite handsome hounds

Here's Millie, she loves her local beach and marshland at Cleethorpes.

This is Neave, a 1-year-old Labrador. She is full of energy and loves to play fetch and swim. She also loves to eat everything!

This is Paddington, he loves this beach because he can chase the seagulls, swim after the mackerel and dig holes to bury his ball!

Dumfries & Galloway

White Hill

Fresh air, huge gardens and stacks of Scottish charm. The aged paint exterior is forgotten once you're inside this treasure-trove of history and heritage. The Bell-Irvings are natural hosts; twenty generations of their family have lived here and worn the floorboards dancing. Throw logs on the fire, ramble round the azalea'd gardens or explore the woods, fish the river, and dine opulently under the gaze of portraits of their 'rellies'. Breakfast is a delightfully hearty affair. A very special chance to share a real ancestral home in the Scottish borders with a kind, funny, lovely couple (and their very friendly springer spaniel). *Extensive woodland, tracks and fields to run about in. River nearby for lots of swimming and paddling.*

Rooms	2 twins: £98.
	Singles £54.
	Dogs £5 per dog per night. Max. 3.
Meals	Dinner £30.
	Pubs/restaurants 4 miles.
Closed	Rarely.

Masses of space for walks – even a river to swim in, and towels are available for drying off dogs. Bedtime biscuits too!

Robin & Janet Bell-Irving
White Hill, Ecclefechan,
Lockerbie, DG11 1AL
Tel   +44 (0)1576 510206
Email   johnbi@talktalk.net
Web   www.aboutscotland.com/
         south/whitehill.html

Entry 214 Map 9

East Cambusmoon Holiday Cottages

Swathed by hills and braes, the farm sits between Loch Lomond and the rolling contours of the Campsie Fells. Deborah and Steve are next door and restored the Old Dairy and Curlew Cottage to high eco standards, with slate and wood floors and local red sandstone. Solar panels and underfloor heating keep things cosy all year while rooms zing with natural light; all is crisp and clean. From tots to grandparents, you are welcome here; book the houses together or separately (both have downstairs bedrooms). Indoors you have total privacy but a low patio wall allows for convivial barbecues; in Curlew, there's seating and crockery for 12. A generous host, Deborah provides home-baked bread, marmalade and their own eggs; she can also arrange for meat from local butchers and at-home beauty treatments! On chilly days throw a log on the burner and curl up with a book or a film. Or head out; a small hill (The Dumpling) makes an ideal nursery slope for little climbers, with a dazzling view. The loch has a Sealife Centre, canoe and cycle hire and cafés, and Stirling and Glasgow are not too far – for heritage and shopping. *Short breaks available. Adjacent to fields, walk to the Loch or up hills.*

Rooms	1 barn for 4 (1 double – en suite, 1 twin; 1 bathroom), 1 barn for 8 (1 double, 1 twin, both en suite, 1 double, 1 twin; 1 bathroom, 2 shower rooms): £600–£1,500 per week. Max. 2 dogs.
Meals	Self-catering.
Closed	Rarely.
	Advice on walks and plenty of exercise space from the cottage door.

Deborah & Steve Macken
East Cambusmoon Holiday Cottages,
Gartocharn, Alexandria, G83 8RZ

Tel	+44 (0)1389 830730
Mobile	+44 (0)7905 093997
Email	cottages@eastcambusmoon.com
Web	www.eastcambusmoon.com

Entry 215 Map 8

10 London Street

Wide cobbled streets, manicured communal gardens, vast sash windows affording glimpses into houses one can only dream of living in: welcome to New Town. You enter this lower ground-floor flat down gently curving steps, and open the door to an interior of elegant sophistication; the flagstoned floor, gilt mirror and fresh flowers are just the start. Down the corridor to the sitting room, a soothing space, with original fireplace, fine Victorian and Edwardian furniture, brand-new entertainment system and paintings and prints. The small kitchen to the side is decked in glass, stainless steel and every modern thing; the bathroom is a spectacle of floor-to-ceiling marble, with a drenching shower and a sumptuous mini bath. In the bedroom, one of Pippa's vintage travel cases folds out to reveal a set of drawers and a hanging rail, while stretches of pale stripped floorboards and a window onto the garden create a light and easy feel. The owners, who live on the top floor, have thought of everything, from children's games to milk in the fridge. Impeccable. *B&B or self-catering available. 2 minutes from the nearest park. Please keep pets off the furniture in the house.*

Rooms	2 doubles: £160 (B&B).
	1 house for 4 (1 double, sofabed):
	self-catering £630–£950 per week.
Meals	Continental breakfast.
	Pub/restaurant 500 yds.
Closed	Rarely.
	A Bonio and advice on walks.

Pippa Lockhart
10 London Street,
Edinburgh, EH3 6NA
Tel   +44 (0)131 556 0737
Email   pippalockhart@gmail.com
Web   www.londonstreetaccommodation.co.uk

Entry 216 Map 9

Edinburgh

Blue Hue

A sparkling example of modern style, Blue Hue is part of Scottish Canals' grand plan to help a new audience discover the magic of its traditional waterways, and what could give you a more thorough introduction to canal life than sleeping on the water itself? It's a remarkably comfy experience – all the furniture is custom-built and everything is cleverly designed to feel light and spacious. It's all open plan, with a clean, blue colour scheme both inside and out (giving the boat its name), and it's got a fully equipped kitchen with gas oven, bespoke bathroom with power shower, and a wood-burner for the chillier evenings. Best of all, the tailor-made, raised double bed means you can just lie back and watch canal life pass by your window. A great canal-side pub is conveniently close. Just ten miles from Edinburgh, Blue Hue is handily placed for a city break, whilst being a calm spot to retreat to after a day wandering the old town, visiting the castle or discovering the plethora of attractions the city has to offer. *Babies welcome. Remember to respect other canal users.*

Rooms	Canal boat for 4 (1 double, 1 sofabed, 1 narrow couch): from £85 per night. Max. 1 dog.
Meals	Self-catering.
Closed	Never.
	Great walks along the canal.

Canopy & Stars
Blue Hue,
The Bridge Inn,
Ratho, EH28 8RA
Tel   +44 (0)117 204 7830
Email enquiries@canopyandstars.co.uk
Web   www.canopyandstars.co.uk/bluehue

Entry 217 Map 9

21 Shoregate

This immaculate fisherman's cottage just above exquisite Crail's harbour gives you a warm hug of a welcome. Views from the pretty garden stretch over rooftops to the Firth of Forth; bliss to eat out here on a summer's day. Inside is perfect: cool colours and pretty objets run throughout, while plump armchairs and sofa front the gas-fired stove; roll out the Scrabble, choose a DVD. The ground floor is open plan with a Shaker-style kitchen that holds all you need, and a dining table for four. Upstairs are two bedrooms, not huge but stylish, with thick mattresses, crisp linen, lovely quilts – and a smart bathroom between them. Small but beautifully formed, No 21 would suit close friends or a family, or a couple of romancers. Beach towels and flasks are at the ready... stroll down to the Lobster Store, a hut on the harbour wall that sells just-caught lobster and crab – Crail once supplied London with 20,000 lobsters a year! There are several fish restaurants here, and the best fish and chips in Scotland at Anstruther. Head off for golf along the coast (St Andrews is close) and handsome Edinburgh – under an hour. A real gem. *Children over 6 welcome. Back garden small but secure. Fife Coastal path runs by the door; 2-minute walk from 2 beaches.*

Rooms	1 cottage for 4 (1 double, 1 twin/double; 1 bath/shower room): £480-£800 per week. Dogs £20 per stay. Max. 1.
Meals	Self-catering.
Closed	Rarely.

Treat bag, balls, ball thrower, dog towels, various size dog bowls, biodegradeable poop bags, advice on dog-friendly cafés and pubs and guide to local walks.

Susan Irvine
21 Shoregate,
Crail, KY10 3SU,

Mobile	+44 (0)7879 480529
Email	susan@21shoregate.com
Web	www.21shoregate.com

Entry 218 Map 9

Huntly

A deliciously calm oasis in the bustling West End – grand and intimate at the same time, perfect for couples. A vast, ground-floor dining room of a handsome Victorian terrace has been skilfully converted into three rooms, without losing its sense of space and elegance. Original features – cornicing, shutters and polished floorboards – are the backdrop for sharply modern and minimalist furnishings. And colourful artwork; Stephen is a professional artist. The light-filled living space, with its floor-to-ceiling bay window, leather sofa and dining table, converts to a bedroom by opening the mirrored cupboard to reveal a double bed. A galley kitchen and shower room – both glossy-white, neat and crisply functional – are on the other side. The vast windows look on to the terrace's beautifully landscaped private gardens – you have a key – a lovely space for lunch and contemplation. You're close to bars and restaurants as well as the Botanic Gardens and Kelvingrove Museum. The nearby tube station speeds you to the centre in 8 minutes. A peaceful bolthole. *Minimum stay: 2 nights. On-street parking available. Riverside walk behind the Botanics is a 2-minute walk away.*

Rooms	1 studio for 2 (1 double; 1 shower room): £450–£750 per week. Short stays available £75–£125 per night. Dogs £10 per stay. Max. 2.
Meals	Self-catering. Restaurants less than a mile.
Closed	Never.
	Homemade livercake, blankets, towels, favourite walks and advice on dog-friendly pubs and cafés.

Stephen Skrynka
Huntly,
Huntly Gardens,
Glasgow, G12 9AU

Mobile	+44 (0)7595 219065
Email	skrynk@ntlworld.com

Entry 219 Map 8

Lochan Shepherd's Hut

With spectacular views stretching out over your own lochan, the shoreline and the Sound of Mull it doesn't get much more peaceful than this! All you'll hear are the sheep, the call of the odd eagle and the sound of the waves below you. The area is crammed with history; ancient burial chambers are dotted around and even a Viking boat burial was unearthed in 2011. From this remote vantage point on the coast, with the wild mountains all around, it's not difficult to imagine a real shipload of Vikings sailing past over the sea. Or for more contemporary interest, a short ferry trip will take you to Mull. The hut itself is comfy and functional, with a full-length double bed, wicker chairs and a folding table. As well as a gas ring inside the hut for an evening cocoa, you've got a little kitchenette next to the hut, and there's solar electricity too. The private compost loo is a few steps away, and good public showers 200 metres away. Look out across the sea to spot dolphins or stay warm by the wood-burner, with cup of tea in hand, and use the hut as a hide to spot corncrakes and pine martens. *Babies welcome. Secure field, plenty of walks, sea, burns and beaches to run in. Countryside all around; cattle & sheep so dogs must be kept under control outside fenced area.*

Rooms	Shepherd's hut for 2 (1 double, space for extra 2 in own tent): from £60 per night. Dogs £5 per pet per stay. Max. 1.
Meals	Self-catering.
Closed	Never.

Advice on walks, dog biscuits, fenced field to run in – all to yourself.

Canopy & Stars
Lochan Shepherd's Hut,
Kilchoan, Acharacle, PH36 4LH

Tel	+44 (0)117 204 7830
Email	enquiries@canopyandstars.co.uk
Web	www.canopyandstars.co.uk/lochan

Entry 220 Map 8

Knoydart Hide

Not content with one gorgeous house high on the hill, Jackie and Ian have put up another and it's every bit as lovely. The only difference is size – this is a magical bolthole for two, perfect for honeymoons or just a blissful time away. Inside, walls of glass open onto a decked terrace, where you can soak in a hot tub while screened from the world by pine trees. Inside, there's a contemporary wood-burner in the sitting room, a kitchen with ample cooking stuff, a lovely big bed that looks out to sea, then a bathroom that's hard to beat with a double-ended bath, a walk-in power shower and an infrared sauna. You'll find all you'd want – fancy TV and DVD player, bath robes to pad about in, a bottle of prosecco on arrival – even the lawn is special, sown with 32 species of wild flower, the same turf as Olympic Park. If you don't want to cook, a chef can do it for you – lazy breakfasts, afternoon tea, seafood barbecues. Further afield, the wonders of Knoydart: wild orchids, sea eagles, mountains to climb. You can kayak, cruise the sea loch or do nothing at all. Stars fill the night sky, the Northern Lights come in winter. *Minimum stay: 3 nights at weekends. Short breaks available. Forest trails and gorgeous woodland walks on the doorstep, including the three Munros. Long sandy beach and coastal shoreline 100m away.*

Rooms	1 house for 2 (1 double, 1 sofabed): £275-£1,450 per week. Extra bed/sofabed available £50-£75 per person per night. Dogs £30 per stay. Max. 2.
Meals	Self-catering.
Closed	Never.

 Pet bowls, extra towels for beachy paws, dog treat and advice on local walks.

Ian & Jackie Robertson
Knoydart Hide,
Inverie,
Knoydart, PH41 4PL
Tel   +44 (0)1687 460012
Email   stay@knoydarthouse.co.uk
Web   www.knoydarthide.co.uk

Entry 221 Map 8

Cover Star Competition

Some of our favourite handsome hounds

Sky Pie loves running in long grass in the countryside. She can be energetic but also can be found lying in bed!

Sunny is a rescue Border Collie and his favourite place for a run is along Newton-by-the-Sea beach.

Layla loves children, treats and seaside holidays... preferably all at the same time! She's a bright and cuddly friend, always having fun.

Highland

B&B

St Callan's Manse

Fun, laughter and conversation flow in this warm and happy home. You share it with prints, paintings, antiques, sofas, amazing memorabilia, two dogs, four ducks, 10 hens and 1,200 teddy bears of every size and origin. Snug bedrooms have pretty fabrics, old armoires, flower-patterned sheets and tartan blankets; your sleep will be sound. Caroline cooks majestic breakfasts and dinners; Robert, a fund of knowledgeable anecdotes, can arrange just about anything. Their Highland hospitality knows no bounds! All this in incomparable surroundings: 60 acres of land plus glens, forests, buzzards, deer and the odd golden eagle. A gem. *There are 69 acres of walkies, 25 of which is a fenced forest area.*

Rooms	1 double with separate bath, 1 double with separate shower: £90. Singles £65. Max. 2 big or 3 small dogs.
Meals	Dinner, 2-4 courses, £20-£35. BYO. Pub/restaurant in village 1.5 miles.
Closed	March & occasionally.
	Gravy bones, biscuits, blankets, towels for drying, advice on walkies, and a large pen with kennel.

Robert & Caroline Mills
St Callan's Manse,
Rogart, IV28 3XE
Tel   +44 (0)1408 641363
Email   caroline@rogartsnuff.me.uk
Web   www.spanglefish.com/stcallansmanse

Entry 222 Map 11

Pilot Panther

Pilot Panther is a classic 1950 showman's wagon originally built by The Coventry Steel Company, once renowned as the finest wagon makers in the country. Its journey has been long and rambling, but it has settled in a fine location. The views from every window are of the spectacular loch which seems to change with the weather and provide a new sight every day. Off the main living and sleeping area, which also has the oven and grill, is the double bunk room. The loos and shower are a minute's walk away at the hotel. The great walking and stunning views around the long loch will help you work up an appetite for dinner that's worthy of Monachlye Mhor, an award-winning pilgrimage for Scottish foodies. Or, if you prefer not to worry about breakfast you can arrange to have it at the hotel and fuel up before you go exploring. Rather handily, the family that run the restaurant also manage the farm, which ensures that a good supply of very local produce goes onto the amazing menus. They have their own fishery, bakery and tea rooms too, all of which can provide you with take away ingredients or eat-in goodies. *Babies welcome. In the middle of a glen with plenty of countryside walks and rivers to jump in. There are a number of fields with sheep where dogs will need to be kept on leads.*

Rooms	Wagon for 4 (1 double, 2 bunks): from £125 per night. Dogs £10 per pet per stay, payable on arrival. Max. 2.
Meals	Self-catering.
Closed	October – March.
	Advice on walks.

Canopy & Stars
Pilot Panther, Mhor,
Balquhidder, Mhor, FK19 8PQ
Tel   +44 (0)117 204 7830
Email   enquiries@canopyandstars.co.uk
Web   www.canopyandstars.co.uk/
         pilotpanther

Entry 223 Map 8

The Owl House

You feel as if you are high up in the trees, like one of the owls that hoot in this most beautiful part of Highland Perthshire. And when you look out of the tiny triangular bedroom window, you see an avenue of lime and oak trees that was an ancient walkway for monks. Couples love this 19th-century stone cottage tucked away at the end of a track amid sprawling gardens and woodland. Open plan and filled with light, it is rustically sophisticated with a strong, quirky owl theme throughout, a slim wood-burner, wooden floors, fur throws and candle lanterns flickering on an oak dining table. You can barbecue out on the stone-flagged terrace or cook in a fantastically well-equipped kitchen looking out to lichen-covered trees and snowdrops in spring. Upstairs, the bedroom is soft in whites and duck-egg hues, with a rustic iron-framed bed under sloping eaves and a huge velux window; star-gaze at night, bird-watch by day. There are delis and galleries in nearby Aberfeldy, and friendly Julie is on hand for advice on local pubs and walks. Come for absolute peace, fresh air and perhaps to bag a Munro or two. *Minimum stay: 3 nights at weekends. Short breaks available.*

Rooms	1 cottage for 2 (1 double – en suite): £630-£770 per week. Max. 1 dog.
Meals	Self-catering.
Closed	Never.

Water and food bowl, towel for drying, blanket, a few doggie treat biscuits & advice about dog-friendly eateries and doggie walks in the area.

Julie Baird
The Owl House,
Garth, Fortingall,
Aberfeldy, PH15 2NF

Mobile	+44(0)7963 088112
Email	julesandsnooty@yahoo.co.uk
Web	www.owlhouseglenlyon.co.uk/

Entry 224 Map 8

Cringletie House

Cringletie's splendours are hard to miss. You're wrapped up in 65 acres of beautiful grounds with daffodils that erupt in spring, cows that graze in lush fields and a peaceful walled garden for a game of boules. Pheasants strut, buzzards circle, views roll over nearby hills. As for the house, it dates to 1860, its playful turrets giving it a soft grandeur. Inside, you get the full works: an open fire in the hall, then a fine old staircase that sweeps you up to a striking first-floor dining room that has the feel of an 18th-century gentleman's club; expect panelled walls, vintage wallpapers and a spectacular muralled ceiling. There's a sitting room up here, too – equally grand, with fat sofas in front of the fire. Bedrooms are scattered about. Some downstairs open onto the garden, those at the top have the best views. It doesn't matter which you go for, they're all lovely, with warm colours, crisp linen, comfy beds and excellent bathrooms. Friday night barbecues are held in the walled garden in summer. Take to the hills, follow the Tweed or scoot up to Edinburgh; it's less than an hour by car. *Walled garden, woodlands and Eddleston river. Sheep and Highland cattle in fields.*

Rooms	12 twin/doubles: £135-£245.
	1 suite for 2: £235-£265.
	1 cottage for 6: £235-£465 per night.
Meals	Lunch from £4.50.
	Afternoon tea £18.50.
	Dinner, 3 courses, £35.
	Sunday lunch £22.50.
Closed	2 weeks in January.
	Biscuits, towels, and lots of walks.

Jeremy Osbourne
Cringletie House,
Edinburgh Road,
Peebles, EH45 8PL

Tel   +44 (0)1721 725750
Email   gm@cringletie.com
Web   www.cringletie.com

Entry 225 Map 9

The Potting Shed

Once this housed the heating for the garden glasshouses; now the richly-coloured stonework has been exposed and a floor-to-ceiling glass window allows light to flood in to a crisp, contemporary interior. It's the perfect bolthole and very private, a mile down a bumpy track, with a wildflower meadow between you and the owners. You have your own garden with a table and chairs, and a delightful deck area overlooking the river Leader. Inside find pale oak floors with rugs, a wood-burning stove in the sitting room, reclaimed tables, a state-of-the-art heat storage range cooker and quirky touches such as old wooden wine boxes instead of tiles behind the sink. The bedroom is simply furnished and cosy with a well-dressed bed; red blinds splash colour onto white walls, as does local art work; the bathroom is modern and functional with fluffy towels and Sedbergh Soap Company goodies. A generous basket is yours: home-baked bread, jam, eggs from the hens, logs – what a lovely gift to arrive to. Walks, and fishing, abound but you may find it hard to leave the sylvan setting and the peace. *Short breaks available. Surrounded by woodland walks and a river at the bottom of the garden to jump into. Dog heaven, just please don't eat the free-range chickens!*

Rooms	1 cottage for 2 (1 double; 1 shower room): £300–£450 per week. Max. 2 dogs.
Meals	Self-catering.
Closed	Rarely.
🚶‍🐕	Advice on the many walks surrounding The Potting Shed.

Kate Comins
The Potting Shed,
Cowdenknowes,
Earlston, TD4 6AA

Tel	+44 (0)1896 848124
Email	kate.comins@yahoo.co.uk
Web	www.pottingshedholidays.com

Entry 226 Map 9

Scottish Borders

Fauhope House

Near to Melrose Abbey and the glorious St Cuthbert's Walk, this solid 1890s house is immersed in bucolic bliss. Views soar to the Eildon Hills through wide windows with squashy seats; all is luxurious, elegant, fire-lit and serene with an eclectic mix of art. Bedrooms are warm with deeply coloured walls, pale tartan blankets and soft velvet and linen; bathrooms are modern and pristine. Breakfast is served with smiles at a flower-laden table and overlooking those purple hills. A short walk through the blooming garden and over a footbridge takes you to the interesting town of Melrose, with shops, restaurants and its own theatre. *Parkland in front of house. Fabulous walks up the hill behind; 5-minute walk to a river to jump in. Dogs on leads when the sheep are in lamb and at lambing time.*

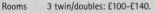

Rooms	3 twin/doubles: £100–£140. Singles from £60. Dogs charged only if there is damage! Max. 1 dog.
Meals	Pub/restaurant 0.5 miles.
Closed	Rarely.

Biscuits, pig's ears, good water and advice on walks.

Ian & Sheila Robson
Fauhope House, Gattonside,
Melrose, TD6 9LU

Tel	+44 (0)1896 823184
Mobile	+44 (0)7816 346768
Email	info@fauhopehouse.com
Web	www.fauhopehouse.com

Entry 227 Map 9

Cover Star Competition

Some of our favourite handsome hounds

Mackintosh is a city dog who loves to travel. Beaches, Sawday's holidays, other dogs and cosy evenings are his top treats.

Harry and Florence are into everything. Walkies o'clock is their favourite time!

The snap of Roxie was taken at one of her favourite places – Port Meadow in Oxford. She loves to play with her ball in the puddles there.

Ben Lomond

A fusion of Kyrgyz design and local materials, there are three yurts here but Ben Lomond is the only one to welcome your canine friend. All the yurts have a homely, earthy feel, with thick rugs, rough tapestries and wood-burning stoves adding comfort. Ben Ledi and Ben Lomond yurts share the woodland just a little way on from Stuc a' Chroin yurt. In each is a double bed, a double futon, and a single 'sleep over' for a child. From the boardwalk leading to the communal kitchen are impressive views across Flanders Moss National Nature Reserve. Arts and crafts courses aplenty too, from willow crafting to Japanese block printing and yoga. There's an abundance of local produce, including veg from the kitchen garden, steaks for the barbecue, local eggs and homemade bread. With all this and the beauty of the Trossachs National Park to explore, you won't be short of ways to create a memorable stay. And for those furry friends looking to curl up beside the wood-burner, blankets are provided for extra comfort. *Babies welcome. Working farm so dogs on leads on farm, but there are no animals in the vicinity of the yurt. Lots of space for a run in the woodland around the yurt.*

Rooms	Yurt for 5 (1 double, 1 double futon, 1 sleepover mat): from £100 per night.
	Dogs £30 per pet per stay. Max. 1.
Meals	Self-catering.
Closed	Never.

Water and food bowls, a blanket and advice on walks.

Canopy & Stars
Ben Lomond,
West Moss-side Organic Farm and Centre,
Thornhill, FK8 3QJ
Tel   +44 (0)117 204 7830
Email   enquiries@canopyandstars.co.uk
Web   www.canopyandstars.co.uk/benlomond

England

Bath & N.E. Somerset

1   Advice on walks and a selection of treats.
2   Advice on walks, a Bonio and a pat on the back.

Berkshire

3   Blankets, dog treats, toys, bed and donation to Battersea Dogs Home.

Cambridgeshire

4   Water and walks.
5   Water and walks.

Cheshire

6   Dog treats and advice on walks.
7   Biscuits on the bar, water bowls, Doggie Beer and good walks. Dogs' dinner menu and dog basket as well for dogs staying in rooms.
8   Dog treats and advice on walks.

Cornwall

9   A Welcome Pack including dog sitting, a dog's own hot/cold outdoor shower, blankets/throws, towels and dog beach guide.
10   Guidance on local walks. Doc Martin's dog Dodger stays here!
11   Advice on walks.
12   Fleecy Chalky's pal blanket, guide to dog walks in Cornwall, personal dog bowls, and 100% natural dog treats from Green & Wilds with selected breaks.
13   Biscuits, bedding and bowls.

14   Bowls, water, biscuits and an information leaflet about dogs at the hotel.
15   Underfloor heating, advice on walks and dog poop bags by the door.
16   Runs on the beach all year round, and advice on other dog-friendly beach walks.
17   Doggie biscuits, blanket, towels, advice on walks, black bags and dog bowls. Very friendly staff too.
18   Towels for drying and advice on walks and dog-friendly beaches.
19   Dog towels, homemade biscuits and a list of dog-friendly activities.
20   Lots of advice for dog-friendly days out.
21   Doggie biscuits, blanket, towels, advice on walks, black bags and dog bowls. Very friendly staff too.
22   Advice on walks, river to swim in, dog-friendly beaches, and lovely dog-friendly pub 5-minute walk.
23   Dog-friendly beach map — there are lots of beaches and walks all year round.

24   Little cupboard filled with tug toys.
25   Coastal, country lane and riverbank walks.
26   Throws for furniture, private fenced garden for dog to play in, empty field for running free. Advice and maps for fantastic dog walks, dog-friendly beaches, pubs and days out.
27   Biscuits and blanket.

28 Treats, biodegradable dog bags, towels for drying and advice on the surrounding walks and some of our favourites.

29 Throws provided, doggy towels and wonderful road-free walks.

Cumbria

30 Towel, dog bowl, biscuits, walking information and dog shower outside for muddy paws.

31 Wonderful walks from the doorstep up and onto the Cumbrian fells.

32 Advice on walks.

33 Doggy welcome pack including treat, map of local walks and doggy bag.

34 Outdoor bed, blanket, water bowl and dog lead.

35 Water bowl and perfect walks from the door.

36 Advice on walks, dog-friendly activities and pubs in the area.

37 Dog treats, toy, bowls, mat and bed.

38 Acres of garden and woodland sniffs; one room has an enclosed garden that's dog-proof for most breeds!

Derbyshire

39 Dog bed, bowls and treats, towels for drying and dog bags. Advice on local dog-friendly cafés, pubs and walks.

40 Dog biscuits at turndown, towels available and lots of walking information.

Devon

41 Towels, water bowl, bedding, dog treats and lovely walks from the door.

42 Edible dog treats.

43 Towels, beds and bowls. Also hose and poo bin provided under lodges.

44 Advice on walks.

45 Lots of advice on dog-friendly walks, beaches and places to eat out. Towels for drying soggy dogs, and plenty of doggy accessories (bowls, crates etc) can be provided if needed.

46 Pig's ears and advice on dog walks and local dog-friendly beaches.

47 Blankets and dog biscuits.

48 Woodland walks, maps and dog towels.

49 Advice on local walks, and fresh water bowl.

50 Advice on walks.

51 Dog biscuits.

52 Towels, bowls and advice on walks. A river to swim in and resident wonder dog Rags to entertain. Plans afoot for special dog-proof run with kennel and shade.

53 Dog snacks, 5-acre gardens, loads of great local walks.

54 Dog bowl, treats, advice on walks and best seat in the house (cushion in front of the wood-burner).

55 Maps and advice on walks, towels for drying on request, entertainment and company from resident Labrador Kasper.

56 Organic dog biscuits, dog towels, and acres of private woodland for walks in your pyjamas and wellies.

57 Advice on walks, dog towels, resident friendly lurchers to play with – and plenty of love and attention!

58 Don't leave your four-legged family member at home! They will have a bed and bowl in the room, and a snooze in front of the roaring log fires in winter.

59 Entertainment from the friendly resident terrier lurcher, Miss Cocofit, advice on walks and a Bonio at bedtime.

60 Lots of long walks in the open country – join the East Devon Way.

61 Homemade biscuits, towels, blanket, pooper scoop bags, shampoo, guides and pet shop voucher.

Dorset

62 Advice on walks.

63 Towels for drying, and advice on walks, dog-friendly beaches and local attractions. Walks through surrounding farmland from the doorstep.

64 Advice for walks – there are many directly from the barn.

65 Water bowl, food bowl and a doggie treat.

66 Advice on walks.

67 Biscuits, blankets, dog-friendly dining area and advice on local walks.

68 Dog-friendly guide to the area, water bowl, towel and treats. Walking map and dog treats in the bar too.

69 Dog treats on arrival. Special menus on request, drying towels and best walks advice.

70 Towels and advice for walking.

71 Towels for drying and protective covers for chairs etc.

72 Village footpaths and 250-acre Woodland Trust wood within easy walking distance.

Durham

73 Dog bed, towel, bowl and suggested walks.

Essex

74 Biscuits, blankets, towels and dog walks.

75 Blankets, towels, advice on walks, doggy dinners, water bowls and treat.

Gloucestershire

76 Advice on walks.

77 Biscuits, advice and walks from the door as well as dog-friendly dining.

78 Dogs treats, and walking maps in an information file. (Please bring your own dog bed, towels and bowls.)

79 Dog bed in room with dog biscuits in a bowl. Pig's ears too.

80 Dog beds in bedrooms, treats and biscuits on request. Towels, water in the gardens and lots of walking maps of the Cotswold Way.

81 Hose for mucky dogs, towels for drying off, stock-proof orchard for dogs to run free. Advice on walks and where farm animals are; attention drawn to Countryside Code.

82 Advice on walks and large dog-friendly garden.

83 Dog-sitting, towels for drying and advice on walks – or walks with Manor Cottage dogs.

Hampshire

84 Lily's Kitchen Bedtime Biscuits, bones, sheepskin rug, water bowl, towels for drying, maps and advice on walks.

85 Advice on walks, and river swims!

86 Advice on the best places for walks and days out.

87 Dust sheets, large dog crate, Aga, wood-burning stove, direct access onto New Forest heathland and woods, and fully fenced 2-acre garden and paddock.

Herefordshire

88 Dog treats, water bowls and advice on walks.

89 Water bowls, doggy treats and advice on walks.

90 A big bowl of water for our thirsty friends.

91 Advice on walks and guided walks, towels, and resident dog playmates!

Isle of Wight

92 Advice on walks, 60 acres to roam and private beach to run on.

Kent

93 Dog bed and dog treats.

94 Home-cooked local sausage. Advice on walks.

Leicestershire

95 Advice on walks.

Lincolnshire

96 Blanket and poo bags.

97 Bowls, biscuits and advice on walks.

London

98 Pig's ears, dog bed, towels for drying and advice on walks.

Norfolk

99 Advice on walks.

100 Lovely walks straight from the cottage – perfect for dogs.

101 Homemade biscuits, towels, blankets and advice on walks.

102 Advice on walks.

103 Locally made dog biscuits, wonderful walks, and occasional dog sitting if owners have to leave their dogs for the day. Dog-friendly beaches nearby.

Northumberland

104 Drying room, towels and Bonedrybed dog bed. Advice on walks, and hose pipe area for muddy paws. Birthday cakes on request and 37 acres to explore.

105 Towels, bowls, and great dog walking from the door.

106 Food and water bowls, and advice on walks through the forest and along the Lakeside Way.

107 Blanket, poo bags, towels, dog biscuits and walks from the front door.

108 Leads, bowls, poo bags, furniture throws, a secure garden and dog-friendly walks away from farm stock.

Oxfordshire

109 Advice on walks, bar treats jar, doggie bowls for water. Doggies allowed in some rooms overnight. Freedom to come and go in garden as long as well-behaved.

110 Advice on walks.

Rutland

111 Advice on walks.

Shropshire

112 Blankets, bowl, treats and advice on walks.

113 Advice on walks.

114 Walks, lots of space and many dog-loving staff!

115 Homemade treats, towels for drying, advice on walks and outside shower tap with hand-hot regulated water.

116 Dog treats, blankets and advice on walks.

117 Dog bones, old towels, dog walks, plays with Copper and a stream for swimming.

118 Butcher's bones, dog-eared towels and accompanied guided walks from resident dog, Copper the Labrador!

119 Throws, dog bowls, towels and advice on walks and places to eat. Downstairs room has direct access to enclosed garden.

120 Advice on walks and maps.

Somerset

121 Black pudding treats, great walks – and towels if needed.

122 Maps and advice on local walks.

123 Towels for drying, pig's ears and advice on walks.

124 Homemade biscuits, pig's ears, blankets, towels for drying and advice on walks.

Suffolk

125 Dog treats, water bowls, doggie breakfast, blanket, map with local walks, dog wash and towels.

126 Dog biscuits, water bowls and maps with local walks.

127 Dog biscuits and advice on walks.

128 Homemade treats, towels, walks, and a bookable "doggie table" in the restaurant.

129 Blankets, towels, walks, bowls and doggy dinners.

130 Towels for drying wet dogs, pooper scoop bags and a bedtime biscuit.

Surrey

131 Water bowls, doggy biscuits, a cosy spot near the open log fire and advice on local walks. Attention and affection too – a warm welcome to dogs and their owners!

Sussex

132 Homemade biscuits, drying towels and drying room. Lots of local walks and places to eat too.

133 Sausages for breakfast.

134 Dog towels, bowls, biscuits and maps for walks.

135 Advice on walks.

136 Towels, advice on walking and walks

from the door. Dog sitting and dog kennel (if you want to go out without your dog).

137 Advice on walks and dog-friendly pubs nearby.

138 Poop bags, dog biscuits and towels for drying.

140 Treats, poo bags and advice on walks.

Warwickshire

141 Plenty of lovely soft towels for drying, and a comfortable bed in front of the fire.

142 Dog biscuits, pig's ears, water, dog beds, blankets and advice on walks.

Wiltshire

143 Maps and advice on walks – and towels if required.

144 Blankets, towels, advice on walks and free range of garden.

145 Dog treats, water bowls, towels for drying, advice on walks – and dog bed if required.

Worcestershire

146 Towels, dog bowl and doggie treats.

147 Towels, water bowls and doggie treats.

Yorkshire

148 Towels for drying and advice on walks.

149 Towels for drying and advice on great walks. Dogs are allowed in the sitting rooms.

150 A lake for dog swimming, lovely walks on site, and a contained 2-acre garden for comfort and safety.

151 Meaty rolls from Pedigree, and a handy guide of dog-friendly pubs and restaurants.

152 Doggie treats upon arrival.

153 Advice on walks, and a lovely nature reserve just 2 minutes from cottages.

154 A guide to local dog-friendly pubs and beaches.

155 Dog bowl.

156 Raw beef bones from the butcher, great dog walks, and towels.

157 Advice on dog-friendly places and walks. Poo bin!

England – pubs

Berkshire

158 Biscuits, advice on walks, doggie bowls – and freedom of the pub (except the conservatory!).

Buckinghamshire

159 Advice on walks.

160 Doggie biscuit jar on the bar. Advice on walks in the nearby beech woodlands of Common and Penn Woods.

161 A huge garden to run around in. Dog biscuits on the bar, fresh water bowls outside and a large OS map by the front door. Lovely circular walk on iFootpath.

162 Homemade treats, blankets, local woodland walks map and Sunday meat treats.

163 Homemade dog biscuits with money raised going to Search Dogs Bucks charity. Water bowls and great walks from the doorstep in the Chiltern countryside.

164 Advice on walks.

Cheshire

165 Dog bowls, dog biscuits and Doggie Beer too. A great pub walk, and extensive gardens and terrace to play in.

166 Biscuits on the bar, water bowls and Doggie Beer. A good pub walk between The Bull's Head and The Church Inn.

167 Dog biscuits, dogs' dinner menu, Doggie Beer and water bowls. Shakerley Mere bird nature reserve walks, and a play in enclosed extensive gardens.

Derbyshire

168 Advice on walks, fresh water in a clean bowl and a dog chew.

Hertfordshire

169 Dog biscuits on the bar, fresh water bowls outside and a large OS map by the front door. Lovely circular walk on iFootpath.

London

170 Water bowls.

Somerset

171 Dog treats and dog beer.

Staffordshire

172 Dog bowls with fresh water.

Sussex

173 Locally made dog biscuits, water bowls – and a friendly welcome!

Wiltshire

174 Scrumptious lovely biscuits, organic treats, towels and a brush. Dogs also get their own champagne buckets full of fresh water.

175 Scrumptious lovely biscuits, organic treats, towels and a brush. Dogs also get their own champagne buckets full of fresh water.

176 Water bowl, homemade doggie treats and advice on walks.

Yorkshire

177 Always water, dog biscuits, towels and advice on walks. Dogs are welcome in the pub if well-behaved. Some owners buy them an ice cream!

Wales

Anglesey

178 Dog biscuits and advice on walks.

179 Advice on dog-friendly pubs, beaches and days out.

Cardiff

180 Towels, and advice on walks and local dog-friendly pubs.

Carmarthenshire

181 Advice on walks.

182 Dog treats in your room.

183 Advice on lots of walks.

Ceredigion

184 Advice on walks and dog-friendly beaches.

185 Towels and good walks.

186 Water bowl and advice on walks.

187 Towels for drying and advice on walks.

188 Dogs truly welcome! Lovely gardens and lots of advice on beaches, local pubs and days out.

Conwy

189 Advice on walks, a dog bowl and a warm welcome.

Flintshire

190 Towels for drying, advice for walks and space for exercise.

Gwynedd

191 Advice on walks, lots of private space and a river on the front doorstep.

192 Advice on walks and 7 acres of garden to play in.

193 Biscuits, special dog bowls and mat, dog towels and wonderful, safe, traffic-free dog walks on the estate.

194 Advice on dog-friendly dining, dog biscuits, dog towel, poop bags and suggestions for walks.

Monmouthshire

195 Pig's ears, and advice on walks and dog-friendly pubs and restaurants.

196 Dog parlour and towels. Dog treats for well-behaved dogs.

197 Specially made dog kennel and advice on walks.

198 Advice on walks.

Pembrokeshire

199 Dog biscuits, towels, walking advice and 3 acres of woodland where dogs can run around off the lead.

Powys

200 Maps of local walks and advice on dog-friendly pubs.

201 Water bowl and tether. Maps and routes for walks around the farm and local footpaths and bridleways.

202 Doggie biscuits, blanket, towels, advice on walks, black bags, dog bowls – and very friendly staff.

203 Lots of information on walks in the area and dog-friendly pubs. Dog bowl, throws for the furniture, 2 wood-burning stoves to sleep by and a utility room for drying dogs off.

204 Biscuits, dog leads, bowls and advice on walks.

205 Sausages for breakfast, towels, dog bowls and walks.

206 Blankets, towels, dog sitting, walk advice – and dog food if you've forgotten to bring some.

207 Great walks from the house.

Swansea

208 Advice on walks.

Scotland

Aberdeenshire

209 Doggie sleepover pack! Includes gravy bones, towel, blanket to put on the sofa, dog bed, dog bowls and lead for use during their stay. (Must keep off the beds!)

Argyll & Bute

210 Biscuits, water and blankets. Expert advice on wild, carefree walks and a special welcome from terrier Boris the Arbuthnott.

211 Dog biscuit.

Dumfries & Galloway

212 Dog basket, acres of garden, beautiful countryside and advice on great walks.

213 Poo bag, map of local dog-friendly walks, bag of treats and dog blanket/bed.

214 Masses of space for walks – even a river to swim in, and towels are available for drying off dogs. Bedtime biscuits too!

Dunbartonshire

215 Advice on walks and plenty of exercise space from the cottage door.

Edinburgh

216 A Bonio and advice on walks.

217 Great walks along the canal.

Fife

218 Treat bag, balls, ball thrower, dog towels, various size dog bowls, biodegradeable poop bags, advice on dog-friendly cafés and pubs and guide to local walks.

Glasgow

219 Homemade livercake, blankets, towels, favourite walks and advice on dog-friendly pubs and cafés.

Highland

220 Advice on walks, dog biscuits, fenced field to run in – all to yourself.

221 Pet bowls, extra towels for beachy paws, dog treat and advice on walks.

222 Gravy bones, biscuits, blankets, towels for drying, advice on walkies, and a large pen with kennel.

Perth & Kinross

223 Advice on walks.

224 Water and food bowl, towel for drying, blanket, a few doggie treat biscuits & advice about dog-friendly eateries and doggie walks in the area.

Scottish Borders

225 Biscuits, towels, and lots of walks.

226 Advice on the many walks surrounding The Potting Shed.

227 Biscuits, pig's ears, good water and advice on walks.

Stirling

228 Water and food bowls, a blanket and advice on walks.

Wheelchair-accessible

At least one bedroom and bathroom accessible for wheelchair users. Phone for details.

England

Bath & N.E. Somerset 1
Berkshire 3
Cambridgeshire 4 • 5
Cheshire 6
Cornwall 12 • 13 • 14 • 16 • 23
Cumbria 37
Devon 41 • 53
Dorset 62
Essex 74 • 75
Gloucestershire 77 • 81 • 83
Hampshire 84
Kent 93
Norfolk 99
Northumberland 107
Oxfordshire 109
Rutland 111
Shropshire 112 • 116 • 119
Suffolk 125 • 126 • 129
Sussex 136 • 137
Yorkshire 148 • 149 • 157

Wales

Ceredigion 184
Gwynedd 192 • 193 • 194
Powys 203 •

Scotland

Argyll & Bute 210 • 211
Dunbartonshire 215
Highland 221
Scottish Borders 225

Pets live here

Owners' pets live at the property.

England

Bath & N.E. Somerset 2
Cornwall 9 • 11 • 27 • 29
Cumbria 38
Devon 41 • 48 • 49 • 51 • 52 • 55 • 57 • 59 • 60 • 61
Dorset 63 • 71 • 72
Gloucestershire 81 • 82 • 83
Hampshire 84
Herefordshire 91
Isle of Wight 92
Kent 94
Leicestershire 95
Lincolnshire 96 • 97
London 98
Norfolk 101 • 103
Northumberland 105 • 107
Oxfordshire 109
Shropshire 115 • 117 • 118 • 119
Somerset 121 • 123 • 124
Suffolk 130
Sussex 138
Warwickshire 141
Wiltshire 144 • 145
Yorkshire 151 • 153 • 156 •

Wales

Carmarthenshire 182 • 183
Ceredigion 184 • 188
Flintshire 190
Gwynedd 193 • 194
Monmouthshire 198
Powys 202 • 205 • 206 • 207

Scotland

Argyll & Bute 211
Dumfries & Galloway 212 • 213 • 214

Quick reference indices

Quick reference indices

Credit cards accepted

These owners have told us that they accept credit cards, most commonly Visa and MasterCard.

England

Wales

Scotland

Alastair
Sawday's

'More than a bed
for the night…'

Britain
France
Ireland
Italy
Portugal
Spain

www.sawdays.co.uk

Self-Catering | B&B | Hotel | Pub | Treehouses, Cabins, Yurts & More

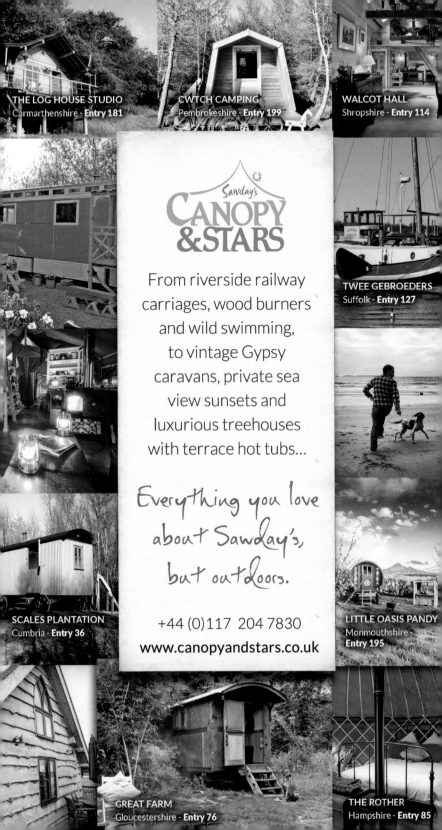

Alastair Sawday has been publishing books for over twenty years, finding Special Places to Stay in Britain and abroad. All our properties are inspected by us and are chosen for their charm and individuality, and with twelve titles to choose from there are plenty of places to explore. You can buy any of our books at a reader discount of 25%* on the RRP.

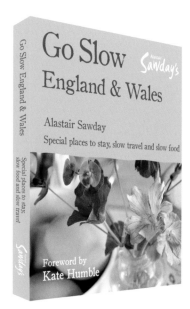
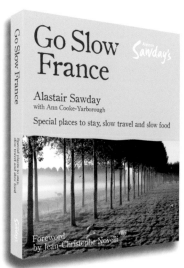

List of titles:	RRP	Discount price
British Bed & Breakfast	£15.99	£11.99
British Hotels and Inns	£15.99	£11.99
Pubs & Inns of England & Wales	£15.99	£11.99
Dog-friendly Breaks in Britain	£14.99	£11.24
French Bed & Breakfast	£15.99	£11.99
French Châteaux & Hotels	£15.99	£11.99
Italy	£15.99	£11.99
Portugal	£12.99	£9.74
Spain	£15.99	£11.99
Go Slow England & Wales	£19.99	£14.99
Go Slow France	£19.99	£14.99

*postage and packaging is added to each order

How to order:
You can order online at: www.sawdays.co.uk/bookshop/
or call: +44(0)117 204 7810

Town index for Dog-friendly Pubs

Photo above: The Westleton Crown, entry 125
Photo right: The Lodge, entry 34

Join us

TIME AWAY IS FAR TOO PRECIOUS TO
SPEND IN THE WRONG PLACE. THAT'S WHY,
BACK IN 1994, WE STARTED SAWDAY'S.

Twenty years on, we're still a family concern – and still
on a crusade to stamp out the bland and predictable,
and help our guests find truly special places to stay.

If you have one, we do hope you'll decide
to take the plunge and join us.

———

ALASTAIR & TOBY SAWDAY

"Trustworthy, friendly and helpful – with a reputation
for offering wonderful places and discerning visitors."
JULIA NAISMITH, HOLLYTREE COTTAGE

"Sawday's. Is there any other?"
SONIA HODGSON, HORRY MILL

WHY BECOME A MEMBER?

Becoming a part of our 'family' of Special Places is like being awarded a Michelin star. Our stamp of approval will tell guests that you offer a truly special experience and you will benefit from our experience, reputation and support.

A CURATED COLLECTION

Our site presents a relatively small and careful selection of Special Places which helps us to stand out like a brilliantly shining beacon.

INSPECT AND RE-INSPECT

Our inspectors have an eagle-eye for the special, but absolutely no check-lists. They visit every member, see every bedroom and bathroom and, on the lucky days, eat the food.

QUALITY, NOT QUANTITY

We don't pretend (or want) to be in the same business as the sites that handle zillions of bookings a day. Using our name ensures that you attract the right kind of guests for you.

VARIETY

From country-house hotels to city pads and funky fincas to blissful B&Bs, we genuinely delight in the individuality of our Special Places.

LOYALTY

Nearly half of our members have been with us for five years or more. We must be doing something right!

The friendly crew

GET IN TOUCH WITH OUR MEMBERSHIP TEAM...

+44 (0)117 204 7810
members@sawdays.co.uk

...OR APPLY ONLINE

sawdays.co.uk/joinus

1 Inn   Gloucestershire **2**

3 | 4 The Royal Oak Tetbury

Resplendent after a full refurbishment this 17th-century coaching inn is abuzz with enthusiasm. Inside, reclaimed floorboards have been artfully fitted together, a salvaged carved oak bar has its own little 'Groucho snug' at one end. Exposed stone and a real fire co-exist with a pretty Art Deco piano whose ivories are often tinkled. Cheery staff will pull you a pint of Uley or Stroud ale – or perhaps an Orchard Pig cider – and on certain days you can even mix your own Bloody Mary. Treats in store on the menu from head chef Richard Simms feature pub classics with a twist: sharing or small plates, hearty salads, 'oak pots' with a veggie or meat option served with crusty bread or brown rice and plenty of choice for vegans. Up in the roof beneath massive beams is a more formal restaurant with a spacious, calm atmosphere. Across the cobbled yard are six bedrooms – three are dog-friendly – with a restful elegance, dreamy beds and bathrooms to linger in. And if a special occasion is the reason for your visit then the Oak Lodge room will not fail to get things off to a very good start. Enjoy the view from the garden, glass of wine in hand. *Minimum stay: 2 nights at weekends & in high season. Secure garden, and great walks on the doorstep.*

5 **6** **7**	Rooms	6 doubles: £75–£160. Extra bed/sofabed available £20 per person per night. Dogs £10. Max. 2.
8	Meals	Lunch & dinner £5–£13.
	Closed	Never.
		Biscuits, advice and walks from the door as well as dog-friendly dining.

Kate Lewis
The Royal Oak Tetbury,
1 Cirencester Road,
Tetbury, GL8 8EY
Tel   +44 (0)1666 500021
Email   stay@theroyaloaktetbury.co.uk
Web   www.theroyaloaktetbury.co.uk

9   Entry 77 Map 3   **10**